"Yeoman Soldiers"

by

"'John Lewis"'

"The Royal Gloucestershire Hussars Yeomanry
1795 - 1920"'

Order this book online at www.trafford.com/07-2149
or email orders@trafford.com

Most Trafford titles are also available at major online book retailers.

© Copyright 2008 John Lewis.

All rights reserved. No part of this publication may be reproduced, stored in a retrieval system, or transmitted, in any form or by any means, electronic, mechanical, photocopying, recording, or otherwise, without the written prior permission of the author.

Note for Librarians: A cataloguing record for this book is available from Library and Archives Canada at www.collectionscanada.ca/amicus/index-e.html

Printed in Victoria, BC, Canada.

ISBN: 978-1-4251-4103-5

We at Trafford believe that it is the responsibility of us all, as both individuals and corporations, to make choices that are environmentally and socially sound. You, in turn, are supporting this responsible conduct each time you purchase a Trafford book, or make use of our publishing services. To find out how you are helping, please visit www.trafford.com/responsiblepublishing.html

Our mission is to efficiently provide the world's finest, most comprehensive book publishing service, enabling every author to experience success. To find out how to publish your book, your way, and have it available worldwide, visit us online at www.trafford.com/10510

Trafford
PUBLISHING

www.trafford.com

North America & international
toll-free: 1 888 232 4444 (USA & Canada)
phone: 250 383 6864 ♦ fax: 250 383 6804
email: info@trafford.com

The United Kingdom & Europe
phone: +44 (0)1865 722 113 ♦ local rate: 0845 230 9601
facsimile: +44 (0)1865 722 868 ♦ email: info.uk@trafford.com

10 9 8 7 6 5 4 3 2 1

Dedicated to the memory of 2305 Sergeant Fred Lewis
and all who served with him in the Royal Gloucestershire Hussars
1914 – 1918

I acknowledge the help and advice I have been given by Lieutenant Colonel Rollo Clifford, who checked the proof and made available the R.G.H. records.

To follow the strategy of the Palestine campaign the author referred to "The Palestine Campaigns" by Lieutenant General A.P. Wavell. For other references see appendix "b"

I am indebted to the Trustees of the Royal Gloucestershire Hussars for permission to use the cover picture. Colonel Cartwright of the Worcester City Museum for permission to reproduce the text and photographs from their Katia display. Mrs Doreen Walwyn-James, Ron Colburn, John Hopkins Brian Welch and John Eaton for making available letters and memorabilia of their fathers'. Stephen Troughton for information about his grandfather and Lord Neidpath for an extract from his grandmother's writings.

I was fortunate in having most of my father's letters, which he wrote from Gallipoli and Palestine, also personal memories of many other "Old Yeomen" with whom he served.

The author apologises for the clarity of some of the photographs, they were taken with a very simple camera and processed in Egypt on indifferent quality paper; the passage of time did not improve them.

The engravings follow original photographs taken by F. Mason Good who travelled through the Holy Land during the nineteenth century.

Place names are those used at the time of the action described, they may have been altered in the world of today.

Previous works by the same author

Foreman of the Fields	a Century of the Cotswold Vale
Three Into One	The History of the Three Counties Agricultural Society
Skokholm the Islanders	Working on a Pembrokeshire Island
Islands – Lovely Islands	Some Beautiful Offshore Islands
Foreman of the Bench	The Experiences of a Swineherd J.P.

Contents

Foreword   8.
        Major General A.G. Denaro C.B.E.

Introduction   11.

Chapter 1   The Birth of the Regiment   12.
Raising of Volunteer Companies – Powell Snell – Fear of Invasion – Gellyhan Colliery – Rioting in Bristol – Troops combine – People's Charter – Moustaches – The Berkeley Quarrel – Horse Fund – Prince of Wales reviews the Regiment.

Chapter 2   South Africa   26.
Queen Victoria's Diamond Jubilee – Boer Settlers in Transvaal. Outlanders – Jameson Raid – Sir Redvers Buller – 1000 casualties – Generals Roberts and Kitchener – 3rd company 1st Imperial Yeomanry, Captain Playne R.G.H. – Thabanchu – Ladybrand – Brandwater Basin – Boer Guerrilla tactics – Standerton, Majuba Hill–Home.

Chapter 3   The Calm Before the Storm.   34.
Anti British feeling in Germany – Yeomanry force reorganised – Field Marshall Roberts inspects the Regiment– rifles issued – Winchcombe Camp – Coronation of King George 5th – Ultimatum to Germany – Mobilisation.

Chapter 4   On Guard   43.
Volunteer training on Oxlease – Schliefen Plan – Contemptible Little Army – Der Tag – 5th Mounted Brigade – Cromer – Shoot hares and pheasants – Zepellin raid – entrain for embarkation at Avonmouth.

Chapter 5   Destination Egypt   51.
R.G.H. arrive in Alexandria – Provide Guards – Gallipoli Casualties – Escort for the Sultan – Native troops strike – Goeben and Breslau bombard Odessa – Turks mine the Dardanelles – The Fleet assaults the Dardanelles – landing at Helles and Anzac.

Chapter 6...........Gallipoli   58.
R.G.H. 2 squadrons dismounted embark for Suvla – Salt Lake – attack Chocolate Hill – wounded loaded in floating stable – Heavy losses – evacuation

Chapter 7   At the Pyramids   71.
Lord Kitchener visits the Dardanelles – R.G.H. embark for Lemnos and Alexandria – bathe in sea – 2nd Lieut Prettejohn and Rev Wilcox – Regiment move to Salhia – officers entertained by the Sheikh – move horses by rail – Kantara.

Chapter 8   Katia   76.
Turks misjudge Egyptian support – Indian Division occupies Basra – Sinai desert – Turks occupy El Arish and advance on Suez Canal – British force established at Romani and Katia – Royal Engineers and two squadrons Worcesters to Oghratina – "A" squadron R.G.H. to Katia – enemy attack – wounded well treated – only 9 R.G.H. get away – R.G.H. lose "A" squadron – Worcesters muster 53 after battle.

Chapter 9   In Captivity   88.

800 mile journey to Afion Kara Hissar - red carpet treatment in Jerusalem - march in twos - feed on dead camel - camel pantomime - "Haidee", get up - prison boredom - malnutrition and dysentery - importance of self discipline - escape impossible - volunteers for lorry driving.

Chapter 10   Romani   93.

Reform of "A" Squadron - Dueidar Hod a shambles - Hill 70 a horrible place - Von Kressenstein attacks Wellington Ridge and Mt Royston with 16,000 Turks - Turks embroiled in the sand dunes - R.G.H. move to Dueidar - Major Turner fills gap in line - Kressenstein ordered to take canal at all costs - terrible scream as Turks attack.

Chapter 11   Avenging Katia   100.

5th Mounted Brigade attack Katia - R.G.H. on patrol work - Brigade Horse Show - Y.M.C.A. Port Said - Cholera amongst prisoners - exercises in bayonet fighting, bomb throwing and use of sword when mounted - Christmas Turkeys - Rafa - Major Clifford killed.

Chapter 12   Gaza   105.

De-lousing - Ali el Muntar ridge - Turkish Divisional commander captured - R.G.H. on sea flank - Green Hill - thick thorn hedges - retire to Wadi Ghuzze - infantry on Mansura Ridge - attack renewed - R.G.H. advance on Wadi el Shira - Anzacs held up - Tanks break down - have to move back to water horses.

Chapter 13   A Change of Command   111.

Relieved by A.L.H. - Lawrence of Arabia goes down into the Hejaz - "Yilderim" force - staff reconnaissance - drive to trap Turk outposts - General Allenby assumes command - intensive training - Lt R.H.Wilson captures Turk patrol - R.G.H. take up outpost line - 30 mile ride in the dark - essential to take Beersheba's wells - Worcesters attacked - Gaza falls.

Chapter 14   Turks in Retreat   124.

Rate of advance limited by water supply - Turk resistance disintegrates - Huj - Turks fear cavalry - large enemy force approach from north - forced to withdraw to Ijseir - all day watering - capture Junction Station - enemy force broken into two separate parts.

Chapter 15   Jerusalem   132.

Forty miles from railhead - country of entanglements - winter rains commenced - Turks make fierce attack - Jerusalem in Christian hands - miserably wet - Sgt Fred Lewis sent for Christmas stores - wadis in flood.

Chapter 16   Training and Recreation   138.

Bring railway up to present position - lower end of Jordan valley cleared - recuperating and re-equipping - R.G.H. hounds - Divisional sports - Intensive training.

Chapter 17   Crossing the Jordan   145.
Army re-organised – Divisions leave for France – replaced by Indian Divisions – camp on west bank of Jordan – 1200 ft below sea level – advance on Es Salt – R.G.H. cross the Jordan – Es Salt taken – let down by Arabs – food and ammunition short – position precarious – withdraw.

Chapter 18   In the Valley of Death   155.
Jordan Valley must be held throughout summer – Turks very active – God forsaken, horrible spot – line on Wadi Auja – high sick rate – very debilitated – scorching hot wind – this month flies die, next month men die – horses lethargic – move to Bethlehem and recovery – the Quartermaster.

Chapter 19   The Final Blow   162.
Turks desertions – R.G.H. move to Solomon's Pools – became 13th cavalry brigade of 5th mounted division – pleasant ride in moonlight – prepare for advance up the coastal plain – opening the gate – Turk army in west trapped – embarking on greatest adventure for cavalry in modern times – opening bombardment obliterates Turk trenches – they cantered along, R.G.H. in vanguard – huge batches of prisoners – R.G.H. gallop into Nazareth.

Chapter 20   Prisoners Galore   172.
Coastal plain cleared – Turkish 8th army captured – 7th army scattered in panic – prepare to march on Acre and Haifa – view Sea of Galilee – held up at Lake Hule – enemy retreat to Damascus – numerous enemy casualties – Golan Heights very cold, 3000 ft up – Lord Apsley's squadron capture wireless station – Turks and Germans butcher Arab village – Turks and British combine to hold off Arabs – Damascus.

Chapter 21   Aleppo and the Armistice   183.
Influenza and Malaria – 5th Cavalry Division marches on Aleppo – feed entirely off the country – beautiful Nahr Zaan valley – invited to feast by local Pasha – R.G.H. enter Baalbeck – enter Homs – hostile villagers – Arab army enters Aleppo – 5th Cavalry Division completes march of 500 miles in less than six weeks.

Chapter 22   Home   188.
Turk detachments troublesome – welcome to 9 Katia prisoners – General Allenby issues stern warning to Turk commanders – farewell dinner to first demobilisation party – lectures to prepare for civilian life – members of R.G.H. transferred to Sherwood Rangers – R.G.H. cadre leaves for home.

Chapter 23   Epilogue   193.
Dedication of R.G.H. War Memorial – old soldiers simply fade away.

Cover picture – Inspection of the Royal Gloucestershire Hussars by H.R.H the Prince of Wales on Cheltenham Racecourse – 13th May 1897
From an original by W.B. Wollen

7.

Battle Honours

South Africa 1900 1901

World War I 1914 - 1918

Suvla	El Mughar
Scimitar Hill	Nebi Samwill
Gallipoli 1915	Jerusalem
Romani	Megiddo
Rafah	Sharon
Egypt 1916-17	Damascus
Gaza	Palestine 1917-18

World War II 1939 – 45

Gubi	Tobruk 1941
Chor es Sufan	Sidi Rezegh 1941
Bir el Aslagh	Gazala
Alam el Halfa	Cauldron
West Point 23	Africa 1941 – 1942

Foreword

by

Major General A.G. Denaro C.B.E., Honorary Colonel
Royal Gloucestershire Hussars Yeomanry

A specific link to a region of this great country, a name that reflects that link, and the family tradition which runs as a strong vein throughout....these are the elements of the Yeomanry regiment. Never were these elements more important in the army and the nation than in today's troubled times. Our yeomanry soldiers are deployed wherever the British army is fighting and they are holding their own and more, with the regular army. In the forefront as I write this, is the Yeoman of Gloucestershire.

This treasure of a book gives a marvellous account of the Gloucestershire Yeomen since their earliest days when in 1795 Mr Powell Snell raised 1st troop in Cheltenham. It recalls so many happy and interesting events, so many terrifying and sad stories....all beautifully expressed in the soft and understated language of the countryman. It brings alive those elements that are so critical to our fighting spirit; the comradeship and courage, the patriotism and self sacrifice, and the sense of adventure and fun which prevailed amongst those fine young men, all bound to do their duty.

These great qualities form the legacy that has been passed down to us by former members of the R.G.H......from men like Fred Lewis, his friends the saddler, the butcher, the fruiterer, the farm hand....and from commanding officers such as one Duke of Beaufort, who commanded for 17 years in the late 1800s and Lt Col Elwes, C.O. during the 1st World War, who both had the confidence to stand up to difficult higher commanders to support their men.

John Lewis has pulled all these threads together; threads that made the tapestry of the regiment strong one hundred years ago and which remain almost identically linked in today's very different world. The hard working civilian, who is prepared to give up so much of his time to make himself into a professional soldier, brings so many of his innate skills to soldiering:

the farmer related his knowledge of the countryside to military tactics; the game shots allowance for wind as he swings, the stalkers eye for the covered approach and the huntsman's use of the lie of the land....all these are as relevant today as they were when the Gloucestershire Yeomen were fighting so gallantly in foreign deserts almost 100 years ago.

Their style and spirit remain the same today; so too does the support that comes from the towns and villages of this uniquely special county of Gloucestershire, for their own Yeoman Soldiers.

I feel honoured to be your Colonel.

Arthur Denaro   10th September 2007
Major General

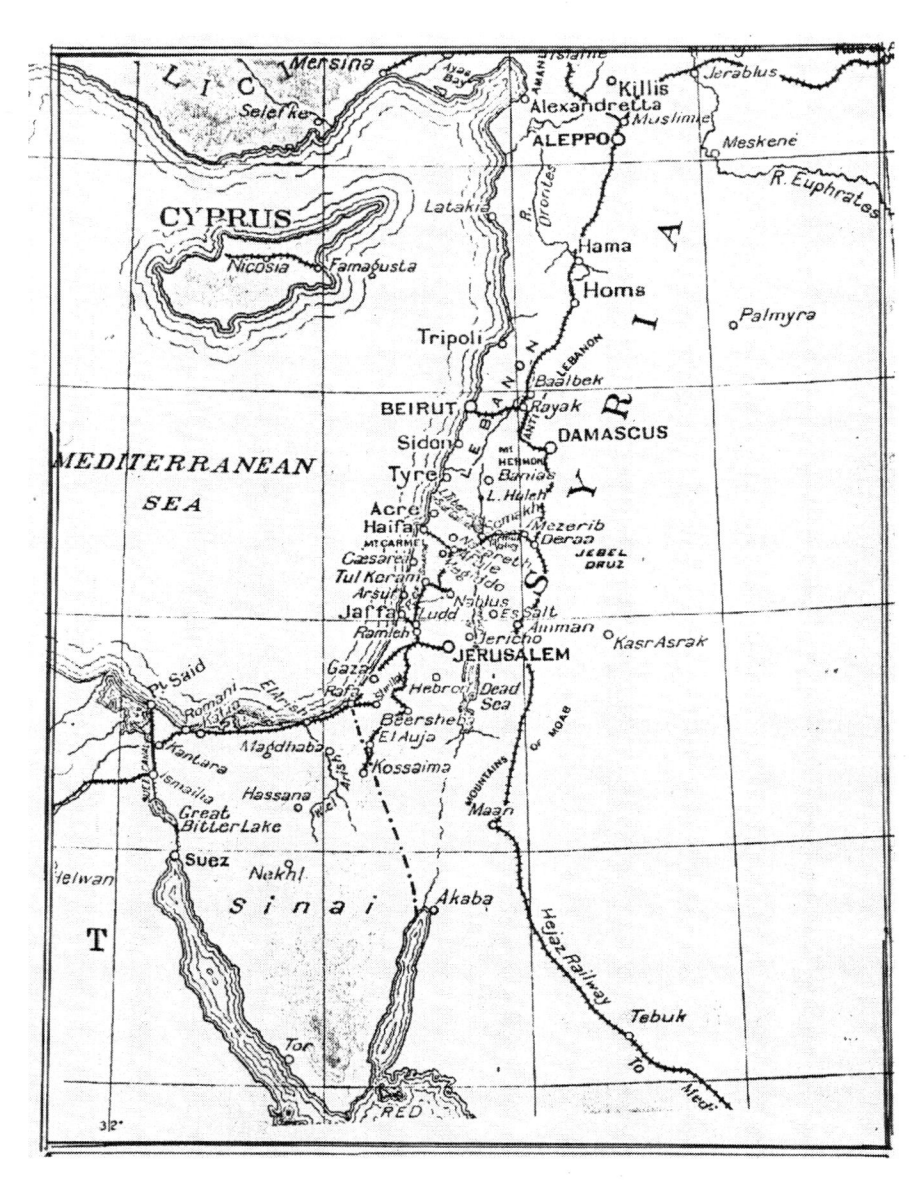

Area covered by the Egyptian Expeditionary Force

Introduction

After attending a most moving memorial service to those who fell at the Battle of Katia, a little oasis in the Sinai desert, I came home and read up the history of the Royal Gloucestershire Hussars Yeomanry. The battle took place on 23rd of April 1916, St George's day, which that year fell on Easter Sunday. On that day 101 Gloucestershire Yeomen and approximately 40 Worcester Yeomen held up a force of some 3,000 Turks for the best part of a day until, running out of ammunition, they were forced to surrender. Some 20 were killed, 9 escaped and the remainder faced a long and harrowing march into captivity.

The 1914 - 18 war is nowadays principally remembered for the carnage on the western front in France, which at the end of four years resulted in a virtual stalemate. The Egyptian Expeditionary Force, in two years covered over 1000 miles; from the Suez canal, across Sinai, up through the Holy Land and Syria, culminating in a 500 miles dash in under six weeks to Aleppo; where the Turks surrendered to an inferior - in numbers - British force. This extraordinary feat, which eliminated the Ottoman Empire has almost been forgotten or ignored.

I felt that this was a tale that had to be told. The men who participated in that momentous advance are no longer with us, but their letters and the tales they told to their sons, daughters and friends have not been forgotten. Inevitably this second generation too will soon be gone and their fathers' memories lost. In gathering up these scraps of information I could not help but be intensely proud of this great feat of arms and the role played by mounted cavalry, especially the Yeomen of Gloucestershire, who more often than not led the advance.

John Lewis
Copse Green Farm
  Gloucestershire

Chapter One

The Birth of the Regiment

Raising of Volunteer Companies – Powell Snell – Fear of Invasion –
a desperate affray – Gellyhan Colliery – Rioting in Bristol–
Troops Combine into one Regiment – People's Charter –
Moustaches – The Berkeley Quarrel – Horse Fund –
Prince of Wales Reviews the Regiment

"I have been a cavalryman for twenty three years and I think I know a good Regiment when I see one and this is a very, very good Regiment indeed".

So spoke Lt Col Charles Birley a 17/21st Lancer. He had been appointed to the Royal Gloucestershire Hussars Yeomanry at the outbreak of war in 1939, it was his job to get it fully trained and equipped for whatever task it was called upon to fulfil. It took him a long time to realise the qualities of the men under his command. He could not understand the easy going, casual way in which they went about their work, he was afraid they would break down and disintegrate when put to the test. He didn't realise until he led them in their first action that this easy going manner disguised a mutual respect and comradeship that cut across rank and welded them together come what may. Intensely proud of 'His Regiment' he commented "nothing can touch them".

So what is the background to this Regiment of part time soldiers that Charles Birley took into action in the western desert in November 1941? They already had an impressive list of Battle Honours gained in the South African and the 1914 – 18 war.

There are records of the militia and 'Hunter Volunteers' going back to the reign of Charles II. But it is generally reckoned that in 1794, when as a result of the government being thoroughly alarmed at the militarist ambitions of the French, they felt that there should be some cohesion of the local militia and the various groups available to bear arms. Letters were sent to the Lords Lieutenant of counties proposing: -

"The raising of volunteer companies of gentlemen and yeomanry or such persons as they shall recommend, according to plans to be submitted and approved by the King or Lord Lieutenants of Counties, under authority from him. The officers to receive commissions from His Majesty, the muster rolls to be approved by the same, the members to find their own horses, and accoutrements to be given by the Crown; only to be exercised at times by the Royal Warrant of the Lord Lieutenant; only liable to be called out of the county or embodied by Royal Warrant of the Lord Lieutenant or by the High Sheriff of the county, for the suppression of riots or tumults within their own or adjacent counties; or by Royal Warrant in case of invasion, to receive pay as cavalry and to be subject to military law".

The first Gloucestershire troop was raised in Cheltenham in 1795 by Mr Powell Snell of Guiting Grange, Northleach. On Thursday 31st of December 1796 the Standard of the 1st troop of Gloucestershire Gentlemen and Yeomanry was consecrated at Cheltenham. The Troop being drawn up in open order, the band played "God Save the King", which ceased on the appearance of the Honourable Mrs Keppel, the sister of the Duchess of Gloucester, at a window in the Plough Hotel. In her hand she held the standard, which she presented to Captain Snell, saying:-

"Gentlemen I have the honour of presenting to you these Colours. I have no doubt you will ever stand by them in defence of your King, your Religion and the Constitution".

The Captain then handed the Standard to the Cornet with these words: -

"Cornet Mathews, receive this Standard into your safe custody, now presented to us by the Honourable Mrs Keppel".

Then turning to the window he said: -

"Accept Madam our united thanks for the great honour now conferred upon us, should there ever be a dreadful necessity for drawing the sword in defence of our beloved Sovereign, the just laws and civil liberties of this realm, we may feel ourselves inspired by redoubled zeal and ardour under this auspicious banner".

The Rev Mr Measham, the Vicar of Cheltenham then took the tassels of the Standard in his hand and pronounced a short benediction and address concluding with the words : -

"'Tis yours kind friends, to guard with tender care,
And shield from brutal insolence the Fair;
The brightest actions from these sources springs,
Truth, friendship, Love, our altars and our King".

The following year two more troops were raised one at Minchinhampton and the other at Wotton-under-Edge, closely followed by one at Henbury and one at Gloucester. These were independent units and it was not until 1830 that they were incorporated into one Regiment, although several of the troops had already found it beneficial to train together.

Instructions were sent to Yeomanry troops in the sea board counties that in the event of the French landing they were to round up all the cattle and sheep and drive them ten miles inland. Afterwards to re-assemble in places to act against the enemy as occasion may demand.

The danger to the country was a very real one, a French expedition some 15,000 strong set sail for Ireland in 1798 to assist the Irish in their war of independence. The invasion ended in a disaster reminiscent of the Spanish Armada, less than 1000 managed to land before severe storms scattered the French fleet and prevented them landing. Another French expedition landed 1200 men near Fishguard in Pembrokeshire. They were mainly French ex army deserters, who had been promised pardons if they could get the local population to join with them and foment insurrection against the Crown. Far from joining them the locals rose against them man and woman, together with the Castlemartin Yeomanry and Fishguard Fencibles they rounded them up. Many of the French having become incapably drunk from looting casks of wine and spirits salvaged from shipwrecks, which they found in some of the farmhouses. For this action the Pembrokeshire Yeomanry have the unique distinction of having been awarded the only battle honour that has been won on British soil.

To add to the government's troubles partly because of the brutal conditions under which ship's crews were expected to serve and partly in sympathy with the French revolution, the Channel Fleet mutinied at Spithead and trouble spread to the Northern Fleet and the Nore. With fears of invasion, panic spread throughout the country and there was a run on the banks by farmers and others for cash. This became so widespread that an order was issued authorising the Bank of England to refuse cash payments until Parliament gave further orders. The government had good cause for alarm.

The "Loyal Gloucestershire Gentlemen and Yeomanry", were kept very much on the alert and manned beacons on commanding heights, to be lit if invasion occurred. Then Admiral Nelson won a resounding victory at Trafalgar, the Peace of Amiens was signed and the danger receded. The House of Commons passed a vote of thanks to the Yeomanry and Volunteers for the services they had rendered and the following is an extract from a letter the commanding officer Lord Berkeley, received from the Speaker : -

"My Lord - by command of the House of Commons I have the honour of transmitting to you their unanimous Vote of Thanks to the several Volunteers and Yeomanry Corps of the United Kingdom, for the promptitude and zeal with which, at a crisis the most momentous to their country, they have associated for its defence --- in communicating this order I have the greatest satisfaction at the same time in bearing testimony to the confidence with which the House is impressed, that the same spirit and exemplary zeal will be exerted throughout the present contest, until with the blessing of Providence, it shall be brought to a glorious issue.

I have the honour to be my Lord, Your Lordship's most obedient servant,

Charles Abbot, Speaker".

The Government initially decided upon a reduction of the volunteer forces in the country but peace did not last very long the Yeomen were recalled and further troops were raised at Dursley, Cirencester, Stow, Bristol, Tortworth, Tewkesbury, Winterbourne, Grumbald's Ash, Bisley and Whitstone. (The different troops throughout the county frequently went through a name change, as did their formation and disbanding)

They maintained a state of readiness until Napoleon was defeated at Waterloo whereupon the country heaved a sigh of relief and orders were given for the various troops to be disbanded, with the exception of the Gloucester troop in case of civil riots. There was no proper police force until it was introduced by Robert Peel in 1830, prior to that the maintenance of law depended on a local Constable or Beadle appointed by the local Justices of the Peace. The Justices administered their district and county with little or no interference from central government, who had no knowledge of local conditions. In extreme circumstance the local militia were called out by the Lord Lieutenant.

In 1810 a "Desperate Affray" took place in Gloucester between a detachment of Irish Militia, en route to the Isle of Wight, and a body of townsmen and others. This led to a large assemblage in the streets by partisans of both parties. The magistrates and civil powers exerted their authority and Colonel Morgan aided by a detachment of Gloucester Yeomanry Cavalry was able to quell the tumult and take a number of persons into custody. The thanks of the magistrates were voted to the Yeomanry for their timely assistance.

In 1822 the Monmouth and Chepstow troops, which were then part of the Gloucestershire force, were called out to deal with a large party of colliers at Gellyhan colliery, who were preventing loads of coal being delivered to Tredegar. The troop cleared the ground with the flat of their sabres, they then escorted 55 wagons to their destination notwithstanding attempts being made by the rioters to break up the road.

The threat of civil disobedience - if not revolution - was still a possibility. An economic depression as a result of the Napoleonic wars had set in and reached crisis point by 1830, this was fuelled in the countryside by the introduction of threshing machines and consequent shedding of labour. Gloucestershire was not so severely affected as the neighbouring counties of Monmouth and Wiltshire, even so it was thought prudent to raise a troop of Yeomen and Mr William Codrington of Dodington Park raised the "Marshfield and Dodington Troop of Yeomanry". This was followed by the Fairford and Cirencester Troop, Stroudwater, Tetbury, Gloucester, Winterbourne and Alveston Troops.

The situation worsened when the Reform Bill which proposed the scrapping of rotten boroughs and the extending of voting rights was rejected by the House of Lords. Serious rioting broke out in cities and towns up and down the country and was especially severe in Bristol. Despite the riot act being read on three separate occasions the mob failed to disperse and attacked the Mansion House forcing the Mayor, magistrates and Sheriff to escape over the roof. This situation had been anticipated and a squadron from the 14th Light Dragoons and a troop of the 3rd Dragoon Guards had been despatched to the city and put under the command of Lt Col Brereton the district commander. Having sacked the Mansion House the mob moved on to the Guildhall and then stormed the city prisons and released the inmates. Fire broke out in several places; many of the rioters taking advantage of freely available liquor from the Mansion House became incapably drunk and perished in the flames. Despite pleas from the Mayor, magistrates and sheriff Lt Col Brereton refused to let his troops disperse the crowds, saying that their appearance would only make things worse. He followed this up by sending the 14th Light Dragoons out of the city to Keynsham and the city was left defenceless.

In desperation a message was sent to the Dodington troop of Yeomanry and later the Tetbury troop. Captain Codrington with his troop of 41 made all speed for the city and placed himself under the command of Lt Col Brereton. What passed between them is not known but it would seem that Brereton refused to accept their help, whereupon Captain Codrington wheeled his troop about and took them home.

By this time the city had been entirely given over to the mob, the Bishops Palace was sacked and any Aldermen, Councillors or Magistrates who put in an appearance had stones thrown at them.

Eventually Colonel Brereton agreed to recall the Dragoons from Keynsham and Major Beckwith their commander arrived with another detachment. After charges through the streets order was restored. Also assisting was Captain Estcourt with the Tetbury Troop of Yeomanry. It was on this occasion that the troop suffered what might possibly be its first casualty, when Quartermaster Playne was sent forward to reconnoitre the position. His horse was brought down by a wire stretched across the road, the horse was uninjured but Playne was rendered unconscious.

Order was eventually restored and the final outcome was that Lt Col Brereton was tried by court martial for incompetence. He pleaded guilty but committed suicide before sentence was passed.

Captain Codrington was indignant at the treatment he and his men received at the hands of the military authorities; the following are extracts from a letter he wrote to the Secretary of State for the Home Department:-

"My Lord - I have the honour to represent to your Lordship, that in consequence of a requisition from the Mayor of Bristol, between two and three o'clock yesterday, I collected my troop of Yeomanry with as little loss of time as practicable. When your Lordship considers that I had to send some miles in different directions, you will I think, admit the alacrity of my men when I state that we were enabled to march from Doddington with scarce a man missing by seven o'clock. Having however fifteen miles to go and the night being very dark, we could not reach Bristol till after nine, when I lament to say we found the city on fire in many places, the gaols emptied and the town in the greatest confusion. Having paraded through the principal parts of the city for more than two hours, without being able to find a magistrate; hearing that they had in fact left the town after withdrawing both His Majesty's troops and the police; finding ourselves unsupported I had no alternative but that of withdrawing my men and we returned home about five o'clock in the morning.

I feel it my duty to state that no men could have come forward with more alacrity, and although, though they may not have acted with the discipline of His Majesty's regular troops, they would not have been exceeded by them in zeal, loyalty or a determination to have done their duty; and had they had an opportunity, to have shown themselves not undeserving of His Majesty's approbation –

I have the honour to be, My Lord, your Lordship's most humble servant.

C.W. Codrington
Captain of the Dodington and Marshfield
Yeomanry Cavalry

Dodington, October 31st 1831".

A few days later Colonel Horner, who had been Commandant of the

Yeomanry Brigade in Bristol forwarded the following note he had received from the Mayor of Bristol to Lt Col Lord Edward Thynne, Captain Codrington and Captain Estcourt: -

Council House Bristol
November 6th 1831

"Sir - I am requested by the Magistrates of this city to convey to yourself, the Officers, Non Commissioned Officers and Privates of the Brigade of Yeomanry Cavalry under your command, their most grateful acknowledgements for the promptitude, alacrity and zeal manifested by them in repairing to this city and for their valuable and efficient services in aid of the civil power, in preserving the lives and property of the Citizens and restoring tranquillity".

Charles Pinney, Mayor.

At this time The Yeomanry force in the United Kingdom consisted of ninety four corps, or county Yeomanry, with an establishment of 19,047 all ranks. The largest of these was the Cheshire mustering 727; twenty three corps were over 300 in strength. There were two systems on which Yeomanry Corps were usually formed. The one was by being available for service throughout Great Britain and Northern Ireland, the other was to limit their service to the county or district in which they resided. In both cases arms were supplied and £9 per man was allowed for equipment, for which sum army contractors supplied uniforms, saddle, bridle, holsters etc.

Most troops followed the Doddington troop under Captain Christopher Codrington and signed up as follows:-

"We the undersigned have enrolled ourselves to serve His Majesty as a corps of light cavalry, to go to any part of Great Britain in case of actual invasion to preserve order; and to suppress at any time any rebellion or insurrection arising in any part of the county of Gloucester".

There then followed a long list of "do's and dont's", the gist of which was that members were liable to be fined if they failed to attend musters without proper excuse. This also applied to officers. Not that their duties were very onerous, namely that corps were to be called out for exercise at least two days every four months, or five consecutive days in the year.

For some time the officers of the various independent troops had been considering combining into one regiment. This met with everyone's approval and in 1834 the command was offered to the Marquis of

Worcester. (The Marquis of Worcester is the title of the eldest son of the Duke of Beaufort and through several generations one or the other assumed command of the Regiment).

The Hon James Dutton, afterwards the 3rd Lord Sherborne was appointed second in command and John Surman, Gent, late of the 10th Hussars, adjutant.

The Marquis of Worcester anxious to see service in the Peninsular War had in 1811, against his parents' wishes, travelled to Spain with three horses and presented himself at the Duke of Wellington's headquarters on his arrival in Lisbon. The Duke appointed him as his A.D.C. and he subsequently saw service with the 10th Hussars at the Battles of Busaco, Salamanca, Vittoria, Nivelle and the Pyrenees. Several of the officers enlisting had similar experiences.

The establishment was fixed at seven troops and consisted of one Colonel, one Lt Colonel, one Major, seven Captains, nine Lieutenants, seven Cornets and 382 N.C.O.s and privates. The Regiment to be known as: "The Gloucestershire Yeomanry Cavalry". The dress consisted of a scarlet double breasted tunic and blue trousers with red stripes, boots and spurs. The undress uniform a blue stable jacket, forage cap and white duck trousers, boots and spurs. At permanent duty each man received seven shillings a week.

Interestingly Yeomen were exempt from paying tolls for their horses at the turnpikes, provided they were wearing uniform. They were also exempt from the very heavy taxes on hair powder, with which every properly dressed yeoman improved his martial appearance.

On September 5th 1835 the newly formed Regiment marched into Clifton for eight days drill under the command of the Marquis of Worcester. The Regiment was inspected by Colonel Faunce who expressed himself amazed that a corps which had so little time for practice could have attained such a high level of efficiency. The horses were in good condition and the appointments remarkably clean.

On their way home, after they had been dismissed, the Gloucester and Stroud troops were entertained to a sumptuous dinner by Lord Segrave at Berkeley Castle. A contemporary account states: - "At about eight o'clock the officers began to think it time to depart and the trumpet having sounded six times at intervals, the troops were at last persuaded to proceed to their horses in the castle yard. After they had all been told off and no-one found to be missing, they marched off in single file to the gate; taking the stirrup cup at the door to the health of the hospitable nobleman who had given them so good an entertainment".

In 1838 the size of the Yeomanry force was reduced nationally with the exception of Gloucestershire. During the winter severe rioting broke out when a group of working class leaders published a "People's Charter". On Boxing Day the Dodington and Winterbourne troops were called out to assist the civil powers in Bristol. No doubt they were apprehensive that there might be a repetition of the riots in 1831. Even though a large meeting of Chartists was held on Brandon Hill it all passed off peacefully and the Duke of Beaufort who had headed his troops, took them home.

In 1840 Lord Segrave sent a circular round his tenants expressing the wish that they join the Yeomanry. Sufficient numbers responded for a squadron some ninety strong to be formed, which was placed under the command of the Hon Grantley Berkeley M.P. for West Gloucestershire. The name of the Stroudwater Troop was changed to the Badminton Troop and the title "Royal" was awarded. So the name of the Regiment became "The Royal Gloucestershire Regiment of Yeomanry Cavalry". Thus originated the colours of the necktie worn to this day in civilian attire, being broad stripes of the hunting colours of the Beaufort blue and the Berkeley Yellow, interspersed with a thin red line, to indicate they were ready to shed their blood if called upon to do so.

In 1846 the Duke of Beaufort issued an order requiring all members to grow moustaches, an order that was not very favourably received in some quarters and caused a great deal of leg pulling. Even though the order was ridiculed in the press and was the subject of a witty piece in Punch, the noble Duke stuck to his moustaches. No doubt this was a contributory factor in the report given by the inspecting officer Lord Rosslyn, who was much pleased with - "the good order of the appointments and soldier like appearance of the Regiment".

In 1847 a bitter quarrel broke out between Captain the Hon Grantley Berkeley and his brother Lord Fitzhardinge, which threatened the future of the whole of the Berkeley squadron. The Duke of Beaufort sent round peremptory instructions to his tenants, who belonged to the squadron, to resign without delay and his cousin Mr Grenville Berkeley was put up to stand against Grantley Berkeley in the coming Parliamentary election.

There was uproar throughout the county and letters appeared in the press about - "the monstrous tyranny both in a civil and military sense exercised by the Lord Lieutenant in coercing his tenantry to desert the Berkeley squadron.

I must send in my appointments with regret, there is a snake in the grass -- you will please accept my resignation as I must surrender my appointments, or I risk losing my tenancy", were typical of some of the letters of resignation received.

In the election tenants were forced to vote for Grenville Berkeley.

Lord Fitzhardinge who had previously paid his brother's not inconsiderable regimental mess bills and other expenses, now refused to do so. The Lord Lieutenant sent his agent Mr Ellis round the non commissioned officers, who were his tenants, requesting them to sign a paper saying that they wished to resign because Grantley Berkeley was unpopular. Sergeant Ellis acting as spokesman for the others said: "I would rather chop my right arm off than set my name to such a lie".

Most of those who feared losing their farms resigned, but not before they had found someone to fill their saddles and a full muster were on parade at the drills. An order from the Duke to Grantley Berkeley to pay up his arrears of mess bills and troop expenses and if he did not do so he was not to attend the muster of the Regiment failed; when a Mr Clayton offered to advance him some money. He was thus able to ride at the head of his squadron to the muster at Bristol, many of the local dignitaries riding alongside him to show support. Thornbury turned out to welcome the Berkeley squadron and along the road banners of welcome were hung out and he was considerably amused to see the Duke of Beaufort studying them.

When the parade was over Captain Berkeley dismissed his squadron and broke his sword over the pommel of his saddle and resigned his commission.

In 1852 the Regiment now named the Royal Gloucestershire Hussars received the resignation of the Duke of Beaufort in an acting capacity and the actual command was assumed by Lt Col Browne. The Cirencester troop was disbanded and a new one at Cheltenham was raised in its place.

Around this time a regimental horse fund was instituted, officers paying ten shillings or 50 pence per annum and other ranks three shillings or 15 pence. This was to remunerate any Yeoman whose horse was injured or died whilst on regimental duty.

In 1855 the Regiment provided a guard of honour for the body of Lord Raglan, the commander in chief before Sebastopol, who had died in the Crimea. The body was brought back to Bristol and escorted to Badminton. It lay in state in the Great Hall before being interred in the family vault.

In 1860 they adopted the Busbie headress in place of the chaco, which they had previously worn. The form of dress adopted was very similar to the present day full ceremonial dress.

In 1874 the Regiment was placed under the direct command of the War Office instead of the Lord Lieutenant. As the latter was the Duke of Beaufort, who was also the commanding officer, I suspect this made little difference. Except on one occasion when he had a blazing row with the

War Office and the command passed to Lord Fitzharding.

Commanding Officers in those days and other officers for that matter were very much a law unto themselves. On one famous occasion the Regiment was taking part in a brigade exercise on Salisbury Plain which lasted three days. Towards the end of the third day it became apparent that the success of the exercise, or its turning into a complete disaster very much depended on action taken by the Royal Gloucestershire Hussars. To General Roberts, who was commanding the exercise, it became apparent that the R.G.H. didn't intend doing very much at all, so he cantered over to the Duke who was C.O. and asked him what action he was going to take and got the reply: -

"What action am I going to take General, I'm going to get off me 'oss and have a piss", and so saying he did so.

National and domestic politics were relatively quiet during the latter half of the nineteenth century. Even so the Regiment maintained an average roll of some four hundred strong at the annual camps and drills. These were organised into four squadrons of two troops each, which in 1888 include one troop from Monmouth and in 1893 one from Chepstow, thus forming a separate squadron.

A succession of bad harvests in the 1880's caused a drop in the number of saddles filled. Times were difficult for farmers, many of them could not afford the expense or time incurred keeping a hunter and attending the requisite number of drills. This was no doubt responsible for the different troops either splitting or disbanding, the strength of the individual troop being very much dependent on local farming fortunes. The dates of training camps for permanent duty frequently had to be altered or cancelled altogether because of a late harvest. This happened in 1871, when the War Office anxious to test whether Yeomanry Regiments could be relied upon to muster in a hurry, also whether the expense of their maintenance was justified; arranged a fourteen day camp in the second week of September. Active preparations were made and everyone looked forward to attending. Unfortunately the harvest was abnormally late that year and as most of the Yeomen were farmers, attendance would have caused great hardship; so the camp had to be cancelled.

In 1861 the Duke of Beaufort offered two cups one for shooting with the new Westley - Richards breech loading carbine and the other for the muzzle loading carbine. At that time there were only twelve of the more modern carbines per troop. Tent pegging and splitting the Turk's head were some of the other competitions organised, also prizes for the best turned out horse and best kept accoutrements. Interestingly old county and farming family names still known and in many cases still active have

23.

Officers standing left to right Lieut Beresford Heywood, Major Mathews, Captain Calvert, Captain Miller, Major and Adjutant Wyndham Quinn, Surgeon Major Wickham. Lieut Taylor, Lieut Lindsay, Major Sir G. Codrington,
Seated:- Captain Barry, Lieut Sir P. van Notten Pole, Major Palairet, Captain Sandeman, Colonel the Marquis of Worcester, Lieut Col Henry, Major Lord Edward Somerset, Lieut Cardwell

N.C.O.s. The Key to the names of the above are given in Appendix "a" Many of their descendants are still active in Gloucestershire life.

been passed down through the successive generations. The Yeomanry was very much a part of the countryside, the officers were the sons of the landlords of the farmers, or their sons, on their estates. At one time there were four masters of foxhounds and one field master in the Regiment, a tradition still maintained in that it is unusual not to find at least one M.F.H. on the strength.

At times it must have been difficult to know whether they were out hunting or taking part in an exercise. The command "hold hard gentlemen", or "hold by" and "gone away", frequently being heard as was "the charge", when a fox was sighted. This was no doubt why the opening bars of "D'ye ken John Peel", was adopted and is used to this day as the Regimental call.

The Regiment had its full share of high spirited young officers who when on permanent duty were not averse to keeping late hours, often requiring a quick change of clothing for riding school in the morning. On one occasion they filled the early hours by painting the tail of a senior officer's Charger bright scarlet, prior to an inspection. It was kept covered until he was mounted, when it caused great amusement to his troop. Fortunately for those concerned the inspecting officer either didn't, or what was most unlikely, pretended not to see the decoration.

1895 being the centenary of the Regiment's founding an invitation was extended to the Prince of Wales. Unfortunately because of a previous engagement he was unable to attend. An outbreak of smallpox the following year meant that he had to postpone the review until 1897. The Regiment mustered at Cheltenham Racecourse where after being inspected, His Royal Highness rode at its head through the town and up the Promenade to the Queens Hotel, where luncheon was served. After lunch, and before leaving, the Prince presented Quartermaster Limbrick with a marble clock, which had been subscribed for by the officers. It was inscribed as follows: -

"Presented by Colonel the Marquis of Worcester
and Officers of the of the Regiment, to Quartermaster Isaac Limbrick,
Dodington Troop on the completion of his fiftieth training with the
Royal Gloucestershire Hussars.
May 1897".

Such devotion and length of service was not unusual.

Also on this occasion a very small boy who afterwards became Sergeant Fred Lewis, who served in the Royal Gloucestershire Hussars

1914 - 18 and was the author's father, got his first sight of the Regiment as it processed up the Cheltenham Promenade.

OOOOOOOOOOOOO

The two leading figures on the left are King Edward VII, (then Prince of Wales) and Colonel the Duke of Beaufort, with his hand raised, leading the Regiment up Cheltenham Promenade after their being reviewed at Prestbury Park on 13th May 1897. Following are General Luck C.B.; Lieutenant General Sir Forestier Walker K.C.B.; General Sir F. Grenfell; Major General Russell M.P. C.M.G. Viscount Valentia (Oxford Yeomanry) Colonel Southeron Estcourt (Wiltshire Yeomanry) and Lord Lonsdale (Westmoreland Yeomanry)

Chapter 2

South Africa.

Queen Victoria's Diamond Jubilee – Boer Settlers in Transvaal – Jameson Raid – Sir Redvers Buller – 1000 casualties – Field Marshall Roberts and General Kitchener – relieve Kimberley and Mafeking – call for volunteers – 3rd Company 1st Imperial Yeomanry, Captain Playne R.G.H. – Thabanchu – Ladybrand Brandwater Basin–Boer Guerilla tactics–60 day trek –Majuba Hill – Home.

In the closing years of the century the role of the army was very much taken up with ceremonial duties. In 1897 eighteen members of the R.G.H. were called upon, with other territorial regiments, to line the route between Whitehall and Buckingham Palace for Queen Victoria's diamond Jubilee celebrations. Two years later on November 15th 1899 the Regiment paraded in Bristol together with two other Yeomanry Regiments. The occasion was a visit by Queen Victoria, together with Princess Beatrice and Princess Christian, to open the Jubilee Convalescent Home. The Duke of Beaufort as A.D.C. to Her Majesty acted as Brigadier to the three Regiments and headed the procession.

Again on November 16th "A" squadron R.G.H provided an escort for Princess Beatrice when she visited Cheltenham to unveil a bust of Queen Victoria at the Ladies College.

Frank Fox in his "History of the Royal Gloucestershire Hussars Yeomanry, says: -

"A very magnificent appearance the regiment made on parade in those days and very proud they were of their splendid accoutrements, it is wholesome and sound that a regiment should take pride in the pomp of chivalry. Whatever we hold to be the original motive of fine uniform for soldiers - - - experience of warfare shows that a fine uniform helps courage, discipline and humanity in the soldier. The good soldier in peace and in war takes pride in a fine uniform as a symbol that he is devoted to the highest service of his country and that his devotion will not stop short at the sacrifice of his life".

All very well but it took another forty years for the army to learn that an efficient, fighting soldier wanted a uniform that was comfortable and blended into the background.

If the second half of the nineteenth century had been relatively peaceful, the first half of the twentieth century was to see the whole world torn apart by fearful conflicts, the like of which had never been seen before. Slaughter, destruction and cruelties on an unimaginable scale debunked fantasies anybody held on the glories of war. Weapons were developed that had the ability to wipe out whole cities, contaminate vast areas and affect the unborn for untold generations to come.

The opening shots of a century of conflict and half conflict were fired in South Africa in 1900. It wasn't apparent at the time but this was a limbering up for a life and death struggle that was to engulf Europe and eventually the world.

The South African war was a war that should not have happened, or it need not have been so bitter but for ambition coupled to bungling, stubborn diplomacy on both sides. The original Boer settlers anxious to develop the country had trekked north to The Republics of the Orange Free State and the Transvaal. The Cape Dutch by and large accepted the rule of the British but the further they got to the north the more tenuous that allegiance became. All would probably have been well but for the discovery of diamonds at Kimberley and more especially vast gold deposits in the Witwatersrand. This brought in crowds of "Outlanders", mainly British with their commercial interests. Johannesburg mushroomed into a big city, much to the alarm of the simple, God fearing, Boer farmer; who feared the influence of the forces of Mammon.

Although the British South Africa Company, as it was known, contributed by far and away the bulk of the country's economy, President Kruger and the Boers were determined to preserve the independence of the Orange Free State and Transvaal Republics from foreign domination. They allowed the outlanders no voting rights, even though they may have been domiciled in the country for some years. The South Africa Company was extending its influence into Rhodesia - now known as Zimbabwe to the north, and Bechuanaland - now known as Botswana - to the west. Cecil Rhodes the South African President had ideas of running a railway line from the Cape to Cairo entirely through British territory. To consolidate his position Rhodes made plans for an uprising of the British in Johannesburg to coincide with a raid to the south from Rhodesia. This was unfortunate timing because the Boers were coming round to the view that the outlanders could get the franchise, if they had been resident for five years.

Before the Johannesburg rising took place Dr Jameson, the governor of Rhodesia, jumped the gun and moved south into the Transvaal with 500 men. The Jameson raid as it became know was a disaster, the raiders were all captured and the raid immediately alienated the whole of the Dutch in South Africa. Then in 1897 Sir Alfred Milner was appointed High Commissioner for South Africa. A very capable administrator he unfortunately lacked the gift of diplomacy and was the last person with the ability to arrange a peaceful deal with the stubborn President Kruger.

Kruger believed, with considerable justification that the British wanted to rob the Boers of their freedom and deny them access to Durban and ports on the east coast. With an army of some 35,000 men armed with Mauser rifles and artillery pieces supplied by the Germans in German West Africa he crossed the border into Cape Colony. Before the British had time to send in reinforcements, Ladysmith, Kimberley and Mafeking were surrounded. Ladysmith fell but the other two managed to hang on for ten months until they were relieved.

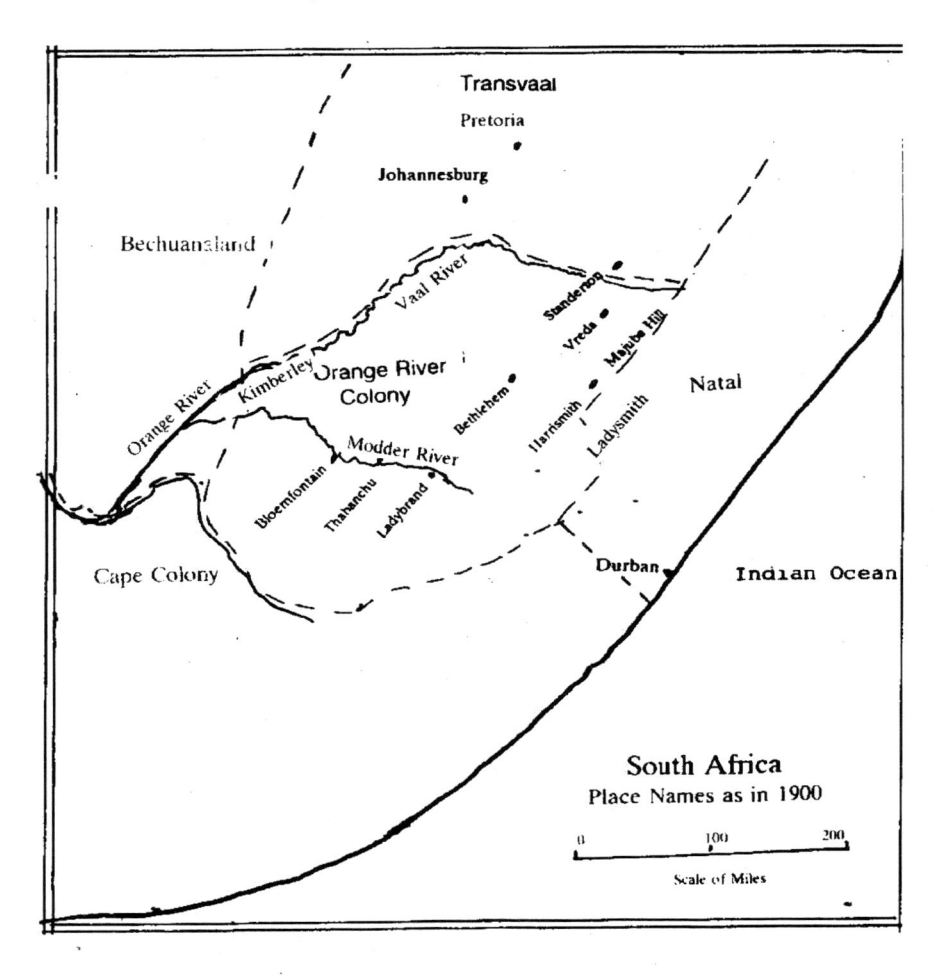

South Africa
Place Names as in 1900

An army corps was formed under General Sir Redvers Buller to hold the line and drive the Boers back. Winston Churchill, who was war correspondent for the Morning Post formed the opinion as soon as he arrived, that it was going to want very many more troops to subdue the Boers. His opinion of Buller was very briefly expressed: -

"Sir Redvers Buller said little and what he said was obscure. He was a man of considerable scale. He plodded from blunder to blunder and from one disaster to another, without losing either the regard of his country or the trust of his troops, to whose feeding as well as his own he paid serious attention".

These comments just about sum up the British military position; in the opening stages of the war. Utterly failing to appreciate the Boer tactics of unexpected quick cavalry strikes followed by withdrawal; Buller made the mistake of splitting his forces, one division was sent to relieve Kimberley, one was sent to Natal and one to the north east of Cape Colony. They were repulsed at Colenso, at the Modder River and at Stormberg in Cape Colony with over a thousand casualties. The nation was profoundly shocked at the scale of the defeat and demanded action against the Boers.

Field Marshall Lord Roberts of Kandahar, who had distinguished himself in the Afghan wars, was sent out as the new commander in chief, together with General Lord Kitchener who had won fame at Khartoum. Sergeant George Harris of the Cape Colony Police, who was convalescing from wounds, recorded that he was picked up by Kitchener to act as his guide. One of his first actions was to visit the Cape Town hotels and round up all the officers up to the rank of Major General, who had awarded themselves extended periods of leave. They were given the choice of taking the first train up country or returning home, where they would run the risk of facing court martial for desertion. This action electrified the British force and together with fresh newly arrived troops they made a two pronged advance on the Boer capitals of Bloemfontein and Pretoria. Repulsing the Boers, they relieved Kimberley and Mafeking; General French's cavalry taking 4,000 prisoners in an encircling movement.

In December 1899 the call went out for volunteers to serve in an "Imperial Yeomanry" force in South Africa. Members of the Royal Gloucestershire Hussars were amongst the first to volunteer, seventy members were medically examined and fifty six were eventually sent. Other volunteers came forward sufficient to make up a full squadron of one hundred and twenty five. A county committee under Earl Ducie the Lord Lieutenant was formed to equip them in the role of mounted infantry. Armed with Lee-Metford rifles, dressed in khaki with slouch hats they embarked on the transport "Cymric" on February 28th 1900. They formed the 3rd company of the 1st Battalion Imperial Yeomanry, which was made up of the 1st and 2nd Wiltshires and the 4th Glamorgan Company under Colonel R.G.W. Challoner. The R.G.H. contingent was under the command of Captain W.H. Playne. Other officers were Captain E.T. Hill, Captain C.G.M. Adam, Captain A.L. Graham Clarke and Lieutenant the Hon R.B. Robertson.

They reached Cape Town on March 19th and marched directly to Maitland camp. Some days were spent being issued with and organising their equipment, interestingly this included spare horse shoes and nails. The camp was very overcrowded with nine regiments where there was room for only three. Dysentery and enteric fever were rife. Colonel Challoner fell ill and was invalided home and Major Wyndham - Quin, late adjutant of the R.G.H. took command.

After a fortnight they were glad to get out of that disease ridden hole and travelling by rail and road they reached Bloemfontein on May 1st 1900. Here they were inspected by the Commander in Chief Lord Roberts - affectionately known as 'Little Bobs' - and ordered to join General Rundle's division which was pursuing the Boers in the direction of Ladybrand.

Leaving Bloemfontain they advanced some fifty miles to Thabanchu where on May 5th the squadron had their first encounter with the enemy and one trooper was wounded. They then advanced in pursuit of the Boers to Ladybrand which they found had been evacuated by the enemy. The R.G.H. were the first to enter the town and they found it to be a land of plenty, not having been previously occupied by British troops. Here Captain Adams was invalided home, Lieutenant Robertson was appointed quartermaster and Sergeant H.F. Clifford (afterwards Major Clifford, killed at Rafa in 1917) promoted to command No 4 troop.

They remained in Ladybrand for the next few weeks, daily expeditions being made into the surrounding country reconnoitring. The regiment left Ladybrand on June 7th doing patrol and convoy escort duties during which they had some warm skirmishes with the enemy. Rations became short then on June 13th they met up with the Grenadier Guards and discovered that their cook knew one of the Gloucester Troop, so they all had a good dinner that night.

Towards the end of July the greater part of the battalion, including the R.G.H. assisted in the operations in the Brandwater Basin. Captain Playne's troop were engaged in the south holding Commando's Nek, the remainder were engaged in holding a post at Hammonica. Sickness and short rations badly affected the troop and out of 28 men only 14 remained with 4 of the original English horses.

The Boer tactics reverted to guerrilla warfare, so the country was divided up into sections and the Boers - men, women and children swept up into huge concentration camps. General Kitchener and the Boer commander General Botha met and agreed the fighting could cease if the Boers were granted a general amnesty. Sir Alfred Milner and the British government refused to endorse the agreement and Kitchener had no alternative than to adopt a scorched earth policy. Blockhouses were erected across the country, it was impossible for anyone to move, but the Boer commandoes were able to find sympathetic refuge in the remote farmsteads.

Sergeant George Harris recorded many years later how they approached a big farm when about thirty rifle shots came from one of the farmhouses. They had a seven pounder attached to them and the order was given to turn about and take aim, but before they could fire a white flag appeared at the window and a bunch of women and children walked out. The officer galloped up to them and asked the women where the men were and got the answer, "gone to the hills to fight".

He then asked "where are the guns", there was no reply and so he ordered the house to be searched and under the floorboards discovered a dump of rifles and ammunition. It had been the women who had fired on the patrol. The arms and ammunition were loaded on to one wagon and the women and children on another. The matriarch of the house refusing to be loaded, showed fight with her arms flailing around and no-one was keen to get near her. The officer thought he might persuade her and walked up and gently took hold of her arm. She looked at him quietly, then suddenly swung her arm and knocked him flying and then she rushed at him while he lay flat on the ground. They had to rush in and haul her off. Still refusing to be pacified they tied her legs together and loaded her on to the wagon.

In August the 3rd (R.G.H.) company joined the 16th Brigade and marched to Elandsfontein, where they captured a large number of cattle. For the next month they operated between Harrismith and Bethlehem and on the Vaal River rounding up more of the enemy's cattle. On September 17th a troop of the company together with one of the Wiltshire companies located the enemy at Hartbeeste, they were engaged and Lieutenant Gifford (as spelt in Fox -- misprint?) was severely wounded.

On September 25th the 1st Battalion were in action again, Captain Playne's troop, escorting the guns, remained in touch with the enemy till the 28th. The whole of General Rundle's force, known as the "Starving

Eighth Division", marched on October 2nd to Tefal Kop and the 1st Battalion were successful in outflanking the enemy and surrounding Vreda and on October 7th they moved on to Standerton. The company then escorted a convoy to Vreda, with the R.G.H. squadron under Captain E.T. Hill in the lead. They were attacked by the Boers and Sergeant J. Reeve of Cheltenham was killed. For their work protecting the convoy General Campbell, who was in command of the 16th Brigade, reported very favourably on the work of the Yeomanry.

On October the 11th the 1st battalion pursued the enemy for eight miles and on the 14th the Boers were again pushed back. There were stiff fights at Vlakfontein and Teransfontein before they arrived in Harrismith on October 30th.

On December 3rd General Rundle began a sixty day trek with his whole force, by the time the operations were over there was only the strength of a squadron left out of the four who originally comprised the 1st Battalion. In February 1901 the Battalion of which the R.G.H. 3rd company formed the rearguard arrived in Standerton and on the 13th they entrained for Harrismith. The Boers blew up the railway line and the Yeomanry together with two companies of Grenadiers drove the Boers off towards Majuba Hill. After some more desultory fighting in May they mobilised for home, returning in July 1901, having been in service for eighteen months and being under fire sixty five times.

Reports in the Cheltenham Chronicle on September 6th 1902 stated that the balance of the 3rd company (Gloucestershire) of the 1st battalion Imperial Yeomanry returned to England on the S.S. Aurania on August 26th. We are glad to report that the great bulk of the men who went to the Gloucesters have returned safe and sound, it speaks well for the personnel of the company that no undesirable had to be expelled from it.

It goes on to make especial mention of Trooper F.H. Davis, son of Squadron Sergeant Major Davis of Newent. He was met at the station by his father and mother and driven home in a carriage and pair. When within a mile of Newent, the returning hero was met by a large and enthusiastic crowd which included members of the Ledbury Yeomanry. The horses were taken from the vehicle, ropes were attached and he was pulled round the town headed by the band. Behind the carriage were about twenty members of the Gloucester Squadron of the Yeomanry, which had been driven over with Regimental Quartermaster A. Perris, to take part in the rejoicings. After a parade round the town some 150 of the principal residents sat down to a dinner given by Squadron Sergeant Major Davis in honour of his son's safe return. Dr Marshall occupied the seat of honour with Trooper Davis on his right and the Rector of Newent Rev

Bentley on his left. Others present were Regimental Sergeant Major Allitt, Squadron Sergeant Major Robins, Regimental Quartermaster A. Perris and a good number of troopers of the Gloucestershire Yeomanry. At the conclusion of the meal toasts were drunk to the Army, Navy and Auxiliary Forces and responded to by the Rev Bentley and R.S.M. Allitt. The toast of the "hero of the day" met with a most enthusiastic reception, the company singing most heartily "For he is a jolly good fellow". Trooper Davis was presented with a silver cigarette case from the members of the Gloucester Squadron who attended the gathering.

On July 26th His Majesty the King on Horse Guards parade awarded the officers and men of the Yeomanry their medals, forty one officers and men R.G.H. being present. Squadron Sergeant Major W. Gregory being awarded the Distinguished Conduct Medal. N.C.O.'s of the 3rd company who wished to join the R.G.H. were told they could retain their rank and be held supernumery until they could be absorbed into the establishment.

Captain Playne remaining in South Africa doing mopping up operations had only five Gloucestershire men in his squadron. Guerrilla warfare continued for some time, herding the Boers into the concentration camps where conditions were appalling, many dying from disease. "Shep" Sheppard (R.G.H.) of whom we shall hear more later said he felt sorry for them. Starved and ragged they came into the camps, thoroughly worn out. It was not a very creditable episode in Imperial history. When it was all over the British government paid the Boers three million pounds in compensation. Cecil Rhodes was forced to resign as President of South Africa and died shortly after.

Welcome Home Parade for the Imperial Yeomanry Volunteers. The two officers in front are Colonel Calvert and Colonel the Duke of Beaufort

Chapter 3

The Calm Before the Storm

Anti British feeling in Germany – Yeomanry Force re-organised – Field Marshall Roberts inspects the Regiment– rifles issued – Winchcombe Camp – Coronation of King George Vth – Ultimatum to Germany – Mobilisation

The Yeomanry's creditable part in the South African War gave a fresh boost to the regiment and there was no difficulty filling the establishment's quota of saddles. News of German assistance to the Boers coupled to known anti British feeling in Germany, maybe sub-consciously brought about a realisation that the country may one day be engaged in a continental war.

In May 1900 the regiment 379 strong trained outside the Gloucestershire borders at Ross-on-Wye. Temporary stables were constructed of wood and canvas and the camp lasted for 21 days instead of the usual seven. Colonel the Duke of Beaufort A.D.C. commanded the brigade and Colonel Henry the R.G.H.

The following year the war office reorganised and increased what was to be recognised in future as "The Imperial Yeomanry". Each regiment was to be recruited up to 593 of all ranks, organised in four squadrons with a machine gun section. There would be 23 officers including a regimental adjutant and quartermaster. The force to be armed with Lee Enfield rifles and bayonets; instead of as previously with swords and carbines. At the request of the Duke of Beaufort they were allowed to retain their swords for ceremonial parades. The annual training to be for 18 days, all ranks to receive a £5 horse allowance and three shillings (15 pence) a day for musketry practices. Dress would be khaki but they were allowed to have Badminton blue facings on their tunics.

These changes did not find universal favour, their traditional uniform gone, their arms changed and their drill changed, they were fearful they were going to lose their cavalry status and become mounted infantry. They felt they were being downgraded and would lose the cavalry spirit. It was difficult as it was to find suitable recruits and they felt it a waste of material to turn young yeomen into infantrymen. The horse was their natural form of transport, their devil may care approach to fox hunting; point to point racing being their principal form of recreation, all combined to produce the 'daring dash' required in a cavalryman. These attributes were to be required in full measure in the years ahead.

These fears were to some extent allayed when Field Marshall Earl

Roberts attended a field exercise after which he took the salute at a march past and afterwards addressed the regiment. He praised what they had done in South Africa, coming at a time when mounted troops were urgently required. There was a great difference between cavalry that occasionally had to fight on foot and infantrymen who had to get on horses to move around. Yeomanry would often be called upon to take up a position, but that did not make them infantrymen. The only change being made in the drill was that they must occasionally be prepared to attack on foot.

He noticed they had all got rifles in place of carbines and he pointed out that these rifles could kill at 2000 yards; it would be folly for them to expose themselves at this distance and get knocked over. Before he left South Africa - all the cavalry, the Lancers, the Dragoon Guards and the Hussars had come to him and begged they be given rifles instead of carbines. He noticed that they carried swords but it would be better if they had a sword fixed to the rifle. He pointed out that in the type of country they had exercised in that day it would be impossible to carry out a shock cavalry charge with so many walls and hedges around. Despite his comments they still retained the sabre, which they were to use with great effect in the forthcoming conflict in Palestine.

In 1902 the Prince and Princess of Wales visited the Duke of Beaufort at Badminton and "B" squadron under Major Playne provided a guard of honour. At the conclusion of the visit they escorted the Royal party to Yate station. "D" squadron mounted the guard when they arrived in Bristol.

Also in the same year the letters "I.Y", for Imperial Yeomanry were incorporated in the cap badge. In 1903 the Badminton blue uniform was abolished, except for officers attending levees. New orders prescribed regulation service dress for officers and drab service dress with blue collars and shoulder straps with the letters R.G.H.I.Y. for the other ranks. The cuffs of the jacket were braided with a blue Austrian knot. They wore Bedford cord breeches, black boots, blue puttees and slouch hats turned up on the left side to show the bronze regimental badge. Officers' chargers wore a scarlet plume; later in 1906 the historic uniform was restored for ceremonial parades.

In 1904 the Duke of Beaufort resigned the command. He had served for forty years and had been colonel for seventeen. He was the third of his house to lead the regiment; all ranks were delighted when His Majesty the King appointed him honorary colonel. Lt Colonel H.H. Calvert was appointed to succeed and the second in command was Lt Colonel R.P. Sandeman.

The following year the Imperial Yeomanry Long Service and Good

Conduct medal was issued to N.C.O.s and men who had completed ten years service and in 1906 a memorial window in the Chapter House in Gloucester Cathedral was unveiled to the memory of all the Gloucestershire men who fell during the South African war.

The first decade of the century was a time of great social change. The suffragette movement occupied much of the government's time causing divisions in families. The trade union movement gathered strength, resulting in the election of Keir Hardie, the first Labour party member to enter Parliament. An increase in the army estimates did not find universal favour, which is a familiar theme in some quarters to the present day, otherwise little of note occurred.

Many of the men probably joined the Yeomanry out of a spirit of adventure, for comradeship, or because it was "the thing to do". The nobility and landed gentry wielded an influence difficult to comprehend in modern times and tenant farmers would most likely have been 'encouraged' to help make up a troop or a squadron. With holidays unknown amongst young farmers of that era, training days must have made a pleasant change. No doubt the annual camp, under canvas was eagerly looked forward to.

In 1906 the annual camp was held in Cirencester Park and the Regiment was inspected by the G.O.C. Southern Command; Lieutenant General Sir Ian Hamilton, who expressed his delight at the high level of efficiency they had attained. He went on to say that the efficiency displayed by the Imperial Yeomanry in his command, which included nearly half the yeomanry force in the United Kingdom, was a revelation to him. The General further commented that he was more than ever convinced that the country possessed in them a military force of great value. He was to find his opinion abundantly confirmed only a few years later, when he was Commander in Chief at Gallipoli.

Other extracts from the report forwarded by the Brigade Commander go on to say: -

"Of the 13 regiments of Imperial Yeomanry the Lt General C in C feels it is due to them for him to express his satisfaction at their high level of efficiency -- the officers belong to a class fond of energetic country pursuits, they are certainly above average -- the N.C.O.s and men ride boldly and well -- half of them own their horses which are of excellent quality -- nothing could be better than the physique of all ranks -- The Brigadier congratulates the 1st South Midlands Mounted Brigade on the satisfactory work performed - his only regret is he had no opportunity of leading such a fine body of men on active service".

An interesting insight into camp life is given by "Gleaner", writing in the Cheltenham Chronicle for May 1906: -

"After the inspection by Field Marshall Lord Roberts, which was made when the Field Marshall visited Gloucester, the Royal Gloucestershire Hussars Yeomanry will detrain in Cirencester to encamp in Lord Bathurst's fine and commodious Park.

Each year the camp regulations are made more stringent and the Yeomanry training is no longer the easy time it was in the palmy days of the Cheltenham billets. This year there will be a stiffening of the canteen rules in the direction that the troopers will not be served with any drinks between meals and that their beverages at all other open times are to be restricted to ale and stout and minerals. Punch will certainly be taboo and I mention this insidious concoction because I well remember many years ago that Earl Bathurst once entertained our battalion, after we had drilled in his Park, to dinner in the Corn Exchange. It was a blazing hot day and punch was the liquor or liquors served out".

With what result he does not enlighten us and we can only guess!

Two years later the camp was held at Winchcombe and the town went out of its way to welcome the Yeomen by erecting a decorated archway across the main street. The Cheltenham Chronicle has a picture of Bandmaster Hatton aged eighty, who was attending. He is shown sitting up straight as a ramrod, attending his sixtieth training with the Regiment. Also shown mounted on his horse is Farrier Quarter Master Sergeant Spreadbury attending his twenty fifth training. He had won the prize for the smartest turn-out three years in succession.

The late W.H. (Bill) Limbrick told of attending at Winchcombe. He had to go to Sergeant "Fishy" Williams' tent to help pack up at the end of the camp. Presumably the liquor regulations of two years previously had been breached because he found the sergeant cussing his batman for being "up the pole" when he was "up the pole" himself.

Somehow or other he got Williams organised and hoisted up on to his horse and they set off to entrain at Winchcombe station, the sergeant rolling around at the head of his troop. There used to be two lamp posts in the approach to the station and as he approached them he put his arm out and wrapped it round one of the posts, the horse went on and off he came. Some how or other they got the horse boxed and Fishy into a carriage, where he dropped off to sleep and only woke up when they got to Gloucester. So ended that year's camp!

In 1908 the Territorial Decoration was issued for officers completing twenty years service.

On June 22nd 1911 the coronation of their Majesties King George V and Queen Mary took place. The regiment was represented by one officer and 25 other ranks and camped in Kensington gardens for four days. They formed part of the 1st battalion of the Coronation Brigade, the whole of the Yeomanry representation being formed into two battalions. Review dress was worn with rifles and bandoliers. The first battalion extended down Piccadilly to White Horse Street.

The King and Queen visited Bristol Infirmary on June 22nd 1912 and "D" squadron escorted them throughout the visit. The King expressed approval at the military arrangements and especially mentioned the smart appearance of his escort.

The year 1914 up to the declaration of war found the government engaged in seemingly intractable problems. The suffragettes were still demanding the vote and going to extraordinary lengths to achieve their aim, Ireland was in a state of civil war, there was trade union unrest at home and Gloucestershire were having a rotten cricket season. In other words the country was going along in its normal humdrum way.

Life moved to set standards and looked like doing so for the rest of time. Then on June 28th this was suddenly all shattered by an assassin's shot, which killed a little known potentate at a place very few had ever heard of, but the effect was to reverberate around the world. The Crown Prince Franz Ferdinand of Austria had been shot at Sarajevo precipitating the First World War and nothing would ever be the same again.

Austria and Serbia had been at loggerheads for generations and Austria sent the Serbs an ultimatum that they must accept Austrian suzerainty, this the Serbs rejected. Europe was at a flashpoint, if Austria invaded Serbia the Russians would support Serbia, in which case Germany would come to Austria's aid following which France would support Russia.

By chance or design Winston Churchill the first Lord of the Admiralty dined with a group of industrialists, which included Albert Ballin a German shipowner. "What would England do if France and Germany marched", asked Ballin. Churchill replied that he couldn't speak for the government but he didn't think England would stand idly by.

During the next few very short weeks tensions throughout Europe rose rapidly, Britain was pledged to defend Belgian neutrality should Germany invade and on August 4th the Germans crossed the border. An ultimatum was sent that they must withdraw by midnight otherwise a state of war would exist between the two countries.

The Germans never responded and at 7 p.m. on August 4th 1914 the R.G.H. were ordered to mobilise.

39.

Bandmaster Hatton attending his sixtieth training

Farrier Sergeant Spreadbury, noted for the smartest turnout.

Winchcombe welcomes the R.G.H.

Members of the Winchcombe Troop

41.

The Horse Lines at Winchcombe May 1906

Horse Lines at Badminton

Ready for inspection by Field Marshall Lord Roberts

42.

Second and third from the left are Johnny Davis and Jack Burroughs, members of two well known Cheltenham farming families

Inspection by Lieutenant General Sir Ian Hamilton

R.S.M. Heather, Colonel Calvert, Captain Darell the adjutant

Chapter 4

On Guard

Volunteer training on Oxlease – Schliefen Plan – contemptible little army – Der Tag – 5th Mounted Brigade – Cromer – shoot hares and pheasants Zeppelin raid – entrain for embarkation at Avonmouth.

One of the first to report for duty on mobilisation was Sergeant Major George Turk, a Cheltenham saddler, who was seen fully equipped riding his horse to the barracks in Gloucester at 6 a.m. on August 5th. He was quickly followed by Sergeant Ben James a butcher, Sergeant Charles Lovell a fruiterer, Corporal George Hyatt a farmer from Sevenhampton. They came from all over the county to muster at their different squadron headquarters.

The regular army was pitifully small, the disastrous adventure in the Crimea, the relief of Khartoum, the Afghan and South African Wars; these had all happened a long way away. The last time the country had been threatened had been the Napoleonic wars culminating in Waterloo a century ago. For many years the country relied on a strong navy for its defence. When war was declared the call went out for volunteers, such was the rousing of patriotic feeling and demand for adventure that there was no difficulty filling the ranks.

Eddie Tippett, an estate agent, visited his farmer friend Fred Lewis and Rex Horton saying, "Come on you two this war will be over before we get a chance to get into it, if we don't sign on soon".

Together with Hugh Walwin, Harry Colburn, Hugh Lefaux, Frank Hopkins, Bert Troughton they left their farms and business's and joined their other farmer friends in the Royal Gloucestershire Hussars. As with other battalions being formed up and down the country, they made sure of getting in with a good crowd of their own kind, before being drafted into some regiment where they knew no one. "Shep" Sheppard, a typical "old sweat" veteran of the South African War was one of the first to greet the new recruits, becoming their friend and mentor ever afterwards.

In this spirit, they and other young farmers and friends up and down the country hastened to sign up. Wherever possible they tried to stay together so as well as the Yeomanry regiments which were countryside based, there were the "pals" battalions, friends with similar interests and from the same location sticking together. A peculiar national characteristic of the British is that they are generally peaceful and slow to rouse. Their enemies tend to write them off as being decadent and having no will to fight. Too late they realise their mistake, when roused nothing will stop them and so it was in 1914.

It took a few weeks for them to start training after volunteering. Hugh Walwin along with many others was ordered to report to the Gloucester Barracks at midday on August 31st for enlistment. He was informed that he would be billeted at home or at such a place as he was directed, until he was issued with his uniform. It took some time for a sufficient number of uniforms to be made available and for the first few weeks they paraded in civilian clothing. Time was spent drilling on the Oxlease and attending lectures in musketry, elementary tactics, horse handling and all aspects of warfare.

When the uniforms did arrive they were in three sizes, small, medium and large and most people managed to get kitted out. Caps were a bit of a problem. Walter Whitting paraded in a trilby for some time because he couldn't get a hat to fit. Andy Andrews learned what an officer's order meant when the Colonel said, "Andrews put your hat on straight" and got the reply, "can't sir I've got a funny shaped head".

Such was the response and such was the demand for manpower that in September 1914 a second regiment R.G.H., destined for France, was formed under Lt Col R.P. Sandeman. Later on a third regiment, which was little more than a cadre, was formed under the command of Lt Col H.H. Calvert. But it is with the 1/1st R.G.H. under Lt Col W.H. Playne that this narrative is chiefly concerned.

In England nobody could have conceived for a moment that a Germany that was prospering and developing both at home and abroad could possibly risk it all by going to war. In its insular situation the country refused to believe that the catastrophe of a world war threatened civilisation. But German militarism was deeply engrained into the German character. Their attitude seemed to be that war was good and wholesome for a powerful nation; it would somehow make that nation stronger.

Germany reckoned on England keeping out of a continental conflict, in fact that had been this country's policy, not to get involved in a struggle that didn't really concern us. The Entente Cordiale had been signed with our traditional continental enemy France in 1904, but this was more a declaration of friendship, after generations of being at loggerheads. It was certainly not a military alliance or intended as such.

Germany reckoned on being able to defeat France in a few short weeks and to do so they got their old "Schliefen Plan" out, dusted it down and put it into effect. This plan was the strategy used during the Franco Prussian wars and entailed by passing the fortresses of Metz and Verdun, sweeping down through Luxembourg and Belgium into northern France.

This they did in 1871, surrounding Paris and inflicting a humiliating defeat on the French. Crossing the border in 1914 they misjudged the Belgians ability to resist and never expected that England would come to her aid.

In this country the only five divisions available to make up a British Expeditionary Force were immediately sent to France, under the command of General Sir John French. Such was the derision in which England was held by the Germans that the German Kaiser Wilhelm said that they would soon defeat Sir John French and his "contemptible little army", they would be no match for the German military machine; how wrong he was. Together with the French and Belgians, slowly retreating but never breaking, the contemptible little army managed to hold the line until reinforcements arrived. In after years to be an "Old Contemptible" was to be part of an honoured brotherhood, those who survived had a little badge which they used to proudly wear in their lapels.

With the regular army engaged in France the territorials were given the job of defending Britain from invasion, a not unlikely occurrence. The German aim was to invade this country, when they had defeated the French. At the bottoms of their hearts they believed England, with her Imperial ambitions, was the real enemy; they didn't expect us to intervene in the war and accused us of treachery for doing so! It had upset their calculations and made them quickly realise that victory over France was not going to be quite so easy. For years they had been drinking to "Der Tag" in messes and wardrooms, toasting "The Day" when they marched against England, turning it into a "Reichsland". This would involve destroying large sections of the population so that German citizens could be settled in their place.

There had been a slow awakening to the danger ever since the South African war. British shipyards had been working flat out for the previous ten years building a mighty navy and the Germans had been doing the same, trying to keep pace. So much so, that a tentative approach had been made to Germany, without success, to get an agreement to hold back on this race.

The R.G.H. assembled with the Warwick and Worcester Yeomanry at Warwick on August 12th, thus forming the 1st South Midland Mounted Brigade. They moved from Warwick to Bury St Edmunds and were kept alert by false alarms of enemy landings. At the end of August they moved to Newbury racecourse and became part of the 2nd Mounted Division.

After rumours that they were destined for France the R.G.H. were sent to the east coast around Cromer and Overstrand. Fred Lewis writing in an undated letter sent from:- "A". Squadron R.G.H., Overstrand Hotel, Overstrand, Norfolk - tells of how they arrived at their destination.

"We were informed that we had to pack our things at once and be ready to move at 11.30 p.m. Then the bustle and hurry started and guesses were made as to where we were going, the general idea was that we were going to Southampton to embark for France --- at last the saddles were packed and the kit bags loaded on the transport wagon. Bread and ham was served out at 9 p.m. and the order to saddle up was given at 11 p.m. We moved off at 11.30 and rode to Newbury, where the horses were boxed and we were packed into carriages.

We left Newbury at 2.30 a.m. and I went to sleep soon after we started and slept until we got to Hitchin, slept again and woke up at Peterborough. We got to Sheringham about 11.30 a.m. where any amount of tea and buns were given to us by some ladies. We marched on to a common just outside the town where we had some corned beef and bread. We stayed on the common till 3 p.m. and then we had the order to saddle up and move off to Weybourne, where we arrived about 5.30 p.m. and then we had to find our stables, groom and feed our horses and make them comfortable before we had anything.

We had some dog biscuits and ham and after feeding we fell down on some straw in a barn, curled ourselves up in our greatcoats and went to sleep. I slept soundly till 6.30 a.m. After breakfast we exercised our horses down by the sea, it woke us up and made us feel fresh and fit again. After dinner we collected our kit and were told to find beds in the village. We had just found a very clean looking place and found three beds between five of us when the alarm was sounded and we were told to pack up and move at once to some place the other side of Cromer. The vision of a night in a real bed faded away in seconds and we did not feel in the best of moods. We left Weybourne at 3.30 p.m. and got to Overstrand about 7 p.m. and had to find fresh stables and billets. Our stables are the best we have ever seen. They are right on the edge of the cliff and were built by a naturalised German, Sir Edgar Spiers (the twopenny tube chap) who had to clear out in a hurry when war broke out. After doing the horses we came to this place, where we are sleeping and eating. It is a huge place right on the edge of the cliff".

They remained in this area for twelve months guarding against invasion. Walter Whitting, fed up with the boredom and fed up with the everlasting bugle calls filled the bugler's bugle with sand. When he went to blow reveille nothing happened, he blew in vain and to get another breath sucked in. The resulting language expressing the perpetrator's parentage was very educational!

"Shep" Sheppard recalled how he was out exercising the horses with his troop when they came across a troop of "Sharpshooters" a name given to the County of London Yeomanry. The Londoners were obviously unused to horses and were strung out in extended line preparing to jump a hedge. On the command "charge" they all went at it and he said you never saw such a shambles, only two of the troop managing to stop on.

On another occasion they advanced on foot across open countryside with five rounds each, firing at targets which suddenly appeared ahead of them. As luck would have it the country was alive with hares and pheasants. At the end of the "drive" not a single round had hit the target but the cook had a most welcome addition to the day's rations.

They dug trenches along the cliff tops and much to the amusement of the locals found that they disappeared into the sea, due to coastal erosion. They stood guard on the top of Cromer lighthouse and perishing cold it was said Fred Lewis. What we were supposed to see when there was no moon I don't know because it was as black as your hat. In a letter home he wrote that; "the latest thing to keep us fit is a pack of beagles, which meets three times a week".

As the year drew to its close it became apparent that the allies were not going to be the pushover that the Germans had expected. Both sides brought in more troops, they dug in, the mighty fortress of Verdun held and there were fearful casualties on both sides.

On the east coast they held exercises and mounted guard on the cliff tops, they got their first sight of the enemy when a very noisy German Zeppelin passed overhead and generally they prepared for they knew not what. Some of these exercises would seem to have been carried out with an eye to the necessities of life, when they came across a pub they would take a break to refresh themselves. One is bound to wonder what sort of discipline was kept, when after one such visit they got a mile down the road and had to turn back when they discovered that George Turk had left his rifle leaning up against the bar.

They continued doing coastal patrol duties until Fred Lewis in a letter home dated 7th March 1915 says: -

"I don't think there is much doubt about us going abroad soon, we are all going to be served out with hammocks and two sets of drill. The horses' rations from next Thursday are going to consist of 3 lbs of corn, 3 lbs of linseed cake and 6 lbs of bran - I have got four pairs of boots, I don't know what I am going to do with them - I don't know when we embark I am going on the same boat as the horses so I shall have some work to do going out".

The following day orders were received to entrain at Huntstanton for Avonmouth. Passing through Gloucester and Cheltenham, they only had a few brief moments to embrace their friends and families on the platform.

A contemporary account in the Cheltenham paper told of a ten minute stop for the Yeomen to stretch their legs, especially mentioning Squadron Sergeant Major George Turk, Quartermaster S. Shenton and Owen Anthony amongst others. Also that the 129 horses and 14 mules looked quite at home in open cattle trucks.

They thought they were destined for France, but with Turkey entering the war the Middle East was to be their destination and battlefield.

Recruits on the Oxlease and in Barrack Square.
Bob Eaton marked with a X in lower picture

49.

Recruits billeted at the "Bell Hotel"
From Left – Unknown, R.Eaton, A.Byard, Will Boddington, unknown
Owen Anthony, Blofeld

From the left: – unknown, Eddie Tippet, unknown, Rex Horton, unknown
Fred Lewis, unknown seated in front.

50.

Somewhere in England. Sgt Ben James seated middle of front row.
Fred Lewis without a cap third from left in back row.

Filling sacks with straw for bedding.

Chapter 5

Destination Egypt

R.G.H. arrive in Alexandria – provide guards – Gallipoli Casualties – Chatby Camp Escort for the Sultan – native troops strike –Goeben and Breslau – bombard Odessa – Turks mine the Dardanelles – The Fleet assaults the Dardanelles – landing at Helles and Anzac.

The R.G.H. 27 officers, 510 other ranks, 485 horses and 70 mules with Lt Col W.H. Playne in command embarked at Avonmouth on the transports Minneapolis and Saturnia on April 10th 1915. The destination was Malta, on the way they passed the Wayfarer which had been torpedoed and was carrying the horses of the Warwickshire Yeomanry. They were not allowed to stop for fear that an enemy submarine could still be lurking about. They reached Malta on April 21st and were ordered to proceed to Alexandria, which they reached on the 24th and where they disembarked.

Trooper Fred Lewis in a letter home has this to say: -
"At last we have arrived but I am not allowed to say where we are, we arrived at seven in the morning and disembarked about one. We then had to march out to the camp, we had marched about two miles on the flagged roads and under a hot sun when the officer in charge halted us and let us board tram cars for the rest of the way – the other fellows who came with the horses gave us a cheer as we marched into camp – the food is very good in fact I think the best we have had since I joined --the natives bring us boiled eggs for breakfast, 4 for 2d".

The regiment had arrived at Chatby camp near Alexandria in a severe sandstorm, many of the men went down with jaundice and high temperatures, which was felt to be due to an infection picked up in billets in England. They arrived at camp without having lost a single horse or mule on the journey. This showed good horsemanship and was a credit to those officers and men who had had to cover for their comrades overcome by seasickness.

The duties of the R.G.H. whilst at Chatby were chiefly providing guards at various headquarters and camps round Alexandria.

Fred Lewis writes: -
"I have been on guard at a prisoners' camp, they are all civilians, Germans, Austrians or Turks. They have a very good time playing tennis,

bowls and all sorts of other games the food they get is provided by a wealthy Austrian, it is much better than some of the other guards -- some of the officers are buying polo ponies so it looks as though we shall be here some time -- I have heard we have to perform garrison duties -- we know about as much as we did when we landed as to what they are going to do with us".

The Cheltenham Troop at Chatby Camp

He is obviously talking about Gallipoli because he goes on to say: -
"A lot of wounded have been coming in this week, they have got fifty two hospitals in this town alone and they have got between eighteen and twenty thousand wounded on their hands. There is a great lack of attendants, doctors and nurses and I am afraid some of them have rather a rough time. Some of them have told us that from the time they are wounded and have the field dressing put on they are not touched till they get to hospital here. They all say that the worst is over, I tell you that when the casualty figures are published they will open the eyes of the people at home -- -- the Wayfarer arrived yesterday They say that nearly all the horses were saved but fifteen fellows were lost".

Men and horses to the strength of a squadron under the command of Major R.M. Yorke were called upon to provide a mounted escort for the Sultan of Egypt and Fred Lewis has something to say about that: -
"The Sultan arrives here next Saturday and about twenty of our squadron (the tall ones) have been chosen to go and ride behind the old

buffers carriage, they are having a great 'do' in the town, expect we shall be doing guard or mess orderly so we will be out of it – – we get a breeze all day but the things that worry us are the dust and flies – – we had the first mounted drill since we arrived last Monday, (letter dated May 20th), we started off in the morning about half past eight and rode six or seven miles out into the desert, we took our rations with us and by the time we halted we were ready for them – – I shall be on guard tomorrow over prisoners in the compound. We are on for twenty four hours and each do eight hour shifts – – it seems to me that all we came out here for is to do guards, I will be doing guards over the cows and pigs when I come home – – we turned out the other morning at four o'clock to go and round up the native troops who had gone on strike and had escaped. It appears that they were going up the Dardanelles trenching and all sorts of engineering jobs but when they saw some of the wounded coming in they were frightened and struck. They armed themselves with crowbars and picks and tent poles and anything they could lay their hands on. They all kept together and we got them into a square and surrounded them. When they saw we were too many they threw down their "arms". We then marched them on to the ship and they sailed the next day for the Dardanelles. Fourteen of our fellows have gone with them to keep guard. I very nearly went, should very much have liked to go".

Trooper Bob Eaton tells of his time in Alexandria: -
"A few of our fellows who cannot stand the heat, I believe are being sent back to England – – it does not look as though we will be in the fighting line for a while as they have sent all the cavalry back from the Dardanelles and there as many as 40,000 horses and mules lying idle, so that does not look as though we will be going for a while – – our officers seem to be having too good a time here to want to leave, as most of them have bought a couple of racing ponies and we have a meeting here every Saturday, besides playing polo four afternoons a week, tennis, golf etc.
Our horses stood the voyage wonderfully well – – they only get a couple of hours exercise before breakfast every morning and a bathe in the sea, as we are right on the sea front".

Many thousands of words and many books have been written about Gallipoli the next few paragraphs summarise the tactical position and the part that the R.G.H. played in the campaign.
There was some doubt until the outbreak of the war with Germany, which side of the fence the Turks would come down on or whether they would remain neutral. A British Naval mission under Admiral Limpus was

advising the Turk navy and the Germans had a military mission training the Turk army. Both belligerents would have preferred they remain neutral, with possibly a preference on the German side that they would come in with them. Intense diplomatic activity took place in Constantinople. After the allies declared war they learned the Turks had signed a secret Treaty with Germany the day before war was declared.

The Ottoman Empire at that time covered what is now Iraq, Palestine or Israel, Arabia and part of Sinai. The revolutionary government known as the "Young Turks" came into power on a wave of popularity when they deposed the Sultan some five years previously; since when after adventures and defeats in the Balkans the empire was rapidly disintegrating. Morale was low, the country was bankrupt and they were in no fit state to fight a war. Enver Pasha, the Prime Minister and leader was a revolutionary who believed in achieving his aims by violent means and his government's honeymoon period was over. He believed that coming in on the side of Germany would strengthen his position, for the Germans it meant that their sphere of influence was extended from the Baltic to the Persian Gulf.

The Turks had ordered two battleships in British yards; to pay for them collecting boxes had been placed on the bridges over the Golden Horn and in all the little country villages. They were a source of great national pride, they had been paid for and Turkish crews were on the way to Britain to collect them. The British government with Turkey's future aims not to be trusted could not allow these two modern ships to pass into what could be unfriendly hands in a vital area. Winston Churchill the First Lord of the Admiralty gave orders for them to be commandeered. The howls of wrath from Constantinople can be imagined.

By chance or more probably by design the Goeben and the Breslau, two German battleships were in the Mediterranean and the German ambassador von Wangenheim immediately offered them to the Turks. They had been shadowed for some time by the British Mediterranean Fleet and could easily have been sunk but Admiral Carden, the Commander in Chief, had strict instructions not to open fire until the ultimatum to Germany expired at midnight. Although a close eye was kept on them they managed to escape by changing direction and putting on full speed in the hours of darkness. They arrived at the entrance to the Dardanelles on August 3rd 1914. Enver knew that letting them pass through the straits would be construed as an act of war and after some hesitation he eventually said, "let them come in".

The Germans and Turks straightaway set about mining the Dardanelles and strengthening the shore batteries. As an international waterway vital to Russian trade, this was a belligerent act. Russian grain ships had no alternative other than to return to Odessa in the Black Sea. The Goeben and the Breslau anchored in the Golden Horn were got ready for war. Turkey not yet being a belligerent, the German officers went through the charade of running up the Star and Crescent and dressing up as Turks. Admiral Limpus and the British Naval mission were withdrawn. The Mediterranean Fleet patrolled the entrance to the Dardanelles with orders to sink any Turkish boat coming out. The facade of peace continued until October 29th 1914 when the Goeben and the Breslau, accompanied by a Turkish squadron, steamed into the Black Sea and opened fire on the port of Odessa doing considerable damage. At the same time a Turkish force started crossing the Sinai, aiming for the Suez Canal.

The possibility of the fleet forcing the Dardanelles had been a staff study for some time, the generally accepted view being that warships could not compete with shore batteries. In this case it was felt that the risk was worth the prize by possibly sacrificing a few old battleships that were due to be scrapped, but whose guns were still in good working order. After overcoming a good deal of opposition by some sections of the government, it was felt to be a risk worth taking. The thinking behind it being that if part of the most powerful fleet in the world appeared off Constantinople it would cause the Turkish government to fall. It would then be replaced by a government more in sympathy with the allied cause.

A preliminary bombardment at the mouth of the Dardanelles took place on February 19th 1915 and engaged two of the Turkish Forts; the others appeared to be deserted. To be effective it was felt that the ships would have to get in closer, a storm then blew up and went on for five days and the attack was not resumed until a week later when the Turk guns at the mouth of the straits were silenced and the Turks withdrew. Parties of marines went ashore during the next few days, coming and going unhindered. There is one unsubstantiated rumour of a marine having his hair cut by a Turkish barber in the village of Krithia, which so much blood was shed trying and failing to reach in subsequent attempts.

The next attempt was made on March 18th 1915 when the combined British and French Fleets entered the Dardanelles. All day the roar of the guns pounding the forts at the Narrows reverberated along the length of the waterway. Admiral de Roebeck, who had succeeded Admiral Carden in the command of the British Fleet, broke off the action in the late afternoon, after two battleships had been sunk and others damaged by mines. Commodore Keyes, his chief of staff, entered the Dardanelles under the cover of darkness to attempt to tow out H.M.S. Ocean, which had been damaged but not sunk. He later recorded that he had the distinct feeling that he was in the presence of a beaten enemy and they would only have to resume the offensive the following morning and they would be through. Some fifty years later the author spoke to survivors of the bombardment and they said they thought heaven had dropped into hell that day. Despite Keyes passionate demands to continue the attack next day, de Roebeck who expected to be relieved of his command for the losses incurred, refused to continue the offensive. Having over the past month made our intentions obvious it was decided that a land assault on the Gallipoli peninsula to achieve command of the waterway would have to be made.

In high letters on the cliffs of the Narrows is written "March 18 1915", this being the date the mighty British Fleet, the most powerful naval force the world had ever seen, was defeated.

The first two landings, one at Cape Helles and one half way up the peninsula in a place ever afterwards known as Anzac cove took place on April 25th. After a bloodbath lasting ten weeks it resulted in stalemate.

In the meanwhile the R.G.H. remained in Egypt and extracts from Fred Lewis's letters read as follows: -

'An officer told one of our fellows that we should not be wanted before the Narrows were forced, I hope they buck up and get on with it, we are getting sick of doing guards -- -- the horses are looking better but I am afraid we shall find some of them touched in the wind -- -- our troop leader (Cripps) told me that 40,000 of Kitchener's army were on the way to the Dardanelles, the 7th Gloucesters landed here today -- -- twenty fellows from the regiment are going to Lemnos next week, what they are going to do I don't know, six are going out of our squadron".

He was evidently picked to go to Lemnos, which was the advanced base for Gallipoli. Their job was to help bring the wounded off and all too often they had to slip some poor soul, who had died, over the side because on the 9th August 1915 he writes: -

"During our time on the boat Hicks-Beach went ashore and when he came back he told us that we would be going up the Dardanelles as infantry. When we got back to camp after having helped unload the wounded we heard that we had to be ready to go on the 4th, which gave us

(In 1925 when Keyes had become a full admiral and Commander in Chief Mediterranean, he took the Fleet through the Dardanelles into the Sea of Marmara. A companion with him on the bridge recorded that Keyes could hardly speak; at last he burst out: - "it would have been even easier than I thought, but because we didn't try the war went on another three years and cost a million more lives.")

two days to get ready -- -- the Brigadier made a speech to the whole of the brigade after stables on Friday. He told us the reason we did not go was that at the last minute more infantry had been sent out from England and he personally thought it was best we wait a little longer and go as cavalry, we are all fed up".

Visiting Gallipoli in 1967 Fred Lewis looks out from the heights of Anzac to his old battlefield. The R.G.H. landed in the curve of the bay seen in the far distance and advanced across the Salt Lake to Chocolate Hill, which is the low eminence on the extreme right.

Left behind in Egypt

Chapter 6

Gallipoli

R.G.H. 2 squadrons dismounted embark for Suvla – Salt Lake – attack Chocolate Hill – wounded loaded in floating stable – heavy losses – evacuation.

On August 11th unexpected orders came for the yeomanry to proceed to Gallipoli dismounted, each regiment to leave a rear party of four officers and 100 other ranks and all its horses in Egypt. Infantry web equipment was served out to all ranks. The new equipment was unfamiliar and they looked a peculiar sight when they were paraded.

They evidently didn't believe in informing the troops what was going on because in a letter dated 12th August Fred Lewis says: -

"We have been equipped with infantry kit and have left Alexandria. As the orders stand we leave tomorrow but where we are going we don't know and I don't suppose we shall know until we get there. Several of the officers think we shall be back again in a couple of months for the horses -- -- I hardly think they will send us up the Dardanelles as we have had no infantry training -- -- we have had a lot of rumours as to what is happening in the Dardanelles and the general opinion seems to be that the worst is over in that quarter".

On 14th August they embarked on the troopships Haverford and Ascania, the regiment being organised as follows: -
Lt Col W.H. Playne in command
Major H.C. Elwes second in command
Captain and Adjutant J. Godman
"A" Squadron Major A.J. Palmer, 5 officers and 160 other ranks.
"B" Squadron Major R.M. Yorke, 5 officers and 160 other ranks.

They were indeed destined for Suvla Bay on the Gallipoli peninsula to take part in the most appalling muddle of bad planning, no planning, lack of information, no instructions, orders, counter orders and orders altered again that ever was. The initial landing had taken place during the night of August 6/7th and had been largely unopposed. If the R.G.H. didn't know where they were bound neither did a Brigadier General Hill, who had been incarcerated with his Brigade in transports for a month. He woke up on the morning of 7th August and was put down on the beach not having the first idea where he was or what he was supposed to do.

In all some 20,000 troops landed in the first wave under the command of Lt General Stopford, of whom the kindest thing that can be said is that he was too old and miles out of his depth. One of his divisional commanders had a nervous breakdown and the other walked off in a huff; after being asked to waive his seniority when an experienced officer, who was his junior, was appointed to overall command. They were opposed by only 1,500 Turks, for three days they fiddled around by which time Turk reinforcements had arrived.

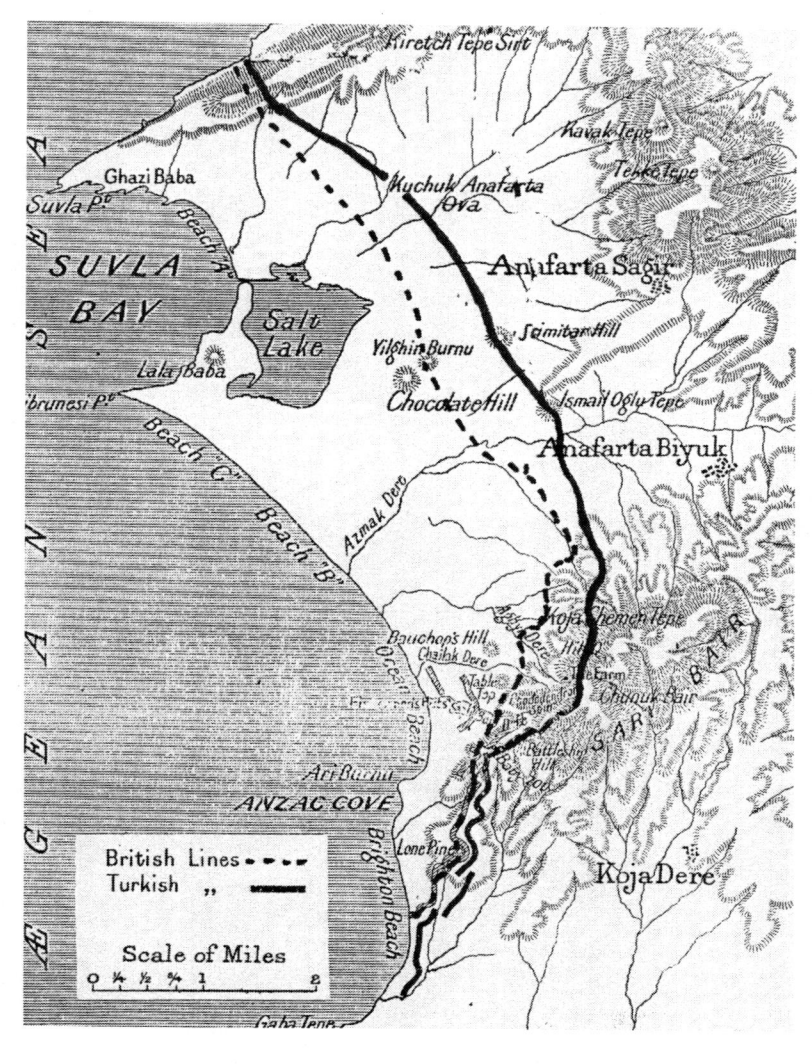

Gallipoli, the Anzac and Suvla beachheads

Suvla is a crescent shaped bay fringed with sand dunes behind which is a large Salt Lake, which tends to dry out in summer. Looked at from the sea the left hand arm of the bay runs back in a ridge to the Tekke Tepe hills on the far side of the lake about two and a half miles away. On the right is a hillock called Lala Baba and from there lowish ground to the right leads to the Anzac position on the Sari Bair hills, the idea being that they would link up with the Anzacs to form one front. The obvious thing to do was to get to the hills and get dug in, but they left it too late and the Turks pushed them back to a line that roughly followed the landward side of the Salt Lake.

The R.G.H. landed on "A" beach at midnight on August 17th. About 2,500 all ranks of Yeomanry left the Transport Ascania and were cheered by the crew. In response an officer sounded "gone away" on his hunting horn. They were to take part in a final effort to reach the hills.

On August 21st the yeomanry division, in support of the 29th division, advanced across the Salt Lake to Chocolate Hill on the far side of the lake. There was no cover and the regiment came under heavy shell fire. As they waited to move off Shep Sheppard commented:- "we ought to be watching county cricket on Cheltenham College ground instead of doing this", while Fred Lewis recalled that his troop officer Viscount Quenington, chose to get into an argument with him about milk marketing. "There we were", said Lewis, "likely to be blown to blazes any moment and we couldn't think of anything better to do than argue about milk".

They reached Chocolate Hill which was held by the 29th Division. With the Worcesters in the front line and the R.G.H. in support they advanced on Green Hill, after a brief pause to get their breath back. Coming under heavy machine gun fire they retired to Chocolate Hill, where they remained until ordered to withdraw to Lala Baba. In the advance one officer was killed, Lt Col Playne and three officers were wounded, 11 other ranks were killed and 44 were wounded.

General Sir Ian Hamilton watched the advance across Salt Lake from his command ship and his despatch reads:-

"The advance of these English Yeomen was a sight calculated to send a thrill of pride through anyone with a drop of English blood in their veins. Such superb martial spectacles are rare in modern war. Ordinarily it should be possible to bring up reserves under some sort of cover from shrapnel fire. Here for a mile and a half, there was nothing to conceal a mouse, much less some of the most stalwart soldiers England has ever sent from her shores. Despite the critical events on other parts of the field I could hardly take my glasses from the yeomen; they moved like men marching on parade. Here and there a shell took toll of a cluster; there they lay. There was no straggling; the others moved steadily on; not a man was there who hung back or hurried".

The author repeated the line of the advance when he visited the battlefield in 1967 in company with some of the veterans of the campaign. Superb martial spectacle it may have been, but one is bound to ask what strategist thought up the idea of ordering them across that open space in broad daylight; no smoke, no cover whatsoever.

Sergeant E.V. Godrich of the Worcester Yeomanry had some very critical comments to make: -
"The 2nd Mounted Division seemed to have got rather out of hand. It seemed to us that the officers had gone into action without any clear orders. The 2nd Brigade (Buckingham, Berkshire and Dorset Yeomanry) attacked Scimitar Hill, which they carried, but found themselves enfiladed from both sides and had to withdraw; losing about two thirds of their strength. One spectacle we saw was of men who had marched two miles under heavy fire, jumping over trenches in which the infantry were sitting and then carrying on with the attack. Everything seemed disjointed; it appears that the Divisional Generals did not carry out General Hamilton's orders. We of the Yeomanry Division happened to be the attackers that day and caught it in the neck. It occurred to us that if the infantry had co-operated with us we might have pushed the Turks right back and in all probability broken through to the high ground commanding the Dardanelles. After floundering around between the British and Turkish trenches all night we were withdrawn and sent all the way back to the sea-shore, from which we had started".

Of course battles always do appear to be a muddle to the participants. Private Potts of the Berkshire Yeomanry, who won a V.C. that day for bringing in a wounded comrade, although wounded himself, confirms Godrich's comments and the lack of co-ordination in the attack. He tells of how his friend Reginald West was hit crossing the flank of Chocolate Hill, he happened to fall on the edge of a dugout occupied by a member of the Gloucester Yeomanry, who said "roll in here mate". This he did and found himself in the company of the R.G.H., who had been ordered to fix bayonets and stand fast. Then Frank Fox tells how Major Palmer, with "A" squadron, advanced to what he thought was a Turkish trench and found it was occupied by the 29th division, he then had some difficulty locating the rest of the regiment.

Also watching the course of the attack was the surgeon on H.M.S. Euryalus and he commented: -

"Towards evening the Yeomanry - dismounted - advanced across the wide expanse of the Salt Lake in close formation to make a last desperate attempt to capture Scimitar Hill. Before they deployed the enemy high explosive and shrapnel found them and - as if on parade they opened out in a slow and dignified manner wonderful to see. Our Syrian interpreter, deeply moved, turned to me as we watched them and said, "I know the armies of Bulgaria, Serbia, Greece, Turkey; nearly all my life I have seen them fighting but I have never seen men of such fine physique as these nor with such bravery under fire".

He goes on to say, "As dusk fell we saw smoke clouds rising from the scrub covered plains and watched stretcher parties searching underneath them for wounded. The flames of the burning scrub stretched for a mile or more and those of our wounded, who could not be rescued perished where they lay". Next day he had to find room for a thousand wounded on three Fleet minesweepers. With an insufficient number of stretchers there was no alternative other than to lay them out on the deck.

Trooper Walter Weston was one of the wounded and he had this to say: -
"I was hit crossing Salt Lake and was put aboard a little tramp steamer that had brought a cargo of mules over. It was a floating stable and there had not been time to clean it out. We set off for Alexandria about 1000 miles away, at a speed of eight knots and had not gone very far before a U boat surfaced and fired a shot across our bows. The officer in charge of the boarding party - seeing our pitiable condition - said they would not sink us and would allow us to proceed, but we must stick to the course he gave us. There must be no deviation otherwise we would be sunk. Food was short and the only sustenance we and the crew were given during the voyage was half a cupfull of Bovril twice a day. My wound was dressed before I was put on the boat and not touched till we got to Alexandria. The doctor who boarded the boat when we docked would not let anyone, wounded or crew do any work, otherwise the exertion would kill us".

Fred Lewis in a letter home described the advance: -
"I expect you will have heard all sorts of rumours and tales concerning R.G.H. and that we lost rather a lot of men in our first action. I can't say

why but can say we had to cross an open piece of ground about two miles wide in full view of the enemy and in broad daylight. When we got about half way across we were shelled by the Turkish guns, we had to sprint for the shelter of the hills we were making for. When we got to the hill we rested for about fifteen minutes and then advanced over the top, the bullets flew past all the time. The fellow next to me went over and I thought he was shot, but he had got his entrenching tool between his legs and was alright. We got into a trench about two hundred yards from the Turks (rear slope of Green Hill) and had the order to fix bayonets. We did not go on any further but retired in the morning to the hill we reached in the afternoon. I am writing this in a dugout in the side of the hill, that I have tried to make as comfortable as possible, it is about four feet wide and about six long. We cook our own food and manage to get plenty of food and drink. We don't get a lot to do and are here in case we should be needed -- it was raining when we woke up this morning, the first we have seen since we left England -- two hostile aeroplanes paid us a visit last night but they were soon driven off by our guns, it was very interesting to see the shells bursting close to the machine. You might send me some more malted milk tablets".

When writing home Lewis probably didn't want to paint too grim a picture of trench life, Sgt Godrich writing some years afterwards tells a very different story: -

"About 6 p.m. we paraded and trekked off into the trenches. This was our first taste of taking up positions in the front line, up and down, tumbling over the legs of sleeping men, kicking over cans of tea that had taken hours to boil. I thought we were going miles but in reality we only went about a mile and a half.

Our first glimpse of trench life was not at all encouraging; imagine a narrow ditch with sandbags on the side facing the enemy, with a dirty, unshaven, hungry looking man about every three yards. Little holes in the sides of the trench with a dirty tin over a small fire; where some poor devil was trying to make a drink of tea. The only occupation: sleeping, eating, making tea and standing up as your turn came to look 'over the top' and watch the enemy. War is a glorious pastime in books when you have the whole strategy explained but to the poor beggars doing it there is nothing but misery. One is just a unit, your job is just to do your turn on the parapet then get down and sleep, if you are lucky. Then you have to start digging or go for a mile or two under fire to fetch, water, rations or ammunition.

The first night we were naturally very jumpy, every time the wind rattled the leaves of the bushes we imagined a Turk attack. Every now and then a rifle would go off, probably a sentry to keep himself awake or to scare the enemy who might be out wiring. Although dead tired we slept with one eye open and the following morning we were able to see our situation better, which is always a satisfaction. The worst job was fetching water, a journey of half a mile to an old Turkish well. The Turks had this place well spotted, they knew it of course, there was always a crowd waiting and they concentrated their fire on it".

Entries from an officer's diary read: -
"Worst job fetching water all of which comes from Alexandria by ship – – we live entirely on bully and biscuit and lime juice – – haven't had my boots off for four days, flies very bad – – Chocolate Hill, we lost several men – – trench very smelly, four dead Turks found buried in a corner – one man lost his sham teeth and had to go to hospital because he can't bite the biscuit, its just like dog biscuit – – ground garnished with dead thistles and dead men – – cuts fester – – poisoning from the swarms of flies – – Horlicks malted milk is the proper diet – – the brigade is now only 250 men, we started with 960".

On September 4th the regiment took over a section of support trenches from the Munster Fusiliers. Casualties were such that the division was reorganised into two brigades, the R.G.H. under Major H.C. Elwes was put into the 1st regiment under Lt Col Wight-Boycott together with the Warwicks and Worcesters. A fortnight later Lt Col Wight-Boycott took over the brigade, Major Elwes took over the 1st regiment and Captain Charles Turner the R.G.H. Casualties from wounds were serious but more so the inroads from sickness - mainly dysentery. On September 29th the strength of the regiment was 169 and of these 10 were "no duty" and 20 "light duty".

Sergeant E.V. Godrich of the Worcester Yeomanry wrote of men going down like flies with dysentery and jaundice. He himself was soon to succumb to enteric fever, but before that he was court martialed for being asleep when on guard; as he explains in the following:-

"Life was uneventful, except for my court martial, which aroused much interest throughout the Brigade. I'm afraid my position as prisoner charged with "Sleeping on Guard" looks very black when regarded from a comfortable chair in England. I can only say that given the same set of circumstances and the same dead tired comrades, I would again tell them to sleep and would again stand up and a hundred to one would fall asleep again. Let a man who has been through the Hell of the trenches judge me and I know what his verdict will be.

My trial took place in a dugout with officers from our own Brigade to try me. Major Hugh Cheape was President, Colonel Coventry was good to me and gave me a good character, which carried a lot of weight. I was reduced to Private and felt that I had the court's sympathy".

He was lucky the penalty for being asleep when on sentry duty was death. His son Dr J.E. Godrich, who carried out much work on enteric fever, says that it was the onset of this which led to the depressed state, which made it impossible for him to keep awake. In the end Godrich wrote: -

"I had a horrible attack of typhoid, I fought against it for five days and never left my dugout, but had to give in -- -- feeling more dead than alive I was helped by a friend to walk the two and a half miles to the hospital ship, after going before a doctor who stuck a label on me. I went on board a barge with about twenty others, who like me were unable to stand and we were towed out to the hospital ship, which was lying about half a mile from the beach. The first thing I did was to go below and get into a warm bath. I stripped and pushed all my clothes through the port-hole -- -- after six weeks in those filthy trenches everyone was covered in vermin. An orderly gave me some pyjamas and I was soon between some beautiful white sheets, which seemed to me to be heaven".

Fred Lewis continuing his story goes on to say: -
"Last night we moved back from the front line to the rest trenches and very glad we are to get somewhere where we can have a good sleep -- -- you can't imagine what its like to be dragged out every two hours to do an hour's guard, that's what we have been doing the last fortnight and we are sick of it -- -- a lot of fellows have gone to hospital suffering from jaundice and dysentery -- -- there are only three of us left in the Cheltenham troop -- we hear all sorts of rumours about being sent back for the horses -- -- I had a bathe yesterday, had to walk four miles but it was worth the trouble -- -- we have had a very lazy time the last two weeks, its about half past two in the afternoon and everything is quiet except for the report of a gun now and again -- -- two of our aeroplanes have just gone up and are making for the Turkish lines, the Turks open fire on them but never hit them, in fact the Turkish shooting is very poor".

The regiment remained in the reserve trenches assisting in evacuating batches of men to the Field Ambulance. On October 8th it marched to the A 63 (sic) front line trench to relieve the 3rd County of London Yeomanry. Heavy losses continued to be incurred from wounds and sickness and it became impossible for the 1st regiment to hold their section of the firing line. The support on one night was represented by one batman and one cook. On October 17th the effective strength of the first regiment was only 95 of which 4 were "no duty" and 23 "light duty". On October 20th the regiment was relieved and marched to the Salt Lake reserve trenches.

Fred Lewis wrote home: -
"We are resting in the reserve trenches and in a few days we are going right away from this place, it will be a treat to be out of hearing of the guns after having the sound of them in our ears for about ten weeks -- they have started a canteen on the beach".

They were indeed leaving on the first stage of their journey back to Alexandria and they were much cheered to receive the following message: -

"The G.O.C. 2nd Mounted Division wishes to convey to all ranks his very great appreciation of the soldier like qualities and fortitude which have been so markedly evinced during the last two months. In the face of heavy losses sustained in the action of August 21st followed by exposure for ten days in a cramped and crowded situation the division has been called upon whilst continually under fire and suffering from the ravages of sickness to carry out abnormal physical and manual exertions. The time has now arrived that the troops should be withdrawn and rested and the G.O.C. feels sure that when the regiments are re-organised they will return with the same indomitable determination".

On October 31st the regiment embarked for Lemnos leaving behind 2nd Lieutenant the Hon E.J.B. Herbert and ten men of the machine gun section, who were attached to the Scottish Brigade. The regiment as it embarked for Lemnos consisted of: -

Lt Col H.C. Elwes, commanding the 1st regiment
Major A.J. Palmer, commanding R.G.H.
Capt M.G. Lloyd-Baker
Lieutenant Viscount Quenington
Lieutenant M.A. Sands
2nd Lieutenant A.G. Wykeham-Musgrave
Lieutenant G.N. Horlick

Capt A.E. Bullock R.A.M.C.
Major S.W. Adderley Brigade Quartermaster
    Machine Gun section   1
    "A" Squadron N.C.O.'s and men 29
    "B" Squadron N.C.O.'s and men 40
        Detached 1st regiment   11
               Total   81

    Gallipoli was one of those chances that occur but rarely, which if it had been successful could well have altered the course of world history. It could have succeeded had fate not put an exceptionally able Turk officer by the name of Mustpha Kemal in overall command of the Suvla/Anzac front. He had an immediate grasp of the strategical situation and was responsible for our defeat.
    He later became President of the Turkish Republic and modernised the state, there is a statue to his memory in Istanbul. When I visited the city with some Gallipoli veterans, Lance Mann ex R.G.H. commented, "there's the bloke who beat us at Gallipoli". To which someone replied, "very ably assisted by our general staff".

Photo by Frank Barker
The Second Mounted Division bivouacked at "A" beach, Suvla

The Salt Lake, Chocolate Hill is in the centre of the picture.

Front line trench on Chocolate Hill

Trenches on Chocolate Hill

Green Hill Cemetery, the resting place of seventeen Gloucestershire Yeomen

70.

Fred Lewis and Lance Mann take up their old position on Chocolate Hill!
Below a typical headstone in Green Hill Cemetery

Chapter 7

At the Pyramids

Lord Kitchener visits the Dardanelles – R.G.H. embark for Lemnos and Alexandria – bathe in sea.– 2nd Lieut Prettyjohn and Rev Wilcox – Regiment move to Salhia.–.Officers entertained by Sheikh – move horses by rail – Kantara

In the first instance the R.G.H. were evacuated to the island of Lemnos, the advanced base some twenty five miles from the peninsula. In a letter from there dated November 12th 1915, Fred Lewis wrote: -

"We get all sorts of rumours here as to how things are going, but what is really happening we don't know – – it looks like lasting a long time yet. We heard today that we were going to return to the flies and dust of Egypt. A very important person was here the other day having a look round, so you may expect to hear of something doing if "he" gets going".

The important person was the Secretary of State for war, Lord Kitchener. He came out to assess the situation on Gallipoli, which was a complete stalemate. After inspecting the three beach heads at Cape Helles, Anzac and Suvla, he recommended withdrawal.

The next letter was written on the troopship Themistocles and he goes on to say: -

"This is a tophole boat, we are supposed to get to Alex some time tomorrow and then I suppose we shall get straight on the train and go to Cairo. All our horses and kit have already gone – – one of the first things I shall do is have a good hot bath somewhere and then a good square meal. We have got nothing to do on this boat except read, sleep and eat – – the regiment that is returning to Egypt is very different from the one that left it, very bad to think of one's pals killed, wounded or ruined in health – – about sixty of the 3rd regiment joined us at Lemnos, they are a lot of kids goodness only knows how they got into the army". (What he failed to realise was that the Gallipoli experience had quickly aged them all, snapshots taken before and after vividly show aging).

He continues three days later: -

"We are back amongst the dust of Egypt again. We got into the train on the docks at Alex and came straight to Cairo. We got on to trams just outside the station and had a ride of about seven miles to Mena camp, close by the pyramids. We had our first ride this morning it did us all good to get on a horse again. It will take a week or two to get the horses pulled together for they look a bit rough".

In another letter Lewis wrote:-

"We get all sorts of rumours that we are going up the Suez, personally I am quite satisfied with our present place. It is quite a camp, over 10,000 horses for a start; it is like a town and a very busy one at that -- -- I was on guard last night, what a change from guards in the trenches where one was straining every nerve to catch the sound of any unusual movement the other side of the parapet".

George Hyett recalled that on one occasion they were travelling by train which halted momentarily on the sea front; within less time than it takes to tell everybody had left the train stark naked and dived into the sea. The engine driver blew his whistle for all he was worth but the Yeomen were not going to be done out of their impromptu bathe!

The regiment was welcomed back by the rear party, who did everything they could to help them recover. The men who had returned from Gallipoli were suffering in health and were generally worn out from the hardships they had experienced so the additional strength was very welcome. Drafts of recruits began to arrive and they had to be welcomed and assimilated into the regiment. One of the new recruits sent out was 2nd Lieutenant R.B. Prettejohn. Also sent out to join the regiment was the new chaplain Rev Wilcox and Prettejohn was told to escort him to the regiment. This was a most unfortunate choice of escort because Prettejohn, in his own words, 'loathed the sight of parsons'.

As he told it to the author, in somewhat sanguinary language, -

"I got this fellow on a horse, all in his black, he obviously wasn't used to being mounted and the horse was acting up, so I brought my riding crop up and gave him a good smack across the arse. Wilcox and horse disappeared into the blue in a cloud of dust and Prettejohn thought, thank God that's the last I shall see of you. I loathed parsons".

Wilcox eventually got to the regiment and as things often turn out he and Prettejohn became the best of friends. Wilcox finished up as chaplain to the Guards Brigade in Wellington Barracks and after the war Prettejohn farmed at Staverton near Cheltenham, becoming a near neighbour of the author's.

The next few weeks were spent equipping again as cavalry. Care and exercise of the horses, the fitting of saddlery and other equipment heavily taxed the resources of the man power available. The sunshine and equable Egyptian winter climate soon got them fit again. For relaxation they climbed the pyramids and had their photographs taken mounted on camels in front of the Sphinx. Wooden huts had been erected and these were first used for their dinner on Christmas day, very welcome the huts were, providing shelter from the heat of the sun.

On December 11th Lieutenant the Hon E.J.B. Herbert and 8 other ranks of the machine gun section rejoined from Suvla. Having been left behind to help cover the withdrawal they had experienced the terrible blizzards in November, when the trenches were flooded and turned into raging torrents so that British and Turks alike huddled in what shelter they could out in the open. They were both too taken up in fighting the elements and generally surviving, than being interested in trying to take advantage of each other.

Early in January 1916 the regiment moved by train to Salhia on the banks of the Suez canal, midway between Ismailia and Port Said. The Arab tribes in the vicinity were friendly and sociable and the chief of the Hanadi tribe, Mohamed Sarudi Tahowi was prompt in calling to pay his respects to the regiment. On January 13th Lt Col Elwes the C.O., Major Palmer, Major Clifford and Lieutenant Viscount Quenington, accompanied by an escort of eight men, the Trumpet Major and Mohamed Said the mess caterer to interpret, returned the call. The arrival of the party at the chief's village was announced by the Trumpet Major; blowing the regimental and cook house calls. The sheikh received them most cordially and introduced them to a large number of his male relatives who were present. He had a splendid collection of hawks, which were paraded with their attendants and at a later date several of the regiment were invited to take part in a hawking expedition on the desert near their camp. An inspection was also made of his Arab stud horses, mares and greyhounds. They also admired a huge Shamiana tent used on state occasions and filled with innumerable carpets and tapestry made by the women of the tribe.

The chief entertained the party to tea, served in several small china pots, home baked bread, desert honey and milk. When leaving the party was escorted on its way by one of the sheikh's relatives mounted on a splendid Arab equipped with full trappings of state.

Cpl Fred Lewis's arrival at the camp did not go so well: -
"We have moved from Cairo to a place about twenty miles from the Suez, it is a very out of the way place but much more healthy than Cairo. It rains about once a year in Egypt and of course it rained the day we moved. When we got to the station we found they had not ordered enough trucks so some of the men and horses had to return about nine miles to camp. We got back to camp about seven in the morning whacked to the wide. We had some breakfast and then groomed the horses and had about two

hours sleep. We moved off for the station again about seven in the evening and got some of the horses boxed by eleven. I got my horse on the train then went to sleep and didn't wake up until we got to the end of the journey around seven in the morning. A seat in a 3rd class Egyptian railway carriage is not the most comfortable seat to sleep on – – the camp is pitched among some palm trees".

Extracts from other letters written about that time: -
"We have been inspected by the General commanding the 6th Army Corps so I suppose we shall soon be moving – – I won't be sorry it gets a bit monotonous – – an Egyptian Camel Corps have been camping close to our camp, they are a sight worth seeing, row upon row of camels lying down in perfectly straight lines, they say another six thousand are coming this week – – we moved from Salhia last Thursday morning and arrived here in the evening a journey of 23 miles across the desert – – we had our first bathe in the Suez and it was grand, the canal is about 250 yards wide, four of us started to cross it and I was the first to reach the other side, I think I can claim to be the first Gloucestershire Yeoman to get across – – I have finished packing up my kit ready to move off tomorrow for some unknown place on the coast, ten of us are going but I don't know what we are going to do".

At the end of January the strength of the regiment was 20 officers, 350 other ranks, 397 horses and 36 mules.
The regiment trained hard at Salhia in cavalry and patrol duties; on March 9th they marched to Kantara where they were inspected by the Prince of Wales and General Sir Archibald Murray, who had recently taken over the command of the Egyptian Expeditionary Force. Lt Col R.M. Yorke took over the command of the R.G.H. when Lt Col Elwes left for England to take command of a regiment bound for France.

With France demanding priority in manpower all available troops in the Middle East had been sent to Gallipoli. Likewise the Turks were primarily engaged with the Russians in the Caucasus. The other British priority in the meanwhile was to safeguard the Suez Canal, so that the oil supplies from the Persian Gulf, by which the Fleet was powered, were not jeopardised. Because of the barren nature of the Sinai Peninsula, which we will discuss later, a staff study concluded that the Turks would not be able to reach the canal with a force much in excess of 3,000. A conclusion that completely ignored the past history of the area. The Turks for their part were confining their activities to nuisance raids, with the aim of sowing mines in the waterway.

With release of the troops from Gallipoli General Murray concluded that the best way to protect the canal was to push his front forward to Katia, about twenty five miles east of the Suez canal, then on to El Arish. Katia lay at the westward end of a line of oases running east to Bir el Abd. They all had a fairly reliable supply of brackish water and could not be by-passed by a force advancing on the canal. The War Cabinet were doubtful about extending as far as El Arish but had no hesitation about the occupation of Katia. General Murray accordingly started the construction of a railway line out from Kantara towards Katia.

Above, the Suez Canal. Below an impromptu bathe.

Chapter 8

Katia

Turks misjudge Egyptian support – Indian division occupies Basra – Sinai Desert Turks occupy El Arish and advance on canal – British force established at El Arish and Katia – Royal Engineers and Worcesters to Oghratina – "A" squadron R.G.H. to Katia – enemy attack – wounded well treated – 9 R.G.H. get away R.G.H. lose "A" squadron – Worcesters muster 53 after battle

When the Turks advanced on the Suez Canal they expected the Khedive, who was pro Turk and owed suzerainty to Turkey, to persuade the Egyptians to rise up in their support. The British had effectively been governing Egypt for the previous thirty years. The Egyptians recognising that their best interests lay with keeping the status - quo, took advantage of the Khedive being in Constantinople and deposed him; electing his pro British Uncle in his place. The Turks certainly misjudged the support they might get.

When the rising failed to materialise, aided and abetted by the Germans, who saw the advantages of blocking the canal and denying us the use of the oilfields in the Persian Gulf, they began preparations to bring artillery across the Sinai desert and mount a full scale attack blocking the canal. They also planned to cut the Sweetwater Canal at Ismailia this would effectively deny drinking water to Port Said, Port Suez, Kantara and the villages in between.

The British had hoped that by the fleet forcing the Dardanelles and bombarding Constantinople, Turkey would quickly sue for peace. When the Gallipoli campaign failed, there was no alternative to defending the canal and the oilfields, other than to fight their way across Sinai up through the Holy Land and beyond.

As an insurance and to protect the oilfields a division from India landed at the Shatt al Arab on November 6th, by November 22nd it had occupied Basra and by December 9th it had occupied Kurna, so any Turk ventures in that direction were forestalled.

Interestingly the campaign was to follow one of the world's oldest and greatest roads between the earliest known cradles of civilisation in the valleys of the Euphrates and the Nile. From Egypt it keeps close to the sea; crossing Sinai it leaves the rocky fortress of Judea to the east, crosses the Carmel range and ascends past the Sea of Galilee to the plateau east of Jordan and so on to Damascus and Aleppo. It then follows the valley of the Euphrates to Baghdad. Along this road the tides of trade, intellect and of war have flowed between Africa and Asia since the dawn of history.

Also along this road travelled the Holy Baby Jesus on His flight to and from Egypt.

The cities of Damascus and Aleppo were the great markets for eastern trade and contained craftsmen skilled in the making of weapons, fabrics and the working of silver and gold. Almost every name along that road awakens the memory of some famous personage or some noted deed. Gaza lies on it, where in 312 B.C. Ptolemy marched with 18,000 infantry and 4,000 cavalry against Demetrius. They were evenly matched but Demetrius pinned his hopes on his 30 elephants, who Ptolemy thwarted by iron spikes on chains thrown in their path. Pelusium was the scene of a great battle between the Persians and Egyptians some 2,500 years ago. Then there was a fierce struggle between Richard Coeur de Lion and Saladin. Caesarea was named by Herod after his patron Augustus.

The Plain of Esdraelon, the traditional site of Armageddon, overlooked by the ancient fortress of Megiddo, lies half way between Egypt and Aleppo. It has seen many wars, from Mount Tabor a wild rush of mountain men destroyed Sisera's host in the plains below. More than 3,000 years ago a host of irregular tribesmen fled in panic from Gideon's three hundred well trained troops, selected in rather a bizarre manner. It was over this ground, soaked in the blood of warriors down the ages, where decisive battles had been fought since the dawn of time that the Yeomen of England were to make their contribution to world history.

When Germany marched against France and Napoleon marched against Moscow they followed a route determined by the topography of the land and so it was with Palestine. General Allenby a very skilled commander carried with him and studied daily the Bible and a work detailing the "Historical Geography of the Holy Land". He studied what had happened in the past and on those studies based his strategy.

The Sinai Peninsula some 240 miles from north to south, 120 miles wide from east to west is the most barren place on earth. As one Yeoman commented 'anyone who wants it is welcome to it, it's certainly not worth fighting over'. In 1916 there was no proper road; in the north it was soft sand, in the middle it was rocky and boulder strewn and the southern part was rocky mountains. Nowhere in the peninsula was there any permanent stream of running water, except for channels in the Wadi el Arish and the Wadi el Muksheib - when it rained. Some of the ancient cisterns, relics of bygone ages that were still unblocked might contain water, but could not be relied upon - if they could be found. The only reasonably sized settlement was at El Arish. In the days of horse and camel transport, a plentiful and reliable source of water was a decisive factor in the movement of an army and so it was to be in 1916.

It was thought that this barren wilderness, impassable to wheeled traffic was a sure protection from the mounting of any sizeable attack from the east. To overcome this, the Turks dug two parallel trenches, the width of a pair of wheels apart, and filled them with brushwood. This way they made a passable track able to bear a gun carriage.

Immediately on the declaration of war the Egyptians evacuated all their frontier posts and fell back behind the canal. Straightaway the Turks occupied El Arish with a light force. Assembling around Beersheba they advanced towards Ismailia with 20,000 men, nine batteries of artillery and one battery of 5.9 inch howitzers. At the same time they made feint attacks to the north and south of the canal.

Knowing that they faced a force of some 70,000 British, who having no knowledge where they would strike, had to defend the length of the canal, with no artillery other than a few patrolling warships. The Turks struck on February 3rd at Tusan between Ismailia and the Bitter Lake. They managed to cross the canal but were repulsed and their commander ordered a retirement on Beersheba.

The Turks reliance on getting help from an Egyptian rising having failed, they pinned their hopes on assistance from the pro Turk Sennussi tribe. With an army of about 5,000 irregulars and a few machine guns they were making themselves a nuisance in the Western desert. To cope with this a British force had to be kept based on Mersa Matruh, to become well known to Yeomen in the Second World War, near the Libyan border. Fighting on this front the R.G.H. lost 2nd Lieutenant J.C. Bengough, who was killed taking part in a cavalry charge when assisting the Dorset Yeomanry.

It was felt that the best way to defend the canal was to establish a force at Romani and Katia, where there was a good water supply. Lines of supply had to be ensured so work was started laying a railway track to the latter oasis which was at the western end of a line of small oases eastward to Bir-el-Abd.

For the latter part of March the regiment was kept constantly on patrol duty. On March 26th Lt Col Yorke and Major Clifford together with two troops made a reconnaissance to Oghratina and back by Katia and Romani, without seeing any signs of the enemy. At the end of the month the regiment assembled at Romani to make an extended reconnaissance to Bir-el-Abd some 22 miles away.

On the morning of April 1st an intelligence report brought news of the presence at Bir-el Abd of a force of 300 Turks, 200 Arab auxiliaries and four guns. The R.G.H. less one squadron and the Worcester Yeomanry less one troop were ordered to march, under the command of Lt Col

Yorke to Katia, six miles away and bivouac there for the night. The force totalled 19 officers, 257 other ranks, 294 horses and mules and native details with ambulance and ammunition on camels.

Next morning the camels were left at the Hod Negiliat with two squadrons of Worcesters and a detachment of field ambulance. All baggage that could be spared was left at Katia and the remainder of the force moved forward, carrying two iron rations and one feed for the horses. An outpost of the enemy was seen near Khirba, but they fled at the sight of the advancing British and Bir-el-Abd was occupied without opposition. Some stores were found and a good well. The military stores were destroyed and the column moved back to Romani via Katia. They had suffered no casualties, except for one horse that fell out with staggers but which was subsequently brought in. They had covered 50 miles in 24 hours through soft sand country.

The C in C of the 52nd division, to which they were now attached, forwarded the following message: -

"The Commander in Chief has expressed his pleasure at the activity in reconnaissance in the Katia area and desires that his appreciation shall be conveyed to the troops. The Corps commander has much satisfaction in communicating the above to the G.O.C. 52nd division, the Gloucestershire Hussars, Worcestershire Hussars, Bikaner Camel Corps and all who have taken part in this successful little enterprise. He recognises the keenness of all ranks and the excellence of the arrangements made".

Reconnaissance from Romani continued, a Worcester squadron went out to Bir el Abd on April 9th and found an enemy force arriving there, the squadron returned with no casualties. A German aeroplane visited Romani and Katia, dropping two bombs on the latter. On April 21st an outpost of our position was attacked at Romani before dawn, but they withdrew when fire was opened.

The next day a party of Royal Engineers was sent to Oghratina, about five miles east of Katia, to dig wells so that a water supply would be available further forward. Two squadrons of the Worcester Yeomanry were sent to cover them and "A" squadron of the R.G.H. under Captain Lloyd Baker was ordered to Katia to take charge of the camp. Also under his command were about 40 Worcester Yeomanry dismounted; detachments of R.A.M.C and a mobile veterinary column. Other R.G.H. were Lieutenant Lord Elcho, Lieutenant Strickland, 2nd Lieutenant C.C. Herbert, 2nd Lieutenant W.A. Smith and 101 R.G.H. other ranks.

On April 23rd, St George's day and also Easter Sunday, Captain Lloyd

Baker sent out a patrol at 4 a.m., which returned at 5 a.m. Shortly afterwards an enemy patrol probed the outpost line and retired; at the same time Oghratina was attacked and repulsed then attacked again at 6.30 a.m., by 7 a.m. it was heavily attacked on all sides and was captured around 7.30 a.m.

At 7.45 a.m. Captain Lloyd Baker sent out another patrol which encountered a large force of advancing enemy about one and half miles from Katia. A dense fog enveloped the country up to about 9 a.m. which all added to the confusion. An hour later the enemy opened fire with a battery of four guns, directing their aim on the horses of the Worcesters. Captain Lloyd Baker had tethered his horses under cover in the Hod, but the Turkish gunners somehow found them and directed their fire on them, quickly destroying them. Corporal Walwin offered to lead a detail down to the Hod and bring them into the squadron position, but permission was refused and it was soon too late anyway.

The enemy infantry attacked in strength but "A" squadron R.G.H. heard that "B" and "D" squadron were coming to their support from Romani and thought they only had to hang on until they arrived. Colonel Coventry with a squadron of Worcesters from Bir-el-Hamish went into action on the left, the enemy were briefly repulsed and it looked as though the day might be saved. However shortly after midday the enemy opened fire again with his artillery, causing severe casualties in the firing line. An infantry attack followed, the squadron hung on expecting relief, but the enemy rushed the camp around 3.30 a.m. and with their ammunition spent it was every man for himself.

Corporal Walwin gives the following account of the battle, unfortunately it is incomplete: -

"On the Saturday after Good Friday, orders came through that one squadron and one machine gun were to advance. There were two machine guns in the regiment, "A" squadron would be going under command of Capt M. Lloyd - Baker -- Sergeant Colburn would be going in charge of one gun section, I was Corporal and No 1 on No 1 gun section, could I go with my section - yes Colburn and I were very friendly and our requests were granted. We all had to be saddled up in marching order at short notice, there was something strange in the atmosphere and just the last look at the remainder of the regiment, that one was almost silent. We moved off winding our way through the desert, our horses seemed so pally and kept good formation until one or two started kicking and we found wires were laid under the sand. Two were so badly cut about the fetlock that it was advisable to return with them to Romani.

We arrived at Katia and tethered our horses at a small oasis a little distance away and placed our horse lines in a little hollow. We erected a few tents but feeling very tired I decided to turn in early and was about to do so when I received a request that Captain Lloyd - Baker wanted to see me. I found him not far away talking with one of the troop sergeants about the positions of the different guards, who would be on duty during the night. He seemed very alert and perhaps a little restless, as if something would happen, but what could happen. We had only seen one or two Turks a few days ago and they had gone back or been shot. When Captain Lloyd - Baker noticed me he dismissed the troop sergeant and said –

Corporal Walwin I understand you are the machine gunner.

Yes Sir.

Well I would like you to have your gun mounted here, ready for action. I will have a guard posted over you so you may sleep by your gun and you will be awakened if necessary, we must take every precaution.

The night seemed very dark, I lay by my gun, tried hard to sleep but frequently woke, only to see the silhouette of the guard standing by me with his bayonet fixed, peering into the desert blackness, the silence only broken by the horses shaking their cow collars.

Daybreak seemed to come mysteriously mingled with mist and fog, which was unusual and presently a few dark objects were approaching us in extended order. Captain Lloyd - Baker immediately enquired if all our outpost guards were in, the reply was 'yes'. Then almost instantaneously from the dark objects there came a few shots and we at the same time received orders to open fire and the dark objects disappeared, either retreated or shot. They were Turk scouts who had penetrated too far or an advance guard of a Turkish army. As the atmosphere cleared a little, some movements were noticed round a small palm grove on our left. I received orders to open fire, visibility was still bad. Lord Elcho who was close by me looking through his field glasses gave the order 'cease fire', believing it was women or children; it was difficult to say for certain. All was quiet, as we had been visited other mornings by a German aircraft we decided to fill a few sand bags ---------".

Unfortunately Hugh Walwin's account ends here.

Corporal A.G.Dabbs of the Worcesters gave the following account of the action at Oghratina: -

"It was just about midday, terribly hot lying in the sand - suddenly I saw the right flank beginning to fall back and saw that the Turks were in amongst them. Then the Turks opposite us leapt up shouting Allah, Allah and charged us. I stood up and fixed my bayonet and waited for the end; hoping it would come quickly. I felt very miserable to think that I had to die, especially in a hole in the desert like this, and I wondered how my people would get to know of it and who would be alive to write and tell them. I wondered which of the advancing Turks would kill me and if I would be able to kill one or two before I was done in. We had almost stopped firing and the Turks too and it was strangely quiet except for their shouting.

Then the Colonel suddenly said "It's no good boys, throw down your rifles". Very gladly I obeyed although feeling very cheap and very much conquered as I held up my hands".

The two squadrons that moved out from Romani engaged the enemy and after suffering heavy losses and losing amongst others Lieut and adjutant Lord Quenington had to fall back on Romani. At Romani Lt Col Yorke not being able to get any assurance that help was forthcoming, moved back to rail-head. The next day the regiment was relieved by the Australian Light Horse and moved back to Kantara.

An unknown member of the Warwick Yeomanry gave the following account of the battle and attempts to relieve the R.G.H. at Katia: -

"Friday April 21st -- Afternoon of the 21st one squadron ("D" squadron) Worcester Yeomanry under command of Captain Leslie Cheape, proceed to Oghratina with the engineer company; the Yeomanry to protect the engineers whilst they carry out "Water Reconnaissance".

April 22nd - Receive news that there is a force of Turks at a place called Mageibra -- we go to Katia, then on to Hamisah and start for Mageibra with two squadrons of Warwick Yeomanry and one squadron of Worcesters at 12.45 a.m. on Easter Sunday morning.

April 23rd -- We got to Mageibra at 4.15 a.m., a small force of Turks there but they had all gone with the exception of six who had been left behind sick. We did not stay very long and marched back to Hamisah, reaching here about 7.45 a.m. We hear that Oghratina had been attacked at dawn and having overwhelmed Captain William Thomas and Captain Leslie Cheape's Worcester Yeomanry squadrons they had come on to Katia. The Worcesters were unlucky, there was a dense fog - unusual in the desert - and but for the braying of a mule the Turks would have missed them. Our force marched on as quickly as possible with the Warwick Yeomanry under Colonel Hugh Cheape to the relief of Katia, where the Gloucester Yeomanry, under Captain Michael Baker was encamped. When within two and a half miles we could see that the Gloucester

Yeomanry under Col R.M. Yorke were very heavily engaged. The Brigadier General decided to try and relieve the Katia garrison on the right flank -- we had soon to recourse to dismounted action as the Turks turned a great deal of their attention on us. In like manner the Gloucester Yeomanry less "A" squadron had come out from Romani to relieve their comrades at Katia. They were held up by a much superior force and could not get on at all. Unfortunately we could not get any lateral communication with them, a belt of trees divided us and our two forces were some seven or eight miles apart. But to return to the Warwick Yeomanry, we soon became very heavily engaged, casualties were becoming very common and the Turks were coming on in continuous lines and I remember being greatly impressed by their wonderful fire discipline and art of concealment. Eventually not more than 200 yards separated us and General Wiggin decided to fall back on Hamisah, fighting a rearguard action. Not long after this we saw flames and a great sheet of smoke and we knew that Katia had fallen".

The regiment as a result of this action, in killed, wounded and those taken prisoner, suffered the loss of virtually the whole of "A" squadron. Lord Quenington was still alive when he was picked up and one of his brother officers galloped back to Romani with him, supporting him on his saddle, to get him to the doctor.

In the words of Cpl Arthur "Johnny" Bull R.A.M.C. attached R.G.H., in correspondence with the author:-

"I assisted the M.O. for almost an hour trying to save him, but we were unsuccessful - he was a fine officer".

After the Oghratina/Katia battles the Worcesters could only muster 54 all ranks, fit for duty.

In letters home starting on April 27th 1916 Fred Lewis wrote: -

"I expect you have heard what bad luck the regiment has had -- -- it appears they were surrounded by a force composed of Turks, Germans and Austrians. They were outnumbered by about five to one -- -- Only (censored but probably nine) of the whole squadron got away -- -- one of the fellows who got back was wounded in the leg, he is in hospital at Port Said, so I hope to get down and talk to him (this is almost certainly Charles Lovell) -- -- we already know three sergeants were killed -- -- the (censored but Worcesters) had heavy losses, so is (censored but most likely "B" or "D" squadron) badly knocked about -- -- we lost one of our best officers Lord Quenington".

On June 6th 1916 he wrote: -

"I went down to Port Said yesterday and went to the hospital to see one of the sergeants (Lovell) who was wounded on Easter Sunday. He told me all about the fight; sorry I can't tell you all he told me. He told me that the Turks treated our fellows splendidly, they took away all those that were lightly wounded on camels after first dressing all the wounds. He was so badly wounded they left him behind, but not before they made a bed for him with some blankets and made him as comfortable as possible. I asked him if he had seen anything of Eddie (Tippet) and Bert Troughton. He did not see Eddie but Bert he said was quite alright, I am sure that those who were taken prisoner will be treated well so that is some consolation".

It was later learned that the attacking Turks numbered between two and three thousand and they were amazed that they had been held up by such a small force.

It was some time before Charles Lovell and the other survivors were rescued. He was visited by some Arabs bent on looting; when they discovered he was alive they tried to strangle him with telegraph wire. Despite their efforts, being a very strong man, he managed to keep his hands up to protect his throat; after a while something distracted them and they left. As a result of this action his leg was badly shattered, gangrene set in and it had to be amputated.

Fred Lewis continues on June 11th 1916: -

"Of course I have heard all about the fight -- -- they were attacked at seven in the morning and managed to hold off till half past three in the afternoon. All their horses were killed and any amount of camels. The Turks got within about sixty yards when the order was given every man for himself and that is when a few of our fellows got away. Thirty two of our fellows were buried at Katia but no-body seems to know who they were, as the Turks had taken all pay books, discs and letters away with them. I am afraid poor old Howard Peacey had a bad time, his body was found about six miles away from Katia; he had evidently crawled until he was exhausted. I have heard of two fellows having written home".

Bert Troughton's bible was picked up in the desert shortly after the action and was returned to his parents, causing them some anxiety, until they heard he had been taken prisoner but that he was safe. Under the impression that he had been killed, a memorial service was held for Corporal Hugh Walwin; but Hughie was very much alive and lived to serve in the Royal Observer Corps in the Second World War.

Those who attended the service to commemorate the 90th anniversary of the battle could not fail to have been moved by a reading from the Countess of Wemyss memoirs, She was the mother of Lord Elcho who was killed; it reads as follows: -

"I had a strange dream vision at Stanway, during the night of April 22nd. The atmosphere of the room seemed to quiver with excitement - I felt the stress and strain and saw, as if thrown on a magic lantern sheet, a confused mass of black smoke with crimson flame: it was like a child's picture of a battle or explosion. The flames and smoke were up high in the right of the picture and to the left I saw Ego (family name for Lord Elcho) standing, straight and tall. I got the impression that he was exercising all his forces with all his might and main. I felt that something had happened, but I knew not what, it was below the threshold of consciousness. I was not anxious nor worried, but stunned. I knew that Ego was dead and through all the weeks and months that followed, before we got official confirmation of his death, the vision had a strangely quieting influence, it helped me to wait and kept me inwardly calm".

Corporal Robert Eaton was one of those who managed to escape and he wrote home as follows: -

"I hardly know how to write to let you know the great trouble that has befallen our Regiment, but I can honestly say that I am one of the luckiest fellows in the world to be alive to tell it.

On Saturday 22nd we moved out our "A" squadron to relieve the Worcesters at a place called Katia, they moving further east. All went well until next morning Easter Sunday (we were sleeping fully dressed that night). At 4 o'clock the order came to stand to arms, we being posted crescent shaped in extended order round our camp in the direction in which we expected the enemy. The morning was very dark and foggy and at 4.30 a.m. we saw something moving straight to our front and the order was given to fire. The enemy opened on us at the same time and at 5 o'clock it began to clear. We could then see a small body of the enemy retiring.

All went well then for a time and a troop at a time fell away, fed and watered horses and had breakfast. By this time it was 9 o'clock, my troop being last to water horses at a well about a mile away. We had hardly got through with this when the enemy guns opened on our camp. We galloped straight for camp, handed horses over and took up a position in the firing line.

No sooner had we got into position than we saw the enemy in two lines of extended order advancing over the ridge about a mile away towards us, covering a front of about a mile. We immediately opened fire and this was kept up without a break, their big guns sending shrapnel and shells over till about 11 o'clock, when they went quiet. The whole time they were advancing and we were firing at them. Between 12 and 1 o'clock their guns opened fire on us again, they having brought up their guns to within about 1,000 yards. By this time the enemy were no more than five or six hundred yards from us and what happened the next two hours is hard to relate.

On our right flank we could see a body of mounted men about 400 strong galloping straight towards us. These dismounted behind a ridge about 600 yards away and lined up in extended order. No sooner had they got into position than about another such number came charging down more to our right flank rear. These also dismounted under cover and came up in the same formation to about seven or eight hundred yards. In the meantime "C" squadron of the Worcesters and "B" squadron came up on our left flank. All this time our "A" squadron about 100 strong had stood before the cruel fire from their two guns and the fire from about 2,000 Turkish rifles.

They still crept up from bush to bush and at about 3 o'clock they were within fifty yards of us we could see their fixed bayonets. We stood it for another ten minutes or quarter of an hour when we could see we were in a hopeless position and the order came 'every man for himself'. I saw all the officers and the majority of the men throw up their arms and surrender and the Turks came on at them with fixed bayonets. What happened to me was a miracle, I started to run back and grabbed a horse which was tied to a post about fifty yards from me and started to gallop away. I had not gone more than thirty yards when they shot the horse from under me causing me to turn about three somersaults. I gathered myself together again and saw another loose horse close by, caught him and made off again. Before I could get to the Worcester led horses under cover they had shot him in four places, neck, knee, shoulder and hindquarter. I got to the horses alright and got another horse off them leaving the other to die. Then made off again for Romani six miles distant, where our headquarters were and reported what had happened. The order was then given to quit that place in a quarter of an hour, loading everything up of any value on camels and make off towards Kantara. All this time our "B" and "D" squadrons were fighting a rearguard action, "C" squadron Worcesters having surrendered with our "A" squadron and the other two squadrons of Worcesters were captured as we have heard nothing of them since.

Two more of the survivors and I kept quietly on and we arrived at

Kantara about midnight having covered about forty miles that evening and I can tell you horses and ourselves were done up.

Up till now there are only eight of "A" squadron out of nearly a hundred that have got here, so you can see that things are pretty bad. I myself, being one of the surviving eight"

Reproduced by courtesy of Worcester City Museum
The camp at Katia before the battle

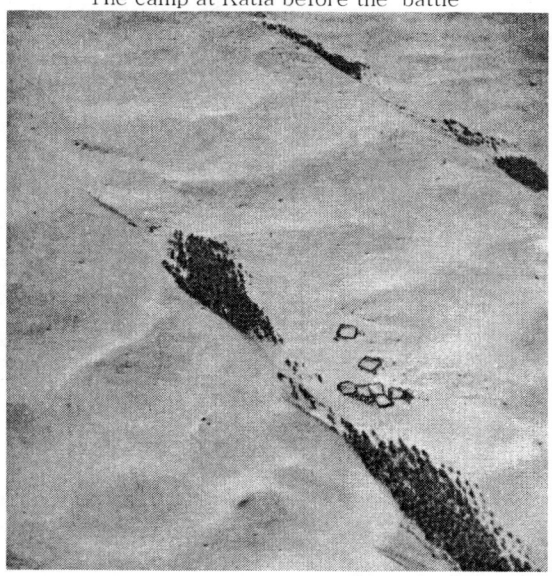

Photo by Brigadier P.R.C. Groves
Aerial view of an unknown Oasis, 40 miles north east of Ismailia; measured off on the map this puts it in the Katia area.

Chapter 9

In Captivity

800 mile journey to Afion – red carpet treatment in Jerusalem – March in twos
feed on dead camel – camel pantomime – Haidee get up – Prison boredom
malnutrition – escape impossible – volunteers for lorry driving

During the battle Hugh Walwin's machine gun had become red hot and he only ceased firing after he ran out of ammunition. He recalled that a big Turk had come at him with his bayonet and he expected to be run through, instead he got struck on the head with the butt of the Turk's rifle and he was knocked unconscious for several moments; when he came round he found he was a prisoner.

The Katia prisoners faced a harrowing march across the desert without proper supplies of food or water to Beersheba and on to Jerusalem. It was the start of an 800 mile journey deep into Turkey to the prison camps of Afion Kara Hissar where they would spend the rest of the war in spartan conditions.

Many of those captured at Katia were reluctant to speak about their experiences as prisoners of war and the author has had to weave together odd comments gleaned from different sources to get an idea of the hardships they suffered. Harry Colburn had been wounded in the arm and was very weak. He was supported by Hugh Walwin and he begged him to go ahead and look after himself; but Hugh would have none of it, comforting and caring for him during the long and terrible journey. His wound got steadily worse and was not properly treated till they reached the hospital in Damascus, when it was found to be full of maggots. There was a happy ending to it all, in that after the war Harry Colburn married Hugh's sister. But there wasn't always a happy ending; many of those captured dying from disease, malnutrition or general neglect during the journey to the prison camp.

The novelty to the Turk of having white prisoners soon wore off and they were constantly being prodded on, thirsty and hungry. Occasionally they were able to buy a sheep or goat from passing Arabs and Frank Hopkins remembered they thought they were in clover, when they came across a camel that had been dead a fortnight. They had to keep marching from one wadi to the next so that they could slake their terrible thirst and fill their water bottles.

The Katia men were fortunate in that the wounded were carried on camels, but they weren't all so lucky. In another party those who had money were occasionally able to buy a donkey from passing Arabs; friends walking alongside the animal holding a sick comrade up. They were silent men determined to keep going and get as far as possible; to fall out was to be neglected and lost. When they at last reached the camping ground they might find no water. After an hour or two of broken sleep they would be aroused by shouts of "Haidee", get up, "Yellah", get on. In the distance a few sandstone hills appeared, their tongues swollen and their throats on fire they reached a river. After a rest of two hours they plodded on again through stony defiles.

One prisoner recorded about a village they passed through: -

"After many false starts and rumours of starts we managed to get going. Early in the morning before starting I slipped out in the confusion of preparing the column and did the rounds absolutely unattended. With the little Turkish I picked up and French here and there, I visited the bank to try and raise some money by cheque. There was no chance of this but I succeeded in changing some notes I had for smaller. The notes were not accepted in the bazaar and one was charged for paper change. I had not the fortune of meeting one likely person or I should not have returned. To attempt to escape without help in such a place with the desert all round was too hopeless".

An officer in another column of prisoners reported that in the larger towns they were happy to take cheques. The Turks would appear to have been very lax in allowing the prisoners to break column when they were halted. Camels that were not properly broken occasionally accompanied them and one of the troopers recorded -

"Each day before dawn broke we were up and after a breakfast of tea, black bread, a small piece of cheese and two figs or generally only raisins, we prepared to leave. Then the camel pantomime started afresh and it was not an uncommon sight to see half our convoy of camels bolting headlong in the wrong direction before a crowd of galloping Turks, disappearing over a sand ridge against the rising sun, leaving their kit distributed over the plain. At last we reached the railhead and heard a locomotive puffing and pulling. No sailor after being tossed amid shipwreck in a frantic ocean ever felt happier to be in port than we do to realise the long march is done. There are other marches ahead over mountains, but they are short we hear, the desert is crossed".

In Jerusalem one party was received in style, they were believed to have the doubtful honour of being the first Christian prisoners to be marched into the city since the Crusades. Corporal Dabbs of the Worcesters described the scene: -

"Suddenly we rounded the corner of a hill and came upon Jerusalem, a beautiful sight, the city within the walls being all white houses with flat roofs and scarcely any windows - very Oriental looking and the whole place full of churches of every style and of mosques.

Here evidently our coming was expected - flags were flying everywhere, a red carpet was down on the platform and many high officials were waiting to meet us. Also what we found very interesting was a large stage erected above the platform and crowded with Turkish ladies - the wives of the officials below - all in black with black veils. As their lords and masters were below them and could not possibly see them many of these ladies became very free, throwing back their veils, smiling and waving their hands at us.

Then we were marched out of the station into the hot sun - steeped road and formed up in two's in order that we should look a longer line. There were hundreds of spectators lining the road, they all looked very sorry for us and we certainly looked very extraordinary objects. Some had lost their helmets and had tied handkerchiefs round their heads, others had lost their jackets and marched in their shirt sleeves and none of us had shaved for a fortnight".

Eventually when they arrived at the prison camp and settled in to interminable days and weeks of boredom, they suffered more from neglect than ill treatment. In a conversation with the author, Hugh Walwin commented that their guards were of low calibre and were ignorant of such things as hygiene and dysentery was rife. Food quality was poor and many of the prisoners suffered from malnutrition. Hugh went on to say that he felt that he would not survive unless he could get some green stuff. He was so weak that he could only crawl down to the rubbish heap where he routed around and found some onion shoots that had been thrown out. He carefully washed and cleaned them before eating them. He was quite convinced this saved his life.

Hugh got the nickname of "scrounger". He used to break out of the prison camp when it was dark and forage for scraps of food. Two guards caught him one night, stood him on a barrel and put a noose round his neck. Whether they intended to execute him or only frighten him he didn't know. Fortunately a Turk officer spotted what was going on and he was cut down. No doubt he hesitated before breaking out again!

Harry Colburn said that it was important for the individual's survival that they imposed a rigid discipline on themselves. He had noticed when they were in the camp, that those who didn't wash and shave regularly, or couldn't be bothered to get up in the morning were always the first to succumb and in many cases died.

Many of the prisoners were employed breaking stone for roadmaking, with Turk guards ensuring that there was no slacking. One day the Turks asked for volunteers who could drive motor vehicles to drive lorries hauling the stone. Eddie Tippett had never driven a motor vehicle before, but anxious to break the monotony of the prison camp said he could and volunteered to drive one of the lorries. He told the guard the lorry was an unfamiliar model and could a friend give him a half hour instruction before he went solo. This was agreed and to Eddie's horror they had to drive up a mountain track with a sheer drop on the one side. To make matters worse he had to negotiate a hairpin bend and reverse before he could get round. He eventually managed and survived to tell the tale.

The Turkish language, poor communications and their obvious northern European origins made escape impossible. Two officers tried to get away by means of an ingenious attempt to bluff their guards, by holding seances with the commandant. They used an ouija board and bluffed him into believing that a 'spirit' could lead him to buried treasure, which "the spirit" conveniently said was in a location from which it would be easy to affect an escape. After a long period over many months, undergoing experiences that drove them to the verge of sanity, they eventually achieved release from captivity, two days before hostilities ceased.

The prisoners were reasonably well treated according to the standards of the day. Harry Colburn commented that the Turkish discipline in the camp was harsh, but they were equally harsh on their own troops.

Prisoners and Guards, Harry Colburn smoking pipe seated second from right

Photo Cheltenham Chronicle
Six unknown R.G.H. captured at Katia, include Trooper A.J. Boswell thought to be standing in the centre.

Photo reproduced by permission of Worcester City Museum

British Prisoners captured at Katia being paraded through Jerusalem

Chapter 10.

Romani

Reform "A" squadron – Dueidar Hod a shambles – Hill 70 smelly –Kressenstein attacks Wellington ridge and Mt Royston with 16,000Turks – R.G.H. to Dueidar Major Turner fills gap in line.–.Kressenstein ordered take canal – terrible scream

On April 26th the regiment moved from Kantara to Ballah, a little village on the eastern bank of the canal, the strength was 18 officers and 314 other ranks. Lieutenant G.N. Horlick was left in Kantara to reform "A" squadron along with Fred Lewis promoted to sergeant, who writes:-
"They have been making up some sort of an "A" squadron and just in the middle of the business the top sergeant is sent off to Cairo for a course of N.C.O.'s instruction. I had to take charge of about fifty men with only two L.Cpls to help, so I have got my hands full -- -- I have been put in charge of the Gloucester troop which has got a record to keep up, they were always thought the smartest troop in "A" squadron. A draft arrives tomorrow so I shall hope to see some familiar faces again".

The 5th Mounted Brigade had been hard hit at Oghratina and Katia, two squadrons of Worcesters and one of Gloucesters virtually wiped out. The unknown member of the Warwicks takes up the tale again: -
"When we got back to Hamisah we just had time to refresh ourselves with any food and drink we could get hold of. Well do I remember a bottle of sparkling cider Smith England gave me, one of the best drinks I have ever had in my life. The veterinary officer has orders to shoot any wounded horses. The Field Ambulance makes the wounded more comfortable and we decide we cannot stop here we must retire on Dueidar, as we do this we see again the same sad sight of our camp vanish in flames and smoke.
Arriving at Dueidar at 11 p.m. we hear they also have been heavily engaged, a Turkish force having made a most desperate attempt approaching from a north easterly direction across the desert. It was only at the point of the bayonet and often with many a bullet in their bodies that this force was persuaded to retire. Charge after charge right up to the Dueidar Hod - and there they all lay, friend and foe, a veritable shambles. I can never quite understand how we missed this force, but the desert is a vast place. What a disastrous day Easter Day 1916 has been, two squadrons of Worcesters and one of Gloucesters wiped out, to say nothing of the company of engineers. Poor Leslie Cheap, the finest polo player I ever saw, Noel Pearson and young Wiggin, nephew of Brigadier General

Wiggin. An exception was Bill Wiggin of the Worcesters, who although severely wounded in the head managed to crawl down to the Hod and made a miraculous escape. At Katia there was Michael Baker, in command of "A" squadron, his body never found and Lord Elcho blown up by a shell from the Turkish guns. Then there were those captured, Colonel Charles Coventry, Captain Tom Strickland and the padre Rev A. Wilcox and many N.C.O.s and men who were to begin that terrible march across the desert to Damascus".

The next three months were spent in training, patrol work and accepting fresh drafts of men, replacements for the Katia losses. A fortnight later the R.G.H. moved five miles to the north east to a place named Hill 70, which we will hear about later. Here they took over the camp of the Anzac mounted division, it was smelly and plagued with flies and they were glad to get out of it when four days later they moved back to Ballah. They then moved back to El Ferdan on the canal, where it was hoped to erect some wooden huts for the men and shelters for the horses, but it was not to be and after a few days they moved to Kantara.

The standard gauge railway had been pushed forward and reached Romani in mid May. This enabled supplies and reinforcements to be brought forward and the 52nd Division was moved there. It was a good defensive position; a line of sand dunes about ten miles in length and three wide runs south and slightly west from Romani to the village of Dueidar, a point opposite the isolated hillock Hill 70, which is about five miles to the west. Another five miles separate the hill from the canal. At the Romani end of the dunes is a ridge running east west, which was named Wellington ridge. To the south of Wellington ridge, about four miles in a south easterly direction was a prominent dune named Katib Gannit. About a mile to the south was another dune called Mount Meredith and another four miles to the west was a similar hillock christened Mount Royston. From the sea to Katib Gannit a line of eighteen infantry posts were built, each holding about 100 riflemen and two machine guns. This is explained in detail so that the course of this important battle may be understood. It was important as being the last attempt the Turks made to reach the canal, from then onwards, although they fought hard and bravely they were unable to avoid being pushed back.

With the defences covering the approach of Romani secured, the construction of the railway toward Katia was continued. Early in July the Turks under the German General von Kressenstein moved forward with a force of some 16,000 made up of some 12,000 riflemen, 30 guns and 38 eight machine guns, reaching Bir-el-Abd and Ogratina on July 19th. These movements had been spotted by reconnaissance patrols and the 42nd

Division was moved up from the canal. Additionally the Anzacs and the 5th Yeomanry Brigade took up position around Hill 70 to wait until the direction of Kressenstein's move became apparent.

    Kressenstein made no move for a fortnight, because he had to wait for the guns and an adequate water supply to be brought forward. General Murray brought 10,500 camels forward to provide transport for his troops, intending to move on August 13th if Kressenstein had not moved by then. The 2nd Australian light horse brigade was sent out on a reconnaissance and on August 3rd Kressenstein followed it back, hoping to surprise the main body of British and seize Wellington Ridge during the night. Despite repeated efforts during the day they never succeeded in crossing the ridge.

The Romani defensive position was well chosen; to the south of the line of dunes was a waterless desert of soft sand. The southern end of the dunes consisted of lines of dunes dominated by Mounts Meredith and Royston, which meant that the enemy had little option then to try and get round the British right through the defile between Wellington Ridge and Mount Royston.

On July 20th Lt Col Yorke commanding a composite regiment of "B" and "D" squadrons R.G.H and one squadron of Worcesters together with a machine gun section moved back to Hill 70. Cavalry patrols had been hanging on to the Turkish forces for the past three months and recent activity had indicated that the Turks were going to make another effort to cut the canal. This had been confirmed by spotting aircraft and sympathetic Arab spies. This constant vigilance paid off; when the attack came the Allied forces were very well prepared.

The enemy developed his attack with great resolution and the cavalry's job was to delay them until the infantry could be got into position where the Turks were making their main thrust. During the morning the enemy got to Wellington Ridge and Mounts Meredith and Royston and from there commanded the Mounted division camp. After midday the battle swung the other way, our reserves had come up and held Wellington ridge and Mount Royston, forcing the Turks to attempt coming round the British right, where they got embroiled in the sand dunes and were held by the cavalry. The Turkish effort was spent, by nightfall most of the high ground had been recaptured, the Turks were falling back all along the line and large batches of prisoners were surrendering. Pursuit was impossible that night because a large part of the fighting had fallen on the cavalry and both men and horses were exhausted.

Next morning August 5th the enemy was pushed off the part of Wellington ridge they still held and forced back toward Katia. Next day they fell back still further, still fighting and taking their heavy guns with them. It was very hot and the infantry could not keep up, so pursuit was left to the cavalry, they tried encirclement but were held off by the Turk artillery at Bir-el-Abd. On August 12th it was found that the enemy had retreated to El Arish and the pursuit was called off.

When the action opened two squadrons of R.G.H. were still at Hill 70 with the composite regiment and one squadron was at Pelusium. On the morning of August 4th Lt Col Yorke was ordered to move to the south west of Royston Hill to support 1st and 2nd Light Horse Brigades. He was then ordered to proceed to Dueidar and take up an out post. There was a danger the enemy would cut through at this point and capture the water pipe line, which had been laid from Kantara and take the railway line to Romani. Major Turner at Pelusium spotted this would leave a gap in the line and brought his force forward into the gap. His quick appraisal of the position had a great deal to do with the final outcome of the battle.

Lt Col Yorke's report on the battle reads as follows: -
"At about 5.45 p.m. on the 4th instant "B" squadron R.G.H. under command of Lieutenant F.A.Mitchell and two troops of Worcester Yeomanry, under command of Major Wiggin took possesion of the highest point of Mt Royston. The four (Turk) guns were immediately east of this position, estimated range about 300 yards. The elevation used on the rifles of Lieutenant Mitchell's squadron R.G.H., owing to firing at a downhill angle, was 400 yards. The guns were in four emplacements. Immediately on our taking possession of the ridge the guns, which had been facing north, were swung round and fired directly at my men lining the ridge. These guns had certainly not been put out of action (there was some argument over this) I personally saw every one of them fire, the shells going just over the top of the ridge or bursting on impact in the sand close to the top of the ridge. At least 25 shells were fired. One of these bursting shells caused Lieutenant Lord Apsley to be completely buried and he had to be dug out. Major Wiggin was sent head over heels, fortunately down the reverse side of the slope. There were several narrow escapes, but with the guns firing at an angle of at least 27 degrees the shells either went right over or buried themselves in the sand.

About 6 p.m. the guns ceased firing, the Turk survivors hoisted a white flag and came running towards us".

Excerpts from the diary of an R.G.H. officer read as follows: -
"Hill 70 in the composite cavalry regiment. Remounts given us are unfit, water is the chief difficulty -- -- the desert is very difficult, covered with camel grass and little clumps. We marched by compass as there are few landmarks -- -- Ants are a trouble - big black ones -- -- nothing to do and being shot at the whole time and no target within range. Then we had a chance to advance, off to a flank on a high skyline. We got on to the ridge which was like a razor back and the Turks evacuated as we advanced. Down below us in the plain, such a scene. We gave them hell. About 500 surrendered to us and four guns -- -- we took them and marched them to camp, the best fight I have been in and Frank (Mitchell?) and I enjoyed it awfully. We got to a Hod at 8.30, awful job to water there, no food except iron rations for the men -- -- the old Yeomen

played up like the men they are".

The following are extracts from a description of the battle, given by a trooper of the 5th Australian Light Horse Brigade: -

"August 5th -- -- Mounted troops are charging for miles along the Romani battle front; the Turkish waves have almost reached the redoubts. Fighting has been severe all night and apparently very uncertain, captured orders say General von Kressenstein was to take the canal at all costs -- -- the regiment had a very lively time holding the Turkish reinforcements up, the main Turkish columns are hammering all along the Romani front, except at the infantry redoubts -- -- word comes that the Turkish attack on Romani is broken, the New Zealanders and Yeomanry crumpled their left flank and they are retiring to Katia. It was a very close thing indeed, some of their battalions actually got to the railway line built behind Romani -- both sides blazed away point blank -- -- their main attack captured Mount Meredith and Wellington Ridge -- -- in the light of the dawn from 383 ridge we gazed back at a grand sight, dawn came with a crimson light, all lit up in pink and Khaki stretching right back to the redoubts of Duiedar; a winding column of New Zealand and Australian troops and mounted Yeomanry, all chirpy and spoiling for a fight.

There are sadder tales too of men beaten in the fighting retirements, by the heavy sand filling their leggings, plodding desperately on only to be overtaken and bayoneted. Of numerous Turks so eager in the attacks that they threw away their boots so they could press over the sands faster. Of the terrible scream when eight thousand Turk bayonets glinted in the starlight and charged Mount Meredith -- -- of the shadow shooting on the precipitous slopes, a handful of men peering over the brink shot the Turks down like wallabies and they rolled over and over down the walls of sand.

Through it all we could sense a battle very, very narrowly won".

With the coming of nightfall the battle ceased, Lieutenant Lord Apsley was the last in action. He had been ordered to take a troop and round up prisoners and in doing so came into touch with the enemy rearguard, remaining in action till dark.

The composite regiment, which now included Major Turner's "D" squadron moved back to Pelusium to water the horses and renew ammunition supplies. It had captured 500 prisoners, four camel guns and two machine guns. It had suffered 13 casualties, Private A.P. Handy died the next day.

Around 4,000 prisoners in total were captured and they had had enough, they said that the Germans kept urging them on when their one idea was to withdraw. Together with casualties the Turks must have lost about half of the 16,000 they started with. The British losses amounted to about 1,100 in all, most of which were sustained by the Anzac Mounted Division.

The following telegram was received from His Majesty the King by the Commander in Chief: -
"Please convey to all ranks engaged in the Battle of Romani my appreciation of their efforts which have brought about the brilliant success they have won at the height of the hot season in the desert country. Please circulate to all ranks".

The commander of the 5th mounted Brigade Brigadier General E.A. Wiggin in his despatch commented;-
"I trust I may be allowed to allude to the exemplary manner in which all ranks performed their duties. In action the young soldiers of the latest drafts were as steady as the veterans of Gallipoli, than which no more can be said --- -- I cannot impress too strongly the work done by Major Turner's squadron on that officer's own initiative, which proved to be a great factor in the successful issue of the day".

For his initiative and leadership during the battle Major Turner was awarded the D.S.O.

After the battle the casualties

Chapter 11

Avenging Katia

5th Mounted Brigade attack Katia – R.G.H. on patrol work – Brigade Horse Show
Y.M.C.A. Port Said – Cholera among prisoners – exercises in bayonet fighting
and use of sword – Christmas turkeys – Rafa – Major Clifford killed.

The pursuit after Romani was left to the 5th Mounted Brigade, including the R.G.H. The Brigade was placed under the orders of the Anzac Mounted Division, operating on the left of the Anzacs, between them and the 3rd Light Horse Brigade.

In the morning of August 5th a machine gun mounted on a camel and some stragglers were captured. In the afternoon the 5th Mounted Brigade co-operated in an attack upon Katia. The sight of all the mounted Brigades attacking must have been a sight to behold. It is a great pity the film crews of those days were not sufficiently mobile to record the event. Perhaps it was just as well because until they opened fire they had no idea that 10,000 Turks were dug in bordering the palm trees. The R.G.H. advanced in column of squadrons, each squadron in line of troop columns. When the leading troops got within about 800 yards, the enemy opened heavy fire with camel guns, machine guns and rifles. The enemy's position was too strongly held for the available forces and the action was broken off. With an officer and five other ranks wounded the regiment moved back to Romani and bivouacked for the night.

Next morning the infantry were brought up supported by the Anzacs with the 5th Mounted Brigade in reserve. When the enemy saw the size of the approaching force they retired to Oghratina for the remainder of that day and the next. Lt Col Yorke was put in charge of a reconnaissance in force working to the north of Oghratina, they came under heavy shell fire and the regiment retired to Katia for the night.

On August 8th the enemy evacuated Oghratina and the regiment moved forward and bivouacked for the night. Next day the Anzacs attacked Bir-el-Abd and the R.G.H. put out a line of outposts for the New Zealand Mounted Rifles, these were later withdrawn and the regiment moved back to Hill 70.

The following are further extracts from the diary of one of the officers:-
"Attacked Katia, we got within 500 yards. It was a beastly position, we withdrew to Romani -- -- came back next morning, awfully beat, half way there we heard the Turks had evacuated -- -- the strain is heavy, working

hard for 21 hours out of the 24, men and horses showing it -- -- Oghratina -- we are fairly on top, men at half rations with two gallons of water a man -- -- the retirement has started, the Australians have been badly hit, we took an outpost line to cover up their retreat but the Turks were too tired to come on -- -- we heard a New Zealander say that they would sooner have a squadron of Yeomanry with them than a Brigade of Australians -- -- diaries of German officers captured say they have a holy dread of our cavalry".

During the next three months the railway and water pipeline was pushed steadily forward across the Sinai desert at the rate of about fifteen miles a month. Labour Corps were formed using Egyptian labour and Camel Transport was attached to each unit. During this time the R.G.H. was kept occupied with patrol work and keeping an eye on the Turks, who appeared to have settled down in El Arish.

On August 19th Captain Horlick with 116 other ranks arrived from Kantara, where he had formed a brigade machine gun squadron, this brought the strength up to 19 officers 413 other ranks 428 horses and 43 mules.

It wasn't all work, there were brief periods of relaxation when the regiment engaged in a rifle match with the Ayrshire Yeomanry and Fred Lewis records:-

"We had a Brigade Horse Show last week and managed to get one first, two seconds and a third out of my troop".

A later letter home read: -

"We have moved camp since my last letter, the first move was inland about thirty miles, the second was back to the coast again. Our camp now is in a palm grove right by the sea and quite close to the town of El Arish. We are now about thirty miles down the coast and while we are here I think we are in for a pretty stiff time. We manage to make ourselves comfortable with the aid of a few blankets, a pole or two and a few bits of string".

Later he writes : --

"On Thursday I am going on ten days leave to Port Said, there is a rest camp down there", -- --then later -- -- "we leave the rest camp tomorrow and re-join the regiment at El Arish and then I suppose we shall be going back up the line again and into the push that will soon be coming off-- -- it has been a perfect rest down here -- -- the Y.M.C.A. have got several huts and tents and they are taken advantage of by the troops, who crowd them out every night -- -- the tent I am writing this in is right by the coast so we get a good sea breeze all the time -- -- I have not been made a full sergeant and I don't suppose I shall be for some time although I have got the

Cheltenham troop and a full sergeant under me and one of the peace time sergeants at that, I don't think he likes it very much, in fact we have got three full sergeants in the squadron who have not got troops, so I don't think that they think too badly of me".

An outbreak of cholera was reported amongst the prisoners taken at Romani and all leave was stopped but thanks to steps taken by the Medics it was contained.

On September 29th the regiment were ordered to the very attractive Hod Nabit where they stayed for some time doing patrol and reconnaissance work. They were not allowed tents because they would show up to hostile aircraft so they made themselves shelters of palm leaves. The officers made a very fine mess until it rained one night and then it was a very fine mess, when they had to hurriedly vacate as palm tree boughs came down on their heads. During this time each squadron took it in turn to do outpost duty. To keep them busy all ranks were instructed in the latest methods of bayonet fighting, bomb detonating and throwing. A track was made with manure hard enough for a horse to gallop on and instruction was given in the use of the sword when mounted.

On November 26th the regiment moved back to Romani and the next day to Dueidar, the strength was 23 officers 319 other ranks 456 horses, 38 mules and 62 camels with native assistants. Lt Col Yorke was taken ill and evacuated to hospital, on discharge he was appointed Brigadier General to command west coast defences; Lt Col Palmer was promoted to command.

The regiment left Dueidar on December 9th and after not having stayed anywhere very long formed the advance guard to the force marching on El Arish. Starting from Maxar in the early morning they found it very dark and very cold arriving at Bittia at 5.45 a.m. The enemy were reported as having left and the water supply being doubtful they were ordered to return to Maxar at 2.15 p.m next day and it was there Christmas day was spent. One of the officers managed to find some Egyptian Turkeys. It rained heavily all afternoon but Frank Fox records that quite a pleasant day was spent. In the evening a most enjoyable concert was held.

The enemy showed no inclination to return to El Arish, the navy cleared a minefield in the approaches, stores were soon being landed and the infantry were brought up to secure the position.

The Turks had retired partly to Rafa and partly to Magdhaba an adjoining fort, where there was a garrison of around 2,000 entrenched behind strong fortifications on a little hill; with a field of fire stretching

2,000 yards. The desert column came under the command of Lt General Sir Philip Chetwode and he decided that Maghdaba had to be taken out before a further advance could be made on Beersheba.

Christmas Turkey!

    Twenty five miles to the east over open country, this had to be a night operation, a quick hit and out before Turk reinforcements arrived. General Chetwoode led the operation in person riding out with the Anzac Mounted Division, the 5th Yeomanry Brigade, the Imperial Camel Corps brigade and six armoured cars. They set out in the evening of January 8th and were ready to put in the attack at 7 a.m. The position was very strongly defended with field guns and machine guns in a redoubt commanding a wide field of fire.

    The R.G.H. were just sitting down to breakfast when orders came for the 5th Brigade to mount up and make for some knolls towards the enemy redoubt. The R.G.H. led the advance coming under machine gun fire. There was some cover in the sand dunes, but it also gave cover for snipers and "B" squadron were ordered to protect the left flank and prevent the enemy getting round, in doing so they got into contact with the New Zealanders. "D" squadron were ordered to move along the foot of the dunes and advance in company with "B" squadron. About 3.30 orders were given for a general advance dismounted, the Worcesters on the right of R.G.H. and the Warwicks in support. The squadrons advanced in quick rushes supported by their machine guns.

The attack lasted for ten hours, there were reports of Turk reinforcements rapidly closing and a detachment was ordered to try and hold them off. The attack looked as though it was going to fail and General Chetwoode gave the order to withdraw but before the command reached them the commanding officers of the New Zealanders and the Yeomanry Brigade ordered bayonets to be fixed and they got into the redoubt, which surrendered. The battle was over, 252 of the enemy were killed and 1,600 prisoners taken. Our losses were 71 killed and 415 wounded.

All ranks of the R.G.H. were very saddened to learn that the very well liked and respected Major Clifford had been killed, together with eight other ranks. Four officers and 33 other ranks were wounded. A very dark night followed the battle and they had difficulty finding the wounded amongst the sand dunes. The Turk reinforcements kept trying to retrieve the position but when they learned the Rafa garrison had surrendered they withdrew.

Shep Sheppard leading a file had a narrow escape when he came face to face with a large party of Turks.

"We quickly turned about and got out at full gallop, I had a nasty feeling between my shoulder blades for what seemed a very long time but was probably not much more than a minute. We soon came up with the squadron and when the Turks saw they were outnumbered they withdrew".

Resting after the battle.

Chapter 12.

Gaza

De lousing – Ali el Muntar ridge – Turk Divisional commander captured
R.G.H. on sea flank – Green Hill – thick thorn hedges – retire to Wadi Ghuzze
Infantry on Mansura ridge – attack renewed – R.G.H advance on Wadi Shira
Anzacs held up – Tanks break down – move back to water horses

The 5th Mounted Brigade had taken a heavy knock during the capture of Rafa, as well as advancing on the fort they had to hold off renewed attacks from Turk reinforcements.

The enemy made no attempt to recapture the position and the R.G.H. retired to El Arish where the camp was extended to give more space between squadrons. They were liable to be shelled from the sea by submarines and they tried to dig dugouts, but this wasn't very easy because they kept collapsing in the soft sand. Enemy aircraft were active overhead, where they had the upper hand because we had very few of our own in that area. The position was eased when an airstrip was built at El Burj and three fighter planes were based there.

On the afternoon of January 11th the regiment was paraded for a Brigade memorial service and letters were read from the G.O.C. desert column and the Inspector of Cavalry, congratulating the Brigade on their conduct at Rafa. It became apparent that they had been successful in completely surrounding the position preventing any of the enemy escaping.

After a fortnight at El Arish the R.G.H. moved to El Burj, which was a much more pleasant camp in a grove of tamarisk trees. It was only about a mile from the sea where they could get fish, which was a welcome change to the rations. Another bonus was large colonies of ants. Constantly on the move with no spare water there was no opportunity to wash their clothes, or get them de-loused. The lice used to lay their eggs in the seams of the men's tunics, their body temperature warmed them up and the eggs hatched out; consequently everyone was lousy and the ants did a good job cleaning up the lice. The preferred method of getting rid of them was to go along the seams of your tunic with a lighted candle, the heat from the candle destroying the eggs.

The lice were no respecter of rank and Shep Sheppard recalled how Lieutenant Wykeham-Musgrave caught him delousing with a candle one evening, "what on earth are you doing", asked the Lieutenant, "getting rid of something I don't want sir", said Sheppard, "what I good idea, could you lend me your candle when you have finished". Evidently they preferred ants to lice in their pants!

> Whilst seated one day in my dug-out,
>   Weary and ill at ease,
> I saw a Yeoman carefully
>   Searching his sunburned knees.
>
> I asked him why he was searching,
>   And what he was looking for,
> But his only reply was a long drawn sigh,
>   As he quietly killed one more.
>   A.M. Park from the Anzac Book

x

Several drafts arrived in January and the strength was brought up to 21 officers, 403 other ranks, 419 horses, 22 mules, 51 camels handled by 28 Arab auxiliaries. Patrol work up the coast to Sheikh Zowaid was the order of the day and preparations were made for the next move, the attack on Gaza. To allow motor cars to pass over the sand, lengths of wire netting were pegged down in two parallel strips. The engineers and labour corps worked steadily bringing the railway and water pipeline foreword and February closed with them at Sheikh Zowaid.

On March 25 the Brigade moved out from Rafa to Deir el Belah, a distanceof twelve miles on the beach road. On arrival the R.G.H. were told to report to the 53rd Infantry Division. The forces we had available for the assault were the Anzac Mounted Division, the Imperial Mounted Division, four infantry Brigades and three artillery Brigades with an infantry Division in reserve. The tactics to be employed were similar to those at Rafa and but for misfortune with the weather they would have succeeded.

The Turks held a strong fortification on a ridge named Ali el Muntar on the outskirts of Gaza, the whole position being held by a force of 4,000. It was known that there were strong enemy forces situated at Huj ten miles to the north east and Abu Hareira fifteen miles away on the Beersheba road. It was hoped to carry the position by a quick surprise assault. On the night of the 25th - 26th March the Anzac Division followed by the Imperial Mounted Division moved out at 2.30 a.m. to take up position to the north and east of the town and hold up Turk reinforcements. Straightaway they got into difficulty by getting tangled up with a body of enemy infantry that had bivouacked in their path, a thick fog then came down which further hindered them. It was 8 a.m. before they reached the

Beersheba road, where they were attacked by Turk camelry, which they managed to beat off, but the element of surprise was lost, if it ever existed.

By 11.30 a.m. the Anzacs had got round in the north and were in touch with the sea and the Imperial Division were in place to the east. The heat was by now excessive and to add to their troubles they were attacked from the air. This might seem a bit incongruous but Frank Fox records that they had to dismount to drive them off, presumably with rifle fire. By this time enemy reinforcements were arriving, the Turk divisional commander, leading from the front, was captured by the Anzac Division but this made no difference to the final outcome of the battle. The enemy began to attack heavily from the east and the north and our attention was divided between attacking the town and holding them at bay.

Meanwhile the R.G.H. attached to the 53rd Division was told to co-operate with the infantry on its sea flank south of Gaza. They crossed the Wadi Ghuzze at daylight under cover of the 2/4th Royal West Kents, their role was to demonstrate and divert the enemy's attention to our left flank, taking care not to become involved in a hostile attack from which they would not be able to extricate themselves, to pay special attention to the seashore and cover a section of the 15th Heavy Battery R.G.A.

The Regiment moved from Deir el Belah at 2 a.m. on March 26th accompanied by the Gloucester section of the Machine Gun Squadron. At daylight they were immediately enveloped in heavy fog but they crossed the Wadi el Ghuzze about 6 a.m. "B" squadron acting as advance guard, was ordered to proceed up the coastline with a patrol on the beach; they encountered an enemy patrol which retired. Because of the fog progress was slow but by now two of the squadrons had reached a point two miles to the north of the Wadi with one in reserve. The 2/4th Royal West Kents were on their right.

The fog cleared around 9 a.m. and Regimental H.Q. was established about 600 yards south west of Green Hill, an advanced squadron was holding the approach to Green Hill with another to their right and on its right were the infantry. "B" squadron was holding the Gaza - Rafa road.

The plan was for the infantry and the mounted divisions encircling the position to attack together, but because of the fog the attack was delayed. There were further delays by thick thorn hedges, worse then barbed wire, which surrounded the town. The Imperial Mounted Division were told to extend round to the north to cover the rear of the Anzacs when they advanced. The Anzacs began their assault at 4 p.m., three hours late nevertheless they got into the northern outskirts of the town and by 6 p.m. the whole Ali Muntar ridge was in British hands.

The position was virtually ours for the taking BUT the horses had been going since daybreak and they wanted watering. The Imperial Mounted Division was being hard pressed by large Turk forces approaching from the north and east and they were in danger of being cut off. A labyrinth of cactus thorn ridges lay between the Ali Muntar ridge and the town with its wells, there was no alternative other than to give the order to withdraw to the Wadi Ghuzze.

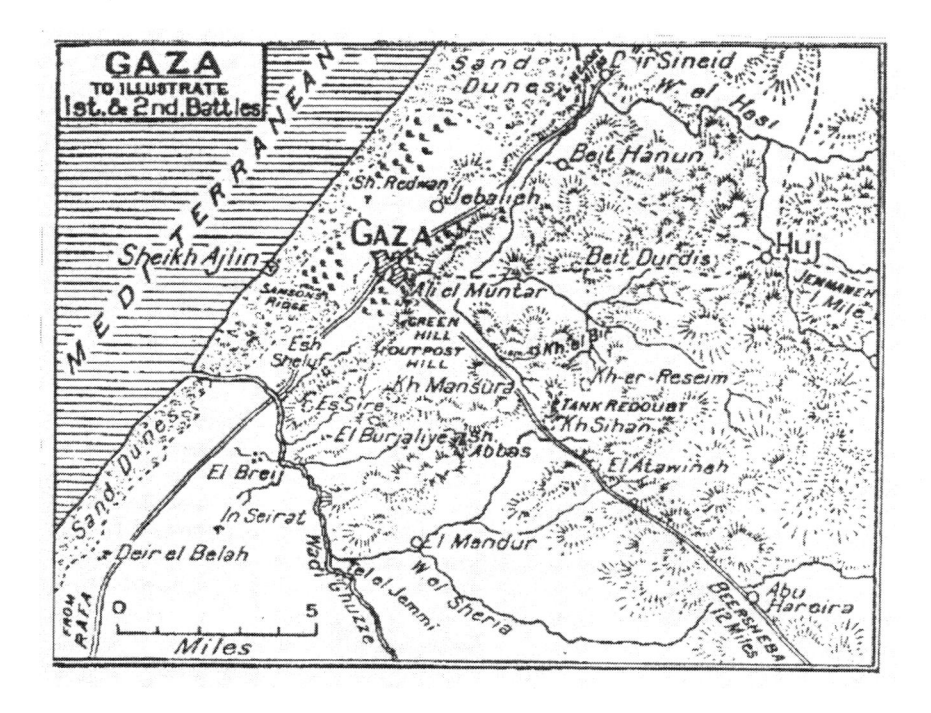

About 2 p.m. the West Kents sent a message that they were advancing and asked the R.G.H. to conform to their movements. This was done but later the infantry fell back drawing in their left flank; this left "D" squadron R.G.H. in advance of the infantry and under heavy fire. "D" squadron were reinforced with the reserve squadron, ordered to hold on till dusk and then retire to the Wadi Ghuzze. The enemy made a half hearted attempt at attack but were dissuaded by our machine guns.

Dawn found the infantry occupying the Mansura ridge about three miles to the south of the town unsupported by cavalry. Lack of communications and misunderstandings made it impossible to renew the attack. They did attempt to take Green Hill but a strong body of Turks counter attacked and pushed them off.

A fortnight later preparations were made to renew the attack. When the infantry withdrew after the first attack they took up position along the Es Sire - Mansura - Abbas ridge and were dug in. The enemy also had not been idle and were holding a strong line from Samson's Ridge on the coast, to Green Hill, Tank Redoubt and another strong position at El Atawina.

For the second battle there were available 32 field guns, six mountain guns with the camel brigade, three divisional artilleries, one of eight 4.5 inch howitzers and 36 eighteen pounders, two of eight 4.5 howitzers and 28 eight pounders and sundry other guns making up the total number of 170 artillery pieces available. In addition three battleships were stationed offshore to bombard the town. For the first time in this theatre of war the infantry were to be supported by a detachment of tanks.

At midnight on April 17th orders were received for the mounted brigade and R.G.H. to march to El Mundur and turn down the Wadi el Shira to clear out some Turks reported to be down there holding the Gaza Beersheba road. The plan was for the infantry to advance on Gaza under the cover of the tanks and artillery fire accompanied by shelling from the battleships off shore. The position of the cavalry was to protect the infantry's right flank.

The artillery bombardment opened at 4 a.m. and by 6 a.m. the brigade had moved into the battle line with the R.G.H. being on the right of the line. "D" squadron was on the left in touch with the Worcester Yeomanry, "A" squadron was on the right and "B" squadron with the machine gun section in reserve. The Anzac mounted division guarded the brigade's right flank but were hindered by Turk artillery fire coming from a prominence named sausage hill. The New Zealand mounted brigade was ordered to clear them but made little headway. The right flank was now dangerously exposed because dismounted yeomanry were advancing up the Gaza road and "B" squadron were brought round to provide cover.

The attack made little progress against the entrenched Turks; the Tanks were either hit by artillery or broke down and early in the afternoon the 3rd and 4th Australian Light Horse Brigades which had reached the Gaza Beersheba road were compelled to retire. The Warwick Yeomanry, which had been held in reserve, was brought up to support the Worcesters on the left. The enemy counter attacked, but were checked. They continued to press heavily and the Australians on the R.G.H. right and left were retiring and the R.G.H. were forced to withdraw. Orders were received for the brigade to withdraw at 7.45 p.m. to Tel el Jemmi to water the horses, they were then ordered to bivouac at El Mundur. Horse lines were put down and everyone except the pickets and sentries fell asleep on the hard ground.

The brigade was kept in reserve then on April 20th ordered to entrench on a line Tel el Jemmi El Mundur, on April 24th the brigade moved back to Khan Yunus where there were horse watering troughs. The battle was over, with nothing having been gained.

Above:- living off the country in true Yeoman fashion
Below:- Gaza, the cacti in both pictures give some idea of the obstacles faced

Chapter 13.

A Change of Command and Gaza Falls.

Relieved by A.L.H. - Lawrence of Arabia - "Yilderim Force" - staff reconnaissance - drive to trap Turk outposts - General Allenby in command - Lt Wilson captures Turk Patrol - R.G.H. take up outpost line - 30 mile ride - essential to take Beersheba's wells - Worcesters attacked - Gaza falls.

Elated at twice repulsing the British the Turks set about consolidating their position along the Gaza - Beersheba road. They were further heartened by the collapse of the Russians, which theoretically made more troops available for them to reinforce their front. For our part after having twice suffered a reverse, bad news from France made us realise the end of the war was still a long way ahead.

The R.G.H. were occupying a position at Esh Sheluf, which had been a Turkish strongpoint. Unfortunately the defences were back to front and they had the tedious job of turning the position round. Caring for the horses occupied a lot of the time, water was short, rations were very basic and the men tended to be affected by sores which turned septic. The water supply was in advance of the position they were holding, so a reserve had to be collected and stored in case the wells were cut off. Added to this was the fear that the Turks would put in a determined attack to try and recover lost ground. The possibility of a summer of trench warfare did nothing to boost morale; however Turkish cavalry patrols that were met showed little offensive spirit.

On May 2nd the regiment was relieved by the Australian Light Horse Regiment and moved back briefly to Beni Sela and then to Tel-el-Marakeb. Here they were by the sea shore and tired out after being continually at work since first Gaza, they quickly recovered their spirits. They were able to wash their clothes and get rid of the vermin which plagued them. The only snag being that they were not allowed to put their tents up. Enemy aircraft were constantly overhead and lights had to be out by 8.30. Being midsummer it was very hot.

Our forces weren't to know it but the Turkish position was extremely weak, her best troops had been taken to fight Germany's battles against Russia and Rumania and those in the Caucasus had been decimated by disease and the severity of the winter. The Arabs advised by Colonel T.E. Lawrence were holding the eastern flank and generally being a thorn in the side of the Turks.

"Lawrence of Arabia" was an Oxford graduate who became a legend in his lifetime. Before the war he had joined an expedition digging for lost civilisations in the valley of the Euphrates. He travelled extensively through the whole area and his knowledge of the terrain stood him in good stead throughout the campaign. He spoke fluent Arabic, dressed in Arab robes and had a thorough understanding of the Arab way of life. As a young Lieutenant in the map department, at the headquarters of the Egyptian Expeditionary Force, he made himself thoroughly unpopular by his criticism of the course of the campaign and lack of support afforded to the Arab revolt. Consequently when he applied for two weeks leave, it was granted with alacrity to get him out of the way.

Instead of going down the Nile, as most officers did, he attached himself to Ronald Storrs; oriental secretary to the high commissioner in Egypt and went down into Arabia to make contact with Shereef Hussein 1, the King of the Hejaz. Hussein had four sons and after assessing them all Lawrence decided that the Emir Feisal was the most likely leader, with the ability to weld the tribes together and pursue the campaign. The Arabs had already liberated the Holy City of Mecca and the Hejaz, which roughly formed the eastern bank of the Red Sea. Feisal was trying to keep the revolution alive, but ammunition was short and they were starving.

Lawrence entered Feisal's tent in October 1916 and after extending greetings over many cups of sweetened coffee he said:

"And when will your army reach Damascus", Feisal replied: "I fear the gates of Damascus are farther beyond our reach then the gates of Paradise".

A few days with Feisal convinced Lawrence that it might be possible to re-organise this rabble into an irregular force which could be of great assistance to the British army in Egypt. He became so absorbed in working out his idea that when his two weeks were up he stayed on in Arabia without sending his apologies to H.Q. in Cairo. From then on Lawrence was the moving spirit in the Arab revolt and in October 1918 the Arabs entered Damascus.

The Turks had built a railway from Damascus down through the Arabian Desert into the Hejaz to Medina and Mecca. There were Turkish garrisons along the route and with the Arabs advised by Lawrence constantly sabotaging the railway, but not completely cutting it, they kept large bodies of Turks held down. Such notoriety did Lawrence achieve that requests kept coming through from Arab tribes to the north to send them a "lurens", so that they could blow up the railway.

The Indian force that had advanced on Basra had been reinforced and was now in the occupation of Baghdad. Anxious to boost the morale of their ally by a spectacular victory, the Germans sent General von

Falkenhayn to advise on the re-conquest of the city. After a tour of the area he advised that Baghdad could be recovered provided the Gaza - Beersheba front was secured. It very quickly became apparent that the Teutonic manner of issuing orders and expecting instant obedience didn't work with the Turks. Furthermore he didn't help himself by ignoring the opinions of those German officers, who had been working with the Turks for the past two years and who understood their ways. The name given to the proposed new force was "Yilderim", which is Turkish for lightening; if it was intended as a lightening strike it was not an appropriate name. The commander chosen for this new army was Mustapha Kemal, the successful Turk commander at Gallipoli. He couldn't stomach the overbearing German manner and resigned the command.

    This force is mentioned because not only did tie up an army that might otherwise have been employed on the Palestine front but it deprived the Turks of their most capable commander, who because of the German influence on all fronts, participated in the war very little more. After the war when Enver, who he despised, had been deposed he became president of the Turkish republic. Changing his name to Ataturk, meaning Father of the Nation, he modernised Turkey. His name is still revered throughout the country and respected by his former enemies.

    The summer months were largely devoted to keeping the enemy patrols in check and to keeping his morale down by minor raids. Kept constantly on the move the R.G.H. took part in an advance at Brigade strength on June 11th, to give cover for a staff reconnaissance, so that Turkish strength and a possible line of advance could be observed. This was interfered with by thick fog, no close contact with the enemy was made but there was an exchange of fire at long range during the day. Shortly after midday the brigade was withdrawn and returned to camp. The next few days were taken up with the regiment finding a digging party to help form a strong point at El Ghabi. Those left in camp had their work cut out with each man having to take care of four horses. Conditions were trying, with cases of heat stroke daily and septic sores were another drain on their vitality.

    At the end of June the regiment took part in a "drive" arranged to trap the enemy's outposts. The Turks were accustomed to come up to our barbed wire under cover of darkness when our day outposts were withdrawn. These movements took on a somewhat "tit for tat" aspect where each side took it in turn to occupy the same post. Booby traps and "welcoming" messages would be left for the other side to read.

    The plan of the scheme was to push out during the night, as far into the enemy country as possible and at dawn to converge inwards on to our barbed wire; driving before them any enemy patrols they encountered. In addition to the R.G.H. the Worcesters, Warwicks and Buckingham Yeomanry were to take part. The net thrown out was to close in on Karm where the expected "bag" was to be sorted out. Each squadron would be entirely on its own and have to provide its own protection during the approach march and the drive. Troops were to march as light as possible and officers were instructed to show dash and initiative.

For this operation the regiment had a marching out strength of 15 officers, 234 other ranks and 271 horses. They moved off at a trot from the start point in extended order and after proceeding half a mile came under enemy shell fire, one officer and three other ranks were slightly wounded and one horse killed. Later about two squadrons of cavalry and fifteen to twenty camelmen were seen approaching from the east. On our opening fire at 1700 yards they immediately retired. The march was continued and contact was made with the Warwicks at about 9.30.a.m.

At 10 a.m. the drive commenced with one troop per squadron acting as rearguard to deal with some Turks seen on the skyline. The combined line of troops advanced at the trot and then at the gallop, no enemy patrols were encountered and the total bag was one Bedouin boy.

At the commencement of the advance from the canal, which had resulted in the advance across the Sinai desert, across the Egyptian border and up into Palestine, General Murray had some twelve divisions at his disposal. It was necessary to keep a force in the Canal Zone and another to deal with any possible rising of the Senussi in the Libyan Desert. Because of casualties and the withdrawal of whole divisions that were fed into the mincing machine in France, by the time of second Gaza the numbers had dwindled to four divisions and six independent brigades. Suddenly the government at home woke up to the fact that this small force had advanced some hundred miles in little more than six months, whereas in France if they advanced a hundred yards they were pushed back two hundred the next day. So the decision was made to reinforce and give priority to the Palestinian front, knock Turkey out of the war and turn the German flank.

The first thing that happened was a change in the command. General Sir Archibald Murray had achieved miracles and General Sir Edmund "the Bull" Allenby, who was chosen as his successor, was the first to acknowledge that fact. Allenby's initial impact in weeding out staff and troops, who didn't seem to be doing much in the rear areas, was reminiscent of Roberts in South Africa. In the forward area a detachment of R.G.H. were one of the first to experience and have contact with the new Commander in Chief. In Fred Lewis's words: -

"I was out on patrol with some kid of an officer, there was nothing much about and we thought we would stop for a break. We carried our rifles in a leather "bucket" attached to the front of the saddle. Anyway we were chatting around smoking, when a motor car appeared from nowhere and out shot a General who came charging at us like a mad bull. The officer stepped forward with his brand new pip and made his snappiest salute.

"How long have you been out here.
Three weeks sir.
What battle school did you go to.
Tidworth sir.
Didn't they teach you never to leave your rifles in buckets in the presence of the enemy"
A mumble.
"If you go on like this you won't last another three days"..

He then turned his attention to Sergeant Fred Lewis.
"How long have you been out here Sergeant.
Two Years sir.
Two years and you don't know better than to leave your rifles in buckets, go on get them out and post sentries, the Turks might appear from nowhere, they may be behind that dune" – pointing to an ant hill – "come on what are you waiting for".

With that he departed and Lewis commented by the time he had finished and lectured me on my duties as troop sergeant, I felt about knee high to a worm.

After considering the problems of supply, re-organisation and of establishing supremacy in the air, Allenby spent the next three months putting in hand a period of intensive training and building up his forces. His estimate of the force required was seven infantry divisions and three mounted divisions. On the basis that new commanders get what they ask for he was sent two new divisions together with Field and Corps artillery, five squadrons of aeroplanes and additional signal and medical units.

So that everybody should be as fit as possible the R.G.H. together with the 5th Mounted Brigade moved back to a rest camp at Marakeb by the sea, where the most popular event of the day was the bathing parade. In addition there was intensive training in the Hotchkiss gun, signalling, musketry and gas drill. The Regiment spent some time at Marakeb and on July 28th they held regimental sports with such events as a V.C. race, a harem race, a tug of war on horse back and a mule race for officers. The band and pipers of the 52nd Division helped to make for an enjoyable day.

Leave was granted for the men to visit a rest camp at Port Said and Fred Lewis wrote home: -

"A" Squadron Sergeants on leave in Port Said.
From left to Right – Sgt Lewis, Sgt Bowl, S.S.M. Smart Sgt Roberts, Sgt Barton

"We leave here tomorrow and rejoin the regiment at El Arish and then I suppose we shall be going back up the line again and into the push that will soon be coming off. It has been a perfect rest down here, nothing to do and all day to do it in. Port Said itself is not much of a place, far and away behind Alex and Cairo. The Y.M.C.A. has several huts and tents here and they are taken advantage of by the troops who crowd them out day and night. The tent I am in is pitched right on the coast so we get a good sea breeze all the time. The fellow who is tickling the piano used to play at the Hippodrome in Cheltenham. I went to the English Church last Sunday evening; I wonder when I shall be in a church again".

The regiment spent some time with the brigade at Marakeb and then moved back along the sea shore to El Arish. On the way they were inspected by Lt General Sir Harry Chauvel commander of the Desert Mounted Corps and Major General Hodgson commander of the Australian Mounted Division; which included the 5th Mounted Brigade.

Intensive training continued and on August 23rd General Allenby visited the camp. They remained at El Arish for the whole of September and then on October 9th the 5th Mounted Brigade took over the outpost line from the 4th Australian Light Horse Brigade.

On October 13th a patrol consisting of Corporal Morgan, Privates Smith, Poole and Smart had the misfortune to be captured by two troops of Turk cavalry. Two days later the regiment got its revenge for this. Under cover of darkness an ambush party under Lt R.H. Wilson pushed forward into enemy territory and occupied two stone huts on a hillock known as Point 720. After they had reached their objective the horses were sent back and the men set about entrenching the houses. At 8 o'clock in the morning an enemy patrol of twelve men approached, some horses and men were accounted for and two prisoners were captured, one of whom had helped capture Corporal Morgan's patrol. For this exploit Lt Wilson was awarded the M.C. and Sergeant Burland Barton and Corporal Lane the M.M.

The R.G.H. were frequently called upon to cover staff reconnaissance, this being part of the C in C's plan that everyone should be familiar with the country they would be advancing over. Prospecting for possible water supplies was another object of these exercises, also to practice communicating with aeroplanes.

Water was to be a constant problem, in a letter home written on October 5th Sgt Fred Lewis wrote: -

"We have been on the move for five days -- you would like to see me now I had all my hair clipped off this morning, I really could not keep it clean for we are not over blessed with water. We are allowed the use of some ablution places once every five days, the remaining four we have to wash in what we can cadge. The thing that worries us is the dust, it is about six inches thick and for about three or four hours in the day a wind gets up and blows it over and into every blessed thing. Mice are also a problem they pay us a visit every night and have a high old time chasing each other round the shack". (Whenever possible they made themselves little shelters with odds and ends of wood, string and coverings of cloth or vegetation).

General Allenby had fixed October 31st as the day for his assault on the Turks. The advance in Palestine very much depended on an adequate water supply, the first battle of Gaza had been successful but our force had to withdraw on the brink of victory, because their horses had to be watered. With a daily requirement of 400,000 gallons this factor was to dominate his future tactics and he decided that his first objective must be the capture of Beersheba's wells.

The Turks held a strong position from the sea at Gaza along the line of the Beersheba road. Gaza was heavily entrenched and wired, the remainder of the line consisted of a series of strong points 1,500 to 2,000 yards apart and finally Beersheba itself; except that there was a gap of some four and a half miles of hilly country between Beersheba and Hareira. He decided to put in his main assault here then roll up the Turkish line to Gaza. To put this into effect he made a double bluff, apparently assembling large forces against Gaza and leading the Turks to think he was bluffing them into thinking that the assault would be on Beersheba, where the cavalry had been making demonstrations. He also got the navy to make soundings to determine the depth of the sea to the rear of Gaza, so that the Turks would think he was going to land troops there. His strategy was eminently successful in that he deceived spies dressed as Arabs, who mingled with stray Bedouin that were always wandering around. In this he was very much assisted by his new squadrons of aeroplanes, which kept Turk planes from observing those preparations that he didn't want them to see.

The country from the Wadi Ghuzze up to Beersheba was completely waterless and the logistical facts of the assaulting force were that the four infantry divisions and two mounted divisions could be supplied with water and ammunition up to Beersheba and for one march beyond. At the same time the two divisions opposite Gaza had to be supplied, they also were going to put in an attack. It therefore meant that Beersheba had to be taken in the first assault. The great bulk of the troops were kept opposite Gaza until the last possible moment. One of the cavalry divisions had been advancing up to Beersheba and back again about once a fortnight. This was part of the deception plan to lead the Turks into thinking we could not succeed in this sector.

Although Allenby was commander in chief of the entire Eastern Expeditionary Force and had his headqarters in Cairo he believed in being up with his troops and he set up his headquarters in Rafa, so as to be near the action. Field Marshall Montgomery's tactics and inspirational leadership in the second war could almost be modelled on Allenby.

Frank Fox records: -- -- to ensure greater mobility for the mounted troops, officers sized saddle wallets were issued to all ranks to carry three days rations. Two nosebags on each saddle carried nineteen pounds of grain this being two days forage. An additional day's forage was carried in limbered General Service wagons, three per regiment. Ration and store wagons were packed each night, nosebags filled after the animals had their last feed and tied on the saddles and all harness and saddlery laid out in order behind the horse. The men's wallets were kept permanently packed, the rations in them being renewed as they were consumed. To keep everyone up to the mark for instant readiness, surprise orders would be given to "mount up". There was keen competition between each troop, as to which would be the first to be mounted.

On October 23rd the 5th Mounted Brigade, including R.G.H. after some heavy fighting took up an outpost line from Hill 630, Hill 720 to El Buggar. The R.G.H. were in the forefront of the battle, "A" squadron met a squadron of enemy cavalry early in the morning, pushed it back and took El Buggar ridge. One troop of "A" squadron under Lt P.H. Morgan then moved on to occupy Hill 720. They were charged by a squadron of enemy cavalry and were forced to retire, suffering one casualty, Private J. Pullin whose horse fell and he was taken prisoner.

Fred Lewis recalling this incident in later years commented: – "we got out as quick as we could, the Turks were coming after us yelling Allah-Allah-Allah and I could almost feel a Turk's lance pricking my behind. One poor beggar's horse fell and he was put in the bag".

"D" squadron was in reserve and three troops under Capt A.H.S. Howard moved out to support and the enemy fell back to Hill 720. Meanwhile "B" squadron under Capt F.A. Mitchell made good at Hill 630 and "D" squadron joined Regimental Headquarters on Imleih ridge. The Berkley troop under 2nd Lt H.P. Ellis was heavily pressed by a squadron of enemy cavalry, aided by the enemy from hill 720. 2nd Lt Ellis by courageous use of Hotchkiss and rifle fire held up the enemy until the Warwick Yeomanry came up in support. Lt Ellis who was wounded received the M.C. and L Cpl Harris and Private Mitchell the M.M.

The enemy on Hill 720 were attacked at 7 o'clock with the help of an H.A.C. Battery, "D" squadron attacked the position and carried it without casualties. The outpost line had now been established.

Later the R.G.H. were relieved by the Warwicks and retired to Karm to be held in reserve. Four days later the 5th Mounted Brigade relieved the Imperial Camel Corps on the line Maalaga to Khalasa.

During the night of 27th/28th and 28th/29th the Desert Mounted Corps less the Yeomanry Division left its position before Gaza. Together with the Anzacs they moved to Khalasa ten miles south of Beersheba, leaving their tents standing and lit up at night. For some days previously the engineers had been digging out ancient wells, relics of forgotten cities, to ensure a water supply at this point.

The main Beersheba defences were to the south west and west of the town and these were to be assaulted by three infantry divisions. The attack went in on the night of October 31st with the two mounted divisions setting out on a thirty mile ride from Khalasa, circling to the east of the town and cutting the road to Hebron, so as to cut off Turk reinforcements. This movement meant a ride of some thirty miles in the darkness, admittedly there was a moon but the fact that they reached their objectives justified their preliminary familiarisation of the country.

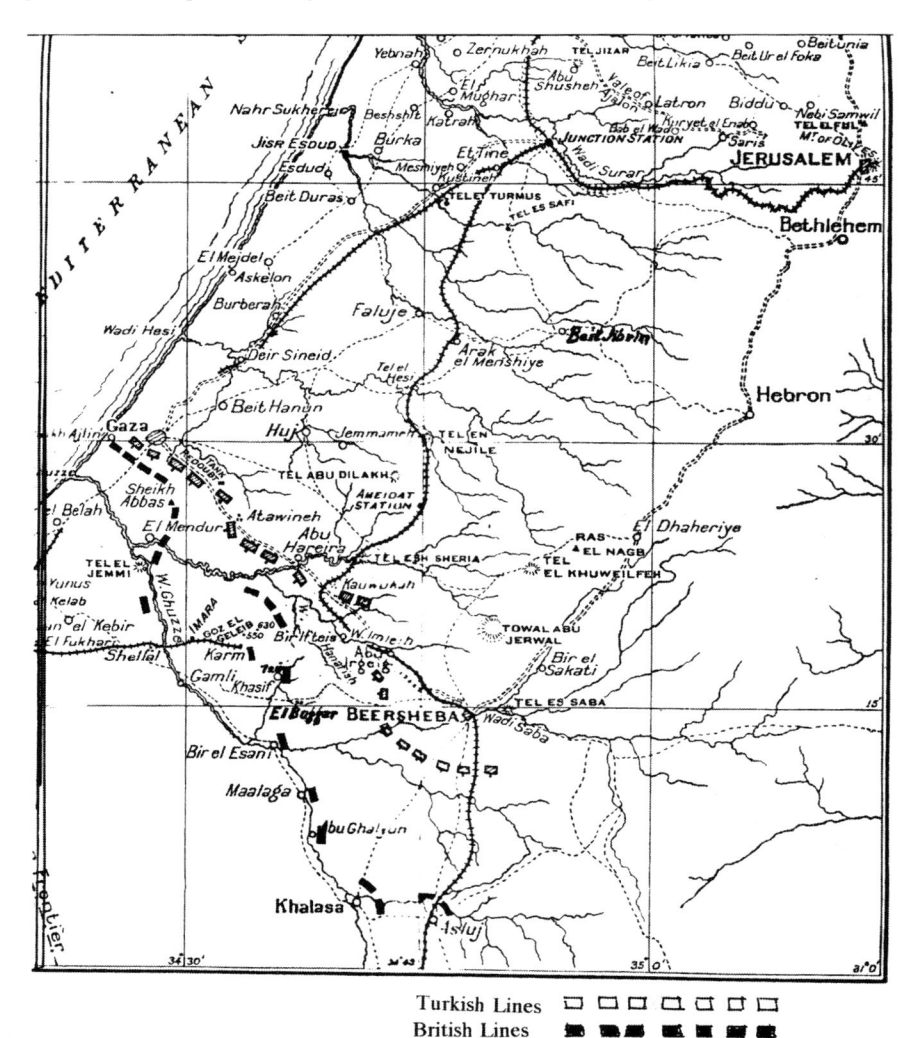

The infantry attack on Beersheba went in very early on the morning of 31st October and at the same time the various units of the Desert Mounted Corps moved in towards the town from the east, south east and north east; cutting the Hebron road. They were eminently successful in threatening the enemy's rear, pinning down his reserves and facilitating the infantry advance from the south and south west.

It was essential that Beersheba and its wells should be taken before nightfall and a Turk strong point at Tel el Saba to the east of the town threatened to hold up the attack. Drastic action had to be taken to force the pace. At four o'clock in the afternoon the order was given to the 4th Australian Light Horse Brigade to charge. Starting off at the trot, soon quickening into a gallop, successive lines of trenches were taken. They reached the wadi just before the town at dusk, after a short pause they dismounted and advanced in a bayonet attack taking 700 prisoners. They then mounted up and followed the fleeing enemy.

At nightfall two enemy planes, the last of the defenders, left the town and attacked the 5th Mounted Brigade transport column inflicting a few casualties. In total 2,000 prisoners were taken and there were about 500 Turks killed. Unfortunately five of the seven wells had been damaged but a heavy rainstorm had left numerous pools of water.

Beersheba having been taken Gaza was successfully attacked on the night of November 1st/2nd, the objective being a line from a feature known as Umbrella Hill to Sheikh Hassan on the coast to the west of the town. At the same time the infantry of the 20th Corps started to attack the strong points at Hareira and Sharia. The mounted troops were given the task of protecting the Corps right flank, entailing hard outpost fighting to the north east of Beersheba. This had the effect of drawing out the Turk cavalry making the work of the infantry that much easier. The Mounted Brigades were given 24 hour periods of duty before withdrawing to water, Beersheba's wells not yet being fully functional.

The R.G.H. on November 1st moved forward from Corps reserve position and bivouacked north of the Wadi Saba where they received orders to be attached to the Anzac Mounted Division. On November 3rd they marched up the Hebron road to join the Worcesters. The strength was 20 officers 349 other ranks, 445 animals under the command of Lt Col A.J. Palmer.

On November 4th several patrols were ordered out, the regiment was relieved in the outpost line by the Worcesters and were just returning for their horses when the Worcesters were attacked and they had to go to their aid. Galloping back over rough country they were successful in relieving the situation.

"A" squadron which was sent to support the Worcesters on the right did not have such heavy fighting as "D", 2nd Lieutenants L.L. Wilkins and T.N. Inglis were both severely wounded. Sergeants Pearse and Insoll carried on with courage and resource and were highly praised. Fighting was heavy until darkness fell and the enemy withdrew. On the arrival of the New Zealand Mounted Rifles the 5th Mounted Brigade withdrew but not before recovering their considerable casualties, which was difficult in the rough terrain. The R.G.H. had two officers and 12 other ranks wounded, one of whom subsequently died. The horses had been without water for 48 hours and could not be restrained when they smelled the water troughs at Beersheba.

At dawn on November 6th a general attack was ordered the Yeomanry reaching the line of the Wadi Sharia, the troops on the left being close to the Hareira redoubt. Some 600 prisoners were taken together with guns and machine guns our casualties were slight. The greatest opposition being encountered by the Yeomanry early in the morning, the enemy's left was being strongly defended. The mounted troops were ordered to take up the pursuit and to occupy Huj and Jemameh; the R.G.H. stood to arms but were not called upon.

Meanwhile the troops on the coast had not been idle and on the night of the 6th they pushed forward with little resistance and next morning it was found that the Turks had evacuated Gaza. The Imperial Cavalry Brigade took up the pursuit and seized the line of the Wadi Hesi. On November 7th the 5th Mounted Brigade, with the R.G.H. in the lead took up a position in the vicinity of Sharia. In the afternoon enemy cavalry approached and the brigade moved forward to charge but the enemy retreated. The battle for Gaza was over.

Exhausted men and horses

123.

Photo by permission of the Imperial War Museum

Watering Camels and Horses at Beersheba

The "Cheltenham Troop", Sergeant Fred Lewis on right of troop leader who is wearing a cap.

Chapter 14

Turks in Retreat

Rate of advance limited by water supply – Turk resistance disintegrates – Huj.– Turks fear cavalry – large enemy force – forced to withdraw – all day watering – capture Junction Station – enemy force broken into two.

General Allenby's plan to surround the Turkish Gaza Beersheba line and eliminate the Turkish army in that area unfortunately failed to materialise. The attacking forces had done wonders but the water supplies could not sustain the advancing army over the country they were entering. This gave the Turks sufficient time to mount a rearguard action and at the same time to damage the wells, temporarily putting them out of action.

As a result of the Turkish counter attack north of Beersheba, General Chauvel's cavalry was compelled to press forward on Jemmameh and Huj instead of north up the railway line to Tel en Nejile, but if they had gone that way they would not have had a sufficient water supply. Therefore the orders to the Desert Mounted Corps on November 8th were to rapidly advance on Huj and Jemmameh and then proceed north west to cut off the Turkish retreat from Gaza.

Though the enemy had escaped immediate destruction his situation was critical. The advance of the infantry had put paid to any hope of his making a stand at the Wadi Hesi. Reports from the Royal Flying Corps showed that the disintegration and demoralisation of the Turkish army was almost complete. General Allenby issued orders on November 9th directing the mounted troops to advance with all speed. But the Desert Mounted Corps was for the moment incapable of any further effort. Only the Anzacs had succeeded in watering their horses during the night of 8th/9th. The Australian Mounted Division had had little water for two days and the Yeomanry Division arriving at Huj on the afternoon of the ninth was also without water. (References to the Yeomanry Division should not be confused with the 5th Mounted Brigade or the R.G.H., this was a separate Division under Major General George Barrow).

One sleepy eyed Camelier had dismounted from his camel to give a drink to a fainting Tommy. Half filling his mess tine the Tommy sat on the ground and slowly swallowed it. The Camelier also sat on the ground and watched him; his head sinking lower and lower and then he fell forward and went to sleep. The Tommy finished his water then he also went to sleep.

Another Australian had poured water from his flask into the crown of his hat and with it washed his aching feet. He was about to throw it away when two men rushed up, took the hat from him and swallowed the water!

On the night of November 8th, officers were sent out to find water for the horses but they were unsuccessful. At 8.30 a.m. next day all horses and mules in the Brigade marched to Jemameh, when they got there they found so many animals waiting to be watered that it was unlikely theirs could be watered that day. They moved on to a wadi reported to contain water and the following entry from an officer's diary gives some idea of what they were up against.

"November 9th - Had an awful night at Sharia, water very scarce, thousands trying to water. The horses are constantly without water for 36 hours, water is like gold. Today spent the most awful time from 8.30 in the morning till 9 at night watering horses".

Sergeant Fred Lewis mentions the water shortage:-

"We got to Beersheba after a 28 mile trek and had a little bit of fun during the day. We stayed here a couple of days and then pushed on about 10 miles. We remained in the front line two days and then returned here, got in about one o'clock this morning just about fed up with Palestine and everything else. I had one bottle of water from the time we left here till we got back again and didn't we drink when we did get to water. Had a jolly good wash and change of clothes, now feel fit to march to Jerusalem".

In a later letter he writes:-

"The country we have come through since leaving Beersheba has been quite a land of milk and honey. Oranges, figs and dates and plenty of corn for the horses -- -- our infantry have been splendid if you could see some of the positions they have taken you would wonder how they were able to do it. Had a taste of what is in front of us, it rained and we got very wet, our troop happened to be near a railway line so we got a dozen sleepers and had a fine fire going that lasted all night".

A large number of prisoners had been captured, if all the mounted forces had been able to advance the greater part of the Turkish army would have been overrun. Kress von Kressenstein related after the war how panic had spread among the Turks, by a report that the British cavalry had broken through. Troops, ammunition columns and transport were scattered in wild disorder and communication between the army staff and the troops was destroyed.

Lt Col R.M. Preston D.S.O., M.R.C.V.S. reinforces this point: -
"Had water been available in abundance throughout the advance our cavalry would have been able to overwhelm the retreating Turks and the capture of Jerusalem would then have been accomplished by a rapid raid of mounted troops. As it was each night was spent by a large part of the cavalry in a heart breaking search for water that too often proved fruitless. The marching powers of the Turks are phenomenal, after fighting all day they would withdraw during the night, destroying the lifting gear of the wells as they went".

Frank Fox records that November 8th was marked by a splendid action at Huj. We had left Sharia and rode through Barata seeking contact with the Turks, who were fighting a rearguard action. The first objective was Zuheilike where the enemy had batteries protected by about 2,000 infantry. The Turks did not wait for an encounter but retired, shelling our forces heavily as they went. The Brigade pressed the enemy hard; galloping from one ridge to another for a distance of about ten miles, rapidly gaining on the guns and passing over country covered with dead Turks and abandoned material. Among this abandoned material were some small water barrels, which were very welcome as we had been without water since the previous night. Soon after midday we were east of Huj and in close contact with enemy artillery.

Major General Shea the commander of the 60th Division saw that the approach to the guns would be a slow and costly operation for his infantry and sought assistance from the nearest mounted troops on his right, which happened to be the 5th Mounted Brigade. Finding Colonel Cheape of the Warwick Yeomanry close by he requested him to charge the enemy guns at once. Colonel Cheape collected one and a half of his own squadrons of Warwicks and one and a half squadrons of Worcesters. Making use of a low ridge he worked round to within about 800 yards then gave the command and the ten troops burst over the ridge and charged at full gallop. The Turks sprang to their guns and turned them round to fire point blank into the charging horsemen. The leading troops of the cavalry dashed into the first enemy battery, the following troops swinging to the right took the three heavy howitzers in their stride, leaving the guns silent and the crews dead or dying they then galloped round the hill to fall upon the mountain battery from the rear. The third wave of cavalry passed the first battery, where a fierce sabre v. bayonet fight was going on and raced up the slope to the machine guns. Many saddles were emptied in that few yards but the charge was irresistible.

Commenting on the action at Huj, S.F. Hatton of the Middlesex Yeomanry had this to say: -

"Towards dusk we reached Huj and here a memorable sight met our eyes. We came across the captured batteries of guns which had been taken at the point of the sword by the Warwick and Worcester Yeomanry. The Londoners of the 60th division had been held up by two batteries of Austrian gunners occupying a fine position on a ridge. Another battery and machine guns at right angles gave enfilading fire. General O'Shea sent for assistance from two and a half squadrons of the Worcester and Warwick Yeomanry who were coming up on the flank. The order was given for the position to be cleared by them. Dividing into two groups the Yeomen charged across an open half mile, right into the teeth of the guns which were firing at them. Through a tornado of shot, shell and machine gun fire these Midland Yeomen rode with full throated cheers, though the Austrian gunners stuck to their guns they were sabred where they stood. Those who saw it say it was magnificent and should rank with Balaclaava".

Most of the Turkish infantry escaped as our force of cavalry was too scattered and cut up by the charge to pursue them. About 70 of the enemy gunners were killed and a large number wounded. Our losses were heavy; of the 170 odd who took part 75 were killed or wounded, all in the space of ten minutes.

This action demonstrated what a fearful weapon the cavalry sword was; the Turkish gunners all had terrible wounds from sword cuts. Little wonder the Turks were afraid of the cavalry. The rapid movement and weight of the charge showed the advantage of this arm as against the cavalryman armed with rifle and bayonet. The latter had to get themselves in position, dismount and then attack; the advantage gained by forward momentum in the charge being lost.

During the 10th and 11th a hot and exhausting wind, the difficulty of bringing supplies up to the front, all added to the water shortage caused the pursuit to slow down. The lack of rolling stock meant that the Turkish line from Gaza could not be fully utilised until our own standard gauge line could be linked in. The navy helped by landing stores at the mouth of the Wadi el Hesi and Wadi Sukhereir, but they still had to be conveyed across the difficult country. Modern satellite images show the country to be very built up and developed, giving a very different picture of the country that the Yeomanry had to fight over in 1916 - 18.

Turkish wireless messages that had been intercepted showed that the Turk seventh army had been ordered to make a counter attack from Hebron. General Allenby was convinced by his air reconnaissance that this was a very small threat, even so in case this threat developed he positioned a brigade of the Camel Corps to cover his right flank at Tel en Nejile. It was apparent that the enemy's resistance was stiffening and that he was going to make a stand to cover the junction of the Jerusalem line with his main railway.

General Allenby decided to hold his eastern flank with the Australian Mounted Division, in which it will be remembered the 5th Mounted Brigade and R.G.H. were incorporated. His infantry and the remainder of his mounted troops would advance up his western flank and turn the right of the enemy front, which was on the line El Kubeiba - Beit Jibrin.

On November 10th the R.G.H. were ordered to take up a line to cover an expected attack by the enemy's Hebron force. The attack when it came was very half hearted and the regiment bivouacked that night at Arak el Menshiye and found that water had arrived for the men, but the horses had to be sent back to Hesi to be watered. Next morning a large number of sick men and horses were evacuated, they had been marching and fighting for 14 days and the horses routinely went without water for 24 hours, saddles were rarely off and the men had not been able to wash or change for a fortnight. Rations were also short but the pursuit had to be continued, the objective being Junction Station thus cutting off the Jerusalem army.

Next morning the Brigade assembled at Arak station, "D" squadron supplied two officers' patrols and the regiment formed the advance guard, to which was attached half a section of H.A.C. and one section of machine guns. The orders were to march on Balin, which was about half way between Arak and Junction station. A hill was occupied to the north of Balin from which our forward patrols could be seen coming back. At the same time a large enemy force was approaching from the north and large numbers of enemy were seen leaving the train at El Tine station.

"D" squadron was holding the right of the line, "B" squadron was north of Balin and "A" squadron was west of the railway. A request was sent back for reinforcements and the Worcester Yeomanry came up in support. Our gun was brought into action against the advancing enemy but did not greatly impede his progress. At first the attack seemed to fade away but then the enemy started to press heavily from the north east. Lieutenant Wilson's troop of "D" squadron met the full force of the attack; they held on with great gallantry but were forced to withdraw about mid afternoon. When they retired the rest of the line withdrew to a ridge about three quarters of a mile to the rear. They managed to hold the enemy off whilst our wounded were evacuated.

Capt O. Teichman D.S.O., M.C. of the R.A.M.C. gives this account: -
"Our regimental dressing station was in a stone walled camel yard and contained many wounded -- -- from our position we could see large numbers of enemy detraining from El Tine station and realised very strong reinforcements were coming up against us. This seemed to be the great danger as we a weak Brigade were ahead of our main body -- -- our H.A.C. battery shelled these reinforcements but were outgunned -- -- after being busy in the dressing station for some time, we came out to see how things were going and were horrified to see strange looking turbaned troops coming down over the ridge which a short time ago had been occupied by our Yeomen -- -- the enemy who were beginning to descend the steep declivity were only about 300 yards away. Luckily we had kept the horses on which our wounded had been brought in, so we hastily mounted all our wounded and galloped them out of the rear of the yard -- -- there were not enough horses to go round and some of us had to escape on foot -- -- some horses were shot and came down but luckily all the wounded managed to escape after galloping about two miles, the horses bearing the serious casualties being led by men who were slightly wounded. This was an occasion when we profited from the exercises and competitions we had held in carrying wounded out of action by various methods -- -- there were some fine rescues that day and a few moments after we had gained the ridge an R.A.M.C. corporal attached to the Gloucester Yeomanry, came galloping in under a hail of bullets, carrying an unfortunate yeoman who had lost his foot, on the front of his saddle".

It appeared that the Brigade had unwittingly bumped into a very strong counter offensive, finding themselves up against thousands of Turkish infantry who had been brought down on the railway from Jerusalem. Before the action commenced in the morning, a troop of R.G.H. with a Hotchkiss gun had reconnoitred El Tine station and taking cover behind a thick cactus hedge watched the enemy detraining. While they watched a Turkish staff car containing two Turk generals passed within 50 yards of their hiding place. They riddled the staff car with their Hotchkiss gun and then got out and rejoined the regiment as quickly as they could. Casualties during the day were two officers and six other ranks killed and thirteen wounded. The attack had been planned by von Falkenheyn as a large scale counter attack and the situation was only saved by the resistance of the Mounted Division and the general weariness of the Turks.

The Regiment withdrew to Ijseir in the evening and bivouacked there for the night. Water was available to fill the water bottles but there was no forage or food. The men and horses were thoroughly exhausted and many of the horses had to be shot.

Next morning the Brigade was relieved by the 7th mounted Brigade and moved back to Hatte, where rations and drinking water were available but the horses still had to go without. "A" squadron managed to get water at a Jewish village for the horses, the first they had had for 48 hours. Extracts from an officer's diary read: -

"November 13th. - Horses are nearly done. Men hungry and tired but cheerful as usual. Half rations yesterday, none today. Open rolling country, rather hot. Flies bad round the villages. A yeoman observed he couldn't see why the Bible made such a rattle about this country. I haven't seen my feet for days and have not had my clothes off for a week.
November 15th - We spent all day yesterday watering 90 horses, only one bucket each. The night before last they had their first water for 56 hours. Horses have gone for three days without water. It is a wonderful sight to march along a line the enemy has retired upon. Dead men, aeroplanes, burnt guns, ammunition lying about".

Our forces were now operating some 35 miles in advance of their rail head and the bringing up and distribution of supplies and ammunition occupied a lot of the time. The route north of Wadi Hesi was good going although there were some difficult Wadi crossings, but the main road through Gaza up to Beit Hanun was soft sand and difficult.

The enemy forces estimated at 20,000 was on a front of 20 miles, the right half about five miles in front of Junction Station. On the morning of November 14th an infantry Brigade of the 75th Division aided by some armoured cars occupied Junction Station. To the north the New Zealand Mounted Brigade successfully attacked Ayun Kara. Next day the Australian Mounted and the 75th Division advance eastwards towards Latron where the Jaffa - Jerusalem road leaves the hills. At the same time the Anzac Mounted Division occupied Ramleh. The enemy army was now broken into two separate parts, which retired north and east respectively in small scattered groups. In 15 days our force had advanced 60 miles on its right and 40 on its left. It had driven a Turk army of nine infantry and one cavalry division out of a position where it had been entrenched for six months. Over 9,000 prisoners, about 80 guns and more than 100 machine guns were taken, as well as a large quantity of stores and ammunition.

131.

Sergeants Reg Bowl and Fred Lewis grab a rare opportunity for a wash and shave.

Jack Burroughs in marching order

Chapter 15.

Jerusalem

Forty miles from railhead – country of entanglements – winter rains commenced
Turks make fierce attack – Jerusalem in Christian hands – miserably wet
Sgt Fred Lewis sent for Christmas stores – wadis in flood.

The British capture of Junction Station and subsequent advance to Ramleh and Jaffa had driven a wedge between the two Turkish armies and complicated their supply problem. Those to the west could still be supplied by the main railway, but those to the east around Jerusalem were dependent on road transport from Nablus or Amman some forty or fifty miles away.

General Allenby had a difficult decision to make. To either hold the line he now held until his strained supply position could be assured, they were now forty miles from rail head. The alternative was to continue the advance and take advantage of the enemy's disarray, before he had time to recover. The winter rains would soon be arriving, the now dry wadis would be turned into rivers and the ground would be a quagmire. His supplies had to be brought up by lorries on indifferent roads and thence by camel to the front line.

He made the very brave decision to advance on Jerusalem realising the difficulties he faced. The main approach to the city through the Judean hills was along a narrow road from Latron to Saris. The remainder were little more than goat tracks leading through narrow defiles, where a handful of men could defy an army. The Romans and Crusaders had failed to penetrate these natural defences and Allenby was fully aware of this from his studies of previous campaigns.

General Wavell writes: - "it is a country of entanglements, ambushes and surprises where large armies have no room to fight and the defenders can remain hidden'. The War Cabinet at home in a telegram counselled caution, having no wish to be embroiled in entanglements expensive in man power; from which they could not withdraw."

Allenby with the genius denoting great commanders took the decision to allow one day's rest for re-organisation and on November the 17th gave the order to advance on the hills.

His original decision was for the Anzac Mounted Division (including R.G.H.) to take up a position in the plain around Junction Station, while two divisions of the Desert Mounted Corps advanced into the hills. These orders were modified after they came up against Turkish resistance around Latron, when it quickly became apparent that forcing the passes was a job for the infantry.

The Anzac Mounted Division was given the job of guarding the supply lines. On November 16th The R.G.H. moved to the banks of the Wadi Sukarier two miles from the sea and about fifteen miles north of Askalon. Here they came across an ample water supply and some good grazing for the horses. On this march they followed the 52nd Infantry Division and came across many Turkish dead. Next day they moved to take up a line centred on El Tine, which was the junction on the railway lines from Gaza to Beersheba; where they found a great dump of enemy stores.

On November 20th the regiment was ordered to rejoin the 5th Mounted Brigade at Enab and marched along the Junction Station road to Latron, where the regiment bivouacked. Winter rains commenced and torrential downpours gave the men and horses more water than they wanted. Next day the regiment was temporarily split, "D" squadron went to Desert Corps H.Q., "B" squadron provided an escort for prisoners and "A" squadron and the regimental H.Q. reported to the 3rd Australian Light Horse Brigade at Junction Station. Next day "B" squadron were relieved by a squadron of the Worcester Yeomanry and for the next five days they bivouacked with the 3rd A.L.H. at El Mejdel.

The advance on Allenby's western flank had gone well and the enemy were making desperate efforts to drive us off the high ground north and north east of Jaffa. On November the 27th the 3rd A.L.H. Brigade, including the R.G.H., marched 24 miles to Deiran and next day they marched a further 14 miles to El Burj, where they prepared for dismounted action, the horses being sent back to Deiran. The regimental strength dismounted was 8 officers and 120 other ranks. They were detailed as support for the 3rd A.L.H. having 8th A.L.H. on their right and 9th A.L.H. on their left.

During the night of November 30th - December 1st the enemy made a desperate attempt to break through and Lt H.P. Ellis was killed leading his troop while plugging a gap in the 8th A.L.H. line. Lt H.V. Hawtrey and Lt E.G. Townsend and their troops were hard pressed filling other gaps in the line until the Royal Scots Fusiliers came up and the Turkish attack was driven back. Later the Turks made another fierce attack which also failed. Dawn found the Turks in a position where they were unable to extricate themselves and what remained of the force surrendered. The unwounded prisoners consisted of a Brigade commander, 105 other ranks and 19 wounded prisoners. There were about 200 Turk dead. The enemy continued shelling the position. If the Turks had broken through they would have been in a position to enfilade the Latron road and jeopardise supply columns to the Jerusalem force.

Sergeant Fred Lewis who had rejoined the regiment having been detailed elsewhere wrote home: -
"I have been back with the Regiment four or five days. When I say the Regiment I mean the horses for all that can be spared are up in the front line, dismounted. We have got some job with the horses, one man to every five; we don't have much time to ourselves after the horses are done. They are having a good rest and want it poor beggars. Our camp is quite close to a town that starts with R and ends with H with an M in the middle. The civil population seem pleased to see us -- the Turks took all their belongings off them -- the last two months have certainly been exciting and full of interest -- I have got a lot to be thankful for having had one or two near touches -- the orange and lemon groves remind me of the orchards around Toddington -- oranges picked straight off the tree are forty for a shilling (5 pence) -- the water supply is very good now, I should think we will not run short this winter. We have not had a lot of rain but quite enough to please me -- what did you think of the charge of the Worcesters and Warwicks (presumably Huj) we just missed it by five minutes. To charge guns that were firing absolutely point blank at you takes a bit of doing – my shack mate has just cooked some porridge for supper so will knock off now".

Frank Fox records that the next few days were comparatively quiet as the regiment did not take an active part in the eastern flank assault on Jerusalem. For the early part of December the rain scarcely ceased and the hills held by the regiment were swept by cold winds and the men still in summer clothing had a miserable time. The roads were impassable for motor transport and rations were almost always short. Those in charge of the horses in the plain below were almost worse off because the plains became a sea of mud, the wadis filling with sludge and water became death-traps for the unwary.

There was a let up in the weather on December 10th, which was a clear warm day and the men were able to dry their clothes and blankets. This was taken as a sign of joy that Jerusalem was once again in Christian hands, because the previous day the Turks had surrendered the city. As a Holy place to Moslem, Jew and Christian it had been mutually agreed that no blood be shed within its walls or in the country immediately surrounding the city. General Allenby humbly entered on foot thus fulfilling a prophecy that when the Nile flowed into Palestine - as it did through our pipe line - the prophet from the west would drive the Turk from Jerusalem.

The enemy did not accept the loss of the city without making a desperate effort at recovery. This had been anticipated and the High Command had been making preparations for advancing our line to secure Jaffa and Jerusalem before the enemy counter attack developed. The 52nd Division on the left of the line had crossed the flooded river Auja, which the Turks had thought un-fordable. They took the enemy by surprise, driving them off with the bayonet and were able to take up a strong defensive position so that Jaffa and the whole left front were secured.

The Turks made a further attempt to break through on the Jerusalem - Nablus road, Allenby's eastern flank. By December 28th his forces were spent and his attempt to recapture Jerusalem defeated. Our whole force moved forward about six miles on a twelve mile front and consolidated their position.

The R.G.H. had rather a dull time during December spending their time in the hills doing guards and reconnaissance and building stone sangars to be held as forts in case of attack. It was all miserably wet on the side of a rocky hill and they either had the choice of bivouacking on the top, or at the bottom. At the top it was colder but at the bottom the water ran down into their beds. Supplies were short and the O.C. 8th A.L.H. took pity on them and sent them some candles and cigarettes, which were so wet they were un-smokable. Everyone was soaked; fortunately there was an issue of rum. Christmas Eve and Christmas day were miserably wet, the supply system was thoroughly disorganised, the railway lines had washed away, roads were impassable and the camel transport broke down with the animals dying in large numbers.

Sergeant Fred Lewis had a rather better Christmas, as he related in a letter he wrote home: -

"I spent quite an exciting Christmas, one I shall never forget for as long as I live. I was sent down the line to buy canteen stores for the regiment. I got the goods alright but had a job to get them on rail as the traffic was pretty heavy and all the truck room was wanted for forage and stores. Eventually I got loaded up after dodging the R.T.O. who told me that I could not take anything because the train was full up. The train started about 5 o'clock on Christmas Eve and landed me at the rail head about nine at night, with the camp fifteen miles away. We got the goods loaded on to the wagon that had come to meet me and then decided we would wait till morning before starting for camp. I slept in a Y.M.C.A. tent, but got flooded out in the early hours of the morning, before we started for camp, quite a cheerful start don't you think? We started off for camp about 8 o'clock, pouring with rain, water up to the horses' knees and nearly wet through but cheerful. We managed to get to a village within five miles of the camp and there we got stuck for the wagon could not cross a wadi that had flooded during the morning. I rode on to the camp and found that the regiment had moved since I left. After making enquiries I found out where they were supposed to be, so started off to find them. I came across them stranded on the banks of the wadi that was holding my wagon up. The O.C. told me to get back to the wagon and wait till they came along in the morning. By this time the wadi had risen another eighteen inches so that I could see that I was going to have a rough time crossing. You can imagine me at four o'clock on Christmas afternoon swimming my horse across the wadi, my - wasn't it cold and horribly wet but I got across. When I got to the place where I had left the wagon I found that they had moved, but where to I was not going to trouble myself to find out till the morning. The next thing was to find a place to sleep and forage for the horse and this is where the best part of the day comes in. I wandered around for a time and came across a camp of the Egyptian Labour Corps. I tied the weary charger up to a limber and made for the first tent I came across and as luck would have it, it was a Q.M.S. and he was one of the best. He got all my clothes dried, a good bed made up and more food cooked than I could eat, plenty of tea and some posh cigarettes. In the morning after a jolly good night's sleep his servant brought me in a good hot cup of tea and some "hot" shaving water. He set me going after a jolly good breakfast and very soon I found the wagon and then we found the camp in a very short time".

An extract from "The Diary of a Yeomanry M.O. is even more explicit and gives some indication of the hardships they went through.

"Christmas day we woke to the usual inky sky and pouring rain -- the plains to the south resembled a great lake with the hill village of Yebna rising from the waters. About 10 a.m. the brigade (5th Mounted) left camp and proceeded towards Yebna. I soon found the wagons of the Field Ambulance could not follow the route traversed by the rest of the brigade. We crossed several small torrents which appeared suddenly, while the rain fell in buckets -- we followed what in dry weather was called a road -- at the bad places we had to put six or eight mules to a light wagon, the road became impassable, mud up to the axles. We turned back to try the sand dunes towards the sea but the water had risen and we thought we would never get out. In one case it was necessary to use twelve mules to move a wagon -- we halted about a mile from Kubeibah village, the horses refused to face the stinging rain -- we found the Warwicks crossing a swollen wadi which had washed away the railway and whose presence could not be discovered until a horseman in two or three feet of water suddenly became submerged -- several horses and men were swimming some of the former disappearing altogether and being drowned in the swift current -- I knew that four or five feet of water with an unknown amount of mud could mean the loss of all my wagons being swept out to sea -- the three regiments after crossing the first flood had found an impassable river beyond – after much swimming they left several abandoned limbers in the stream -- one could actually see the streams rising as the water poured down from the hills -- I gave it up as a bad job and pitched our camp on a hill beyond Kubeibah village -- some of the Worcesters got over after swimming their horses -- several of the men had to be resuscitated after prolonged immersion in the water -- each man carried two days rations. We cut some wood from nearby olive trees, even though this had been expressly forbidden, but I thought the circumstances warranted it. We got a fire going and managed to get some shelter under the wagons. Luckily I had about 30 litres of the native port wine, this worked out at half a litre per man. In spite of their miserable wet conditions it actually made the men break into song, as they sat round the sizzling fire.

During the early morning of December 26th the rain abated and a little blue sky could be seen. After breakfast a friend from the Gloucester Yeomanry came round and said that the floods had subsided and it might be possible to reach Yebna. We rode for about two miles through water a foot deep and found the worst crossings were only about four feet deep -- about an hour later we brought all the transport out with the loss of the contents of one wagon – the camels were very awkward and when they fell down in four feet of water we had great difficulty in keeping them from drowning -- about midday we reached our camping ground between the Warwicks and Gloucesters about a mile south of the town".

The R.G.H. were ordered to set up an observation line north of Suffa and to take up road making fatigues. On December 31st they were relieved by the 29th Brigade and moved to an assembly point south of El Burj.

So ended 1917, between October 31st and December 31st the Desert Mounted Corps had advanced 80 miles, fought nine major engagements and captured 9,500 prisoners and 80 guns. The effective strength of the regiment on this date was 19 officers, 401 other ranks, 403 horses, 42 mules and 17 donkeys.

Chapter 16

Training and Recreation
Bring railway up to present position – lower end of Jordan Valley cleared
Recuperating and re-equipping – R.G.H. hounds – Divisional Sports
Intensive Training

The capture of Jerusalem had frustrated Turco - German ambitions towards Baghdad and given the allies a much needed boost to morale, after three years of virtual stalemate on the Western Front. Opinion in the war cabinet was divided on whether to adopt a defensive approach in France, reinforce the Eastern Front, knock Turkey out of the war and come up through the Balkans. Proponents of this strategy called it "knocking out the props", bringing about a German defeat by eliminating her allies. The pro western front argument was that a defeat in Palestine would not lose us the war but a heavy defeat in France most certainly could.

The pro Western Front lobby won the day with the argument that the Germans were preparing for a heavy thrust in the spring. Logistics of supply to the Eastern Front dictated a long haul before further significant advances could be made. General Allenby was ordered to continue with the forces available, but he was adamant that he must first be given time to bring the broad gauge railway up to his present position. To ensure a regular flow of supplies, two battalions of Canadian railwaymen together with materials and rolling stock were sent to the eastern theatre.

Allenby's plan was to occupy the Jordan valley and establish a line from Lake Tiberias to Haifa, putting him in a position to demolish the Hedjaz railway and cut off the Turkish forces in Medina. This would give great assistance to the Arab revolt, which was effectively acting as Allenby's eastern flank. Iraq was secured, the Arabs were advancing on Maan and the Emir Feisal their leader had been declared King Feisal 1st of Baghdad. A period of intensive training was embarked upon, the basis of which was to lead the enemy into thinking that the attack would come up the Jordan Valley. Thus drawing his forces to the east of Jordan, when his intention was to put in his main punch on his western; coastal flank. In the meantime Allenby had to rest his troops and get his supply position satisfactorily organised. Having done this he hoped to put in maximum effort in the spring and knock Turkey out of the war.

The R.G.H. took no part in the first phase of the operation across the Jordan; this was given to the Anzac Mounted Division and the 60th

Infantry Division, who advanced across the hills from Jerusalem to Jericho. The mounted troops found the ground extremely difficult, having to advance in single file along very rough tracks which were exposed to enemy machine gun fire, while the infantry found it impossible to advance on a wide front. Even so by mid march the lower end of the Jordan valley had been cleared, permitting operations against the Turkish lines of communication to the Hedjaz. Also we were enabled to link up and co-operate with the Arab forces south east of the Dead Sea.

In the meanwhile the R.G.H. starting on January 1st had marched back from Latron, via El Burj, Ramleh and Yebna to a rest camp by a lagoon at Deir el Belah north of Gaza.

Fred Lewis writes of events at the turn of the year: -

"We have had a great time since this last advance started, even if it has been rough. The horses fared even worse than we did, for often they had to go forty eight hours without water and on one occasion three days. We could not always depend on the forage and rations reaching us, so we had often times to live on the country we were passing through. We could generally get a sheep or two and sometimes some beef and on one occasion we struck a lot of poultry in a deserted Bedouin camp. The Turks had left a lot of barley behind in their various camps and of course that is what we feed our horses on out here. The barley was a fine sample and very clean, quite the best that I have seen here. The ground here is not unlike the Uckington (Cheltenham) land -- I am in a village about six miles from Jerusalem, I came across a lot of agricultural implements drills, ploughs, reapers and mowing machines. A lot of them were quite new, of English manufacture and had not been used. They are the first implements I have seen out here; the natives still stick to tools that were used in the year one. A lot of the cattle appear to have a touch of the Hereford about them but not the Hereford size. The rains have started and from what the natives tell us we must not expect many dry days for the next couple of months. As I write this letter the rain is falling down in sheets and is just starting to work its way through the weak places in my shack. Could you send me a rainproof coat, our great coats soak up the rain like a sponge and take days to dry out -- we have been living very well the last few weeks, it is really wonderful how they manage to keep us so well supplied with food -- how I wish you and I could walk round the farm as we used to before the war -- as long as I live I shall never be able to thank you for keeping the farm going so that I have something to come back to after the war".

He then goes on to say that they have been going through a period of intensive training in musketry, riding, troop training, Hotchkiss gun, signalling classes, instruction of junior officers, N.C.O. classes and care of kit, saddlery, arms and equipment. Remaining at Deir el Belah training continued into February and March, some leave was granted during this time to visit Egypt or return to England.

After the hard time they had experienced during the last weeks of 1917, especially the horses, it was imperative they had time to recuperate, re-equip and accommodate fresh drafts of personnel. Fred Lewis tells of how he spends his time during this period: -

"Every other day I get up at 6 a.m., call the roll and see to the horses being fed. Breakfast is at seven, walk down to the stables about eight fifteen, get on my horse which is already waiting for me and go off to exercise and grazing with the squadron. Get back to camp about eleven and watch other people grooming horses till about twelve fifteen. We have lunch at twelve thirty and then have the afternoon off except for an occasional rifle inspection. Water and feed the horses at four thirty, dinner at five thirty, hay up at seven, go to bed any time.

I am orderly sergeant today and have to take the sick and lead swingers to the doctor at 6.30 a. m., 8.15 a.m. inspect the main guard, 11.30 a.m. walk round the camp with the orderly officer and show up the orderly corporals for having untidy lines. 5 p.m. inspect the grub; 5.30 p.m. mount the guard, 8.30. p.m. close the canteen, 10 p.m. lights out and walk round the camp with the orderly officer".

If they trained hard they also played hard, brigade and divisional sports were arranged and to quote Frank Fox, during the stay in rest camp the regiment organised a hunt, "The R.G.H. Hounds".

The "Hounds" consisted of one couple known as "Tripe and Onions". The former was a marvel for nose drive and tongue. He could own to a scent over dry sand on the hottest of days and was always keen. The only thing that caused him to tire was want of water and hunting arrangements had to be made to get a supply before returning to kennels. "Onions" preferred camp life to fox chasing and when the regiment moved forward he deserted.

On February 9th 1918 the R.G.H. hounds met at "St James Park", found a brace of jackal and ran one in a big circle until he swam the Wadi Ghuzze and was lost. Another was found and ran until the hunt changed to a shepherd's dog and had to be whipped off. Three days later the hunt found at Review Hill and Corporal George Castle had a nasty experience when digging for a "fox". Having got into the earth a considerable distance the sand roof fell in and he had to be dug out. He was none the worse and was able to continue hunting. (After the war George Castle became hunt servant to the Duke of Beaufort's hounds at Badminton).

The following account was sent to "The Field" of a hunt that took place on February 24th, when a cap was taken for the Hunt Servants Benefit Society which raised £40.

Fox Hunting in Palestine.

We in Palestine are doing our best, when not employed hunting Johnny the Turk to hunt Charlie the fox. There is more than one bobbery pack in existence and the Cairo Lost Dogs Home is one of the first places where any embryo Master goes to when on leave, sometimes he is able to augment his pack with a useful Hound. Dog though it may be, from the moment of purchase it is honoured with the name of Hound. With the Yeomanry Hounds the Fields are large, generally somewhere around a hundred, increased by second horsemen and casual followers. On a recent outing the fixture was at the Red House on the banks of the Wadi Ghuzze - well known to anyone who participated in the attack on Ghaza. Proceedings opened with hounds drawing a three acre orange grove surrounding the house, generally a safe find for either fox or jackal but today they were not at home. Suddenly the field were awakened by a loud "Halloa" from the first whip; a jackal had broken covert far ahead. A toot on the horn soon had hounds together and over the wadi the field galloped, the hounds throwing their tongues well as they gained the far bank and picked up the scent on the grass, hard pressed by the eager field, who were only restrained by the master's wonderful vocabulary. Turning for the wadi banks he retraced his steps and the hounds got their first view. Fortunately the Field were spared galloping over soft sand because the engineers with commendable foresight had erected a bridge in the right spot. "Hunt Servants First" bellowed the field master, taking the opportunity to get his own back on one or two senior officers, who were inclined to push to the front. Hounds were already across the wadi and heading for that difficult bit of waste land between the Gaza road and the sea. Here again the going was heavy but a disused road helped the followers to keep the flying pack in view without unduly distressing the horses. You could not see all the fun from the road so the task of negotiating the innumerable trenches leading towards Sampson's Ridge was undertaken by many. At last came a check and it was as well too, because the field had got into a maze of old wire entanglements. A few were fortunate enough to secure their second horses before a "Halloa forrard", from a corporal in charge of some natives had the field going again, only to lose the jack on the outskirts of Gaza. A really sporting hunt enjoyed by a field which included many of the hardest riders from the most famous packs at home.

On March 7th the 22nd Brigade held a steeplechase meeting, when the Palestine Grand National was won by a squadron leader of the Warwickshire Yeomanry.

They played hard and Fred Lewis remembered turning out as fly half in a rugger match against the Australians. He wasn't a very big man and a large Australian picked him up by the scruff of his neck and the seat of his shorts and sat him up on top of the scrum.

To keep them up to the mark and remind them they were still soldiers they were inspected by the Corps Commander, the Duke of Connaught and General Smuts. No adverse comment is recorded so presumably they were satisfied that they were fit for action, because on April 1st they moved out arriving on April 5th at Selmeh, where a standing camp was pitched. They were given leave to visit Jaffa, Jerusalem and Bethlehem; being especially struck with the peaceful beauty of Bethlehem. They were not so impressed with some of the other Holy places. An officer commented.

"We walked down the Mount of Olives, across the brook Kedron which runs between it and the town, up to the Garden of Gethsemane. If only the religious bodies who have taken possession of these spots would leave them alone But they build horrible new churches on the sites which take away all the feeling one would otherwise have -- we went to the Church of the Holy Sepulchre and saw inside the tomb of Our Lord and the stone where His body was laid to be anointed. There is much disagreement about the real spot. Outside the city walls was a green mound like a skull and quite what one would imagine -- I cannot believe Calvary is where they say it is, it is so very unlikely that Christ would have been buried within fifty feet of the Cross or that Joseph of Arimathea would have selected his tomb on a spot for public executions".

At Selmah intensive training was kept up to prepare them for the next development of the campaign - the breaking of a gap in the enemy line through which the cavalry would pour towards the enemy's rear.

The marching out strength of the regiment was 21 officers, 403 other ranks, 465 horses, 32 mules and 14 donkeys. In these days of mechanical transport it is difficult to envisage the logistical problems of feeding this number of animals and this was only one regiment. Wherever possible the horses lived off the country, but being pushed hard necessitated long recovery periods.

143.

Bathing at Port Said, presumably there were ladies present!
From left to right - Sgt Roberts, Sgt Lewis, S.S.M. Smart Sgt Bowl, Sgt Barton

A hunting we will go.
Illustration from the Anzac Book - artist unknown.

OOOOOOOOOOOOOOOOOOOOOOOOOOOOOOOOOOOOOOOOO

"A" Squadron Sergeant's mess, somewhere in Palestine.

"A" Squadron Sergeants
Farrier Sgt Morgan, Sgt Bowl, Sgt James, Sgt Nash
Sgt Waters, Sgt Roberts, S.S.M. Smart, Sgt Vines
Sgt Barton Sgt Harding

Chapter 17

Crossing the Jordan

Army reorganised – Divisions leave for France replaced by Indian Divisions
Camp west bank Jordan – 1200 ft below sea level – advance on Es Salt
R.G.H. cross the Jordan – Es Salt take – let down by Arabs – withdraw

On April 18th a farewell parade was held in honour of the Worcestershire Yeomanry. They were leaving the 5th Mounted Brigade to join the 20th Corps in the Jordan Valley as Corps Cavalry. This was a poignant moment because it marked the end of the old 1st South Midland Mounted Brigade, which before the war had consisted of the R.G.H., the Warwick and Worcester Yeomanry, the Warwick R.H.A. and the 1st South Midland Mounted Brigade Field Ambulance. After Gallipoli these had all been incorporated into the 5th Mounted Brigade.

Allenby was going to have to re-organise his whole army because of the critical situation in France. Reverses on the western front, which would bring the Germans within twenty miles of Paris, meant that not only would he get no reinforcements but that he would have to lose many of his seasoned troops. Two infantry divisions, nine Yeomanry regiments, five and a half siege batteries, nine British battalions and five machine gun companies were withdrawn from the front for embarkation. The following month fourteen more British battalions were sent. The two divisions were replaced by two Indian divisions and to replace the Yeomanry, Indian cavalry units came from France. The twenty four British battalions were gradually replaced by Indian battalions direct from India. They had no battle experience and very inadequate training.

In the re-organised army the 5th Mounted Brigade - afterwards officially named the 13th Cavalry Brigade - consisted of the R.G.H., and two Indian cavalry regiments, the 9th and 18th Bengal Lancers. Together with the 3rd A.L.H. and 4th A.L.H. Brigades this made up the 5th Australian Division. The changeover did not happen immediately but took effect after the action detailed in the next chapter.

On April 24th the regiment was ordered to move to Latron, which is the southern entrance to the passes through the Judean hills. For the next three days the regiment moved over rough tracks and through narrow defiles through the mountains to Enab, following the road traversed by armies throughout the ages. On the night of the 26th they moved by night to Telaat - ed - Dumm and so on into the Jordan valley, camping on the west bank of the Jordan about three miles north of Jericho.

Fred Lewis takes up the story: -

"My last letter to you had to be cut short because while I was in the middle of it an order came through that we had to be prepared to move. We passed through Jerusalem in the night so did not have much chance of seeing the town. Our road lay through the Garden of Gethsemane at the foot of the Mount of Olives. We are now camped near Jericho on the banks of the River Jordan. The ground that we are on and in fact for miles around is about the most desolate spot, barren and rugged that we have come through; quite unlike the Jordan valley as I imagined it to be. Expect we shall be off on a short stunt in a day or so, but we don't know for certain. The town or mud village called Jericho is out of bounds and as it looks just like the other villages out here I don't think we shall miss much. You would like to see me crushed into my shack with little more than a pair of shorts and a disc (identity) on. More clothing one does not want to wear, for the climate is to say the least of it more than hot. All the creeping things of the earth seem to find a home here, scorpions, spiders, lizards, ants, snakes, and goodness knows what else. They seem to enjoy our company for we generally find some of the above in our blankets in the morning".

Extracts from an officer's diary paint a further picture of the conditions encountered: -
"Friday 26th - We leave Enab at 7 p.m. and trek twenty one miles through Jerusalem by moonlight and halted at midnight two miles beyond Bethany, in the country known in the Bible as the Wilderness. We arrived at Telaat - el - Dumm at 3 a.m. very tired and dirty. This place is half way between Jerusalem and Jericho, there is plenty of water and otherwise there is nothing to say about it. There are snakes; scorpion and vultures, who are consistent camp followers, forty days and forty nights would indeed be a penance.

To the north you can see a prominent hill overlooking Jericho called Keruntel, or the Hill of Temptation where the Devil tempted Our Lord. Below it in the face of the rock is an Anchorite monastery, where monks are sent as a punishment for their sins. Running near Telaat - el - Dumm is the Wadi Kelt with a good running stream in it and also a few convents or monasteries built into the most precipitous rocks and apparently impossible to approach. One can also see beautifully built Roman aqueducts, still used to carry water down to Jericho.

April 27th - We moved next day to the Jordan valley going down the old road, which was very rocky, rough and precipitous. This road passes by the Tomb of Moses, where he is supposed by the Moslems to have been buried, but according to the Scriptures he died in the Moabite Hills east of Jordan. There is an annual Moslem pilgrimage there from Jerusalem and it happened to be taking place that day, about 1,000 pilgrims going there to worship for three or four days.

We turned north and went up the valley to our camping ground which is nothing but rocks. We had no idea what the position of affairs was or where our outpost line was or where the Turks were. Just as we arrived five shells burst around us, examination of the cases proved them to be British. The matter was reported and the apology of the battery, which was carrying out an experiment, was duly received".

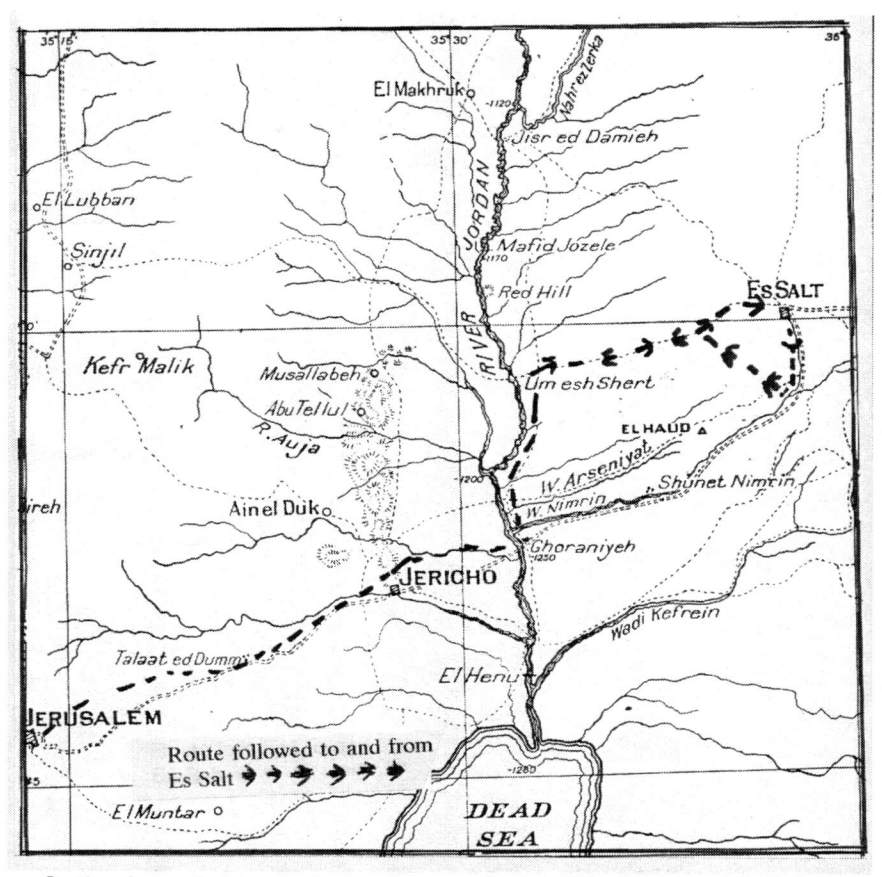

On the above sketch map Amman is approximately 15 miles east of Es Salt.

The British force had effectively cleared the lower end of the Jordan valley and General Allenby's plan was to cut the enemy's railway line to the Hedjaz, this would greatly assist the Arab forces advancing on Maan. The attack was aimed at Amman the most vulnerable point on the railway about thirty miles north east of the Dead Sea where the Hedjaz railway passed over a viaduct and through a tunnel.

From the bridge over the Jordan at El Ghoroniya, 1200 ft below sea level, to Nasur some sixteen miles further east on the edge of the plateau on which Amman lies, the ground rises some 4,300 ft. The intervening country was a maze of rocky footpaths and narrow ravines.

The Turks were defending Amman with as many troops as they could spare. The tunnel and viaduct had been fortified; a defensive line had been prepared at Shunet Nimrin astride the Jericho - Es Salt road, the key to which was a prominent hill named El Haud. A third position was being prepared on the east bank opposite El Ghoraniyeh.

The first attempt on Amman had been made on the night of March 21 - 22nd by the 60th London Division, the Anzac Mounted Division and the Camel Brigade. The 60th Division advanced on Es Salt while the mounted troops were to move directly on Amman, destroy the tunnel and viaduct and withdraw to the Jordan bridgeheads. Heavy rain hampered the advance and the delay enabled the enemy to bring up reinforcements after our forces had crossed the Jordan and penetrated as far as Es Salt. Amman was found to be covered by a strong enemy force, after carrying out some minor demolition work our forces retired to the west bank of the Jordan.

General Allenby decided to take the next favourable opportunity to cross the Jordan and occupy Es Salt, the ancient Ramoth Gilead, and hold it until the Arab forces could come up. The operation was planned for mid May but was brought forward because the Arab Beni Sakhr tribe said they could not co-operate if the advance did not take place before the 4th of May, because their supplies were running short. It was to take part in this attack that the 5th Mounted Brigade (R.G.H) had advanced on the Jordan.

General Allenby's plan was to take Es Salt with his mounted troops thus cutting the enemy's communication with his force at Shunet Nimrin, which would be attacked in front by infantry. It might then be possible with the help of the Arabs to hold the town and adjacent country and spare our troops the ordeal of a summer in the Jordan Valley. The Arabs, thought to be 20,000 strong promised to advance on Es Salt from the south east via Ain - es - Sir, thus making a two pronged attack at the same time covering Allenby's eastern flank.

Some six miles north of the Ghoraniyeh Bridge was a ford at Um esh

Shert; where a road ran direct to Es Salt and nine miles further north to the Jisr el Damieh Bridge. Allenby proposed taking both these crossings with the 5th Mounted and 3rd and 4th A.L.H. Brigades to prevent Turk reinforcements crossing from the west bank.

On April 29th 1918 the R.G.H. crossed the Jordan to enter the land of Moab. An event commemorated for all time by a bas relief bronze plaque on the Regimental War Memorial. The Regiment crossed the river by the Ghoraniyeh Bridge and then turned north to the Wadi Abu Muhir where they rested until dawn. The Regimental strength at that time was 22 officers, 375 other ranks, 421 horses, 39 pack animals and 13 donkeys.

Meanwhile the 4th and 3rd Australian A.L.H. Brigades moved fast up the valley and arrived at Jisr el Damieh by 5.30 a.m. The Turks were too strongly entrenched for the bridge to be taken so the 4th Brigade together with three R.H.A. batteries took up a position astride the Es Salt road facing west, to hold up any Turk reinforcements. Meanwhile the 3rd A.L.H. Brigade which had been following turned up the track to Es Salt, thereby achieving the one tactical success of the day by capturing the town that evening.

The R.G.H. regimental transport less one water cart and one limbered wagon was detached and told to report for headquarters duty at Jericho. One troop of "B" squadron was attached as escort to the Brigade Camel Squadron and another troop as escort to the Brigade Camel Ammunition squadron. The remainder of the regiment was to follow the Um el Shert track to Es Salt. Early in the day the Worcesters and Sherwood Yeomanry, who were in the lead encountered a small body of enemy. The R.G.H. advancing in support lost one man and one trooper wounded. Advancing along the rough mountain track the force reached the plateau above the Jordan Valley and encountered exceptionally difficult mountain country. In many places they had to dismount and lead their horses in single file. In some places the men had to hold the tail of the horse in front and be pulled up the more precipitous banks.

On the plateau the brigade halted for an hour then resumed the march with "A" and "B" squadrons R.G.H. in the lead, with "D" squadron as rear guard. In the late afternoon the enemy were encountered some miles south of Es Salt. The G.O.C. came forward and made a reconnaissance of the position and decided it would be best to bivouac for the night and attack at dawn next morning. The night passed quietly, the enemy making no attempt at an attack.

An unknown writer's diary reads: -
"At 2 a.m. on April 30th we arrived at our position and we filled our

water bottles for the last time. I tried to get off to sleep but it was too cold and just as I was going off the 60th division began their attack and appeared to progress very well judging by the sound. At 4 a.m. we moved off to advance up Track 13, someone remarked that they hoped it wasn't unlucky. We met with some opposition from snipers, a good many bullets were flying around and poor Sergeant Roberts was killed. The Turks were on the hills, it was impossible to climb up; we were just going to make a dismounted attack when it was decided to give them a miss and go up the track. In single file we led our horses up, our column was four miles long and it was beginning to get hot. I have never had such a climb before and I hope I never will again -- there was no fighting but stray shots coming from all directions. We passed a well and a few of us had time for a drink but as it was necessary to push on to Es Salt, we could not stop.

Finally we moved up a deep ravine to within two miles of Es Salt, where the advance guard came upon the enemy and were heavily fired on. The order to dismount was given -- the men were all very exhausted -- it took a long time to reconnoitre the place -- after about an hour troops were seen to our left who turned out to be part of the 3rd A.L.H. Brigade. The Brigadier decided to bivouac for the night and attack Es Salt next morning. We moved up the valley to a large field of barley and lucerne, where we picketed the horses, saving us having to feed them. There was a very high hill in front where we put our outposts; it was not until 10 p.m. that we got our protection troops out.

The Turks had been so engaged watching us that they allowed the 3rd Brigade to come round and take Es Salt from the northwest. When we advanced next morning we found that the town had already been taken".

Meanwhile the 60th Infantry Division attacking Shunet Nimrin had captured the advance works, but was unable to make any further progress. The 3rd A.L.H. Brigade, although held up for a while by an enemy position on the North West of the town had, as has previously been related, reached Es Salt late in the afternoon. The 8th Regiment, which had been held in reserve galloped into the town and by 7 o'clock, had taken 300 prisoners, a large number of machine guns and documents of the 4th Turkish Army Headquarters. One squadron pursued the enemy some distance down the Amman road.

Early in the morning of May 1st the 1st and 2nd A.L.H. Brigades, who had followed the 5th Mounted (R.G.H), moved into Es Salt. The 1st and 2nd A.L.H. Brigades took up position to the north and west of the town. Success appeared to have been achieved but disaster had overtaken the 4th A.L.H. Brigade in the valley around Jisr ed Damieh. Unknown to our intelligence the enemy had crossed the river by a pontoon bridge a little north of Red Hill and by 7.30 in the morning were advancing up the east bank of the river, forcing back the 4th A.L.H. All our lines of supply were cut, except for the precipitous track up which the R.G.H. had advanced. If the Shunut Nimrin position could be taken without further delay the position could be secured. Arrangements were made for an attack next morning, the infantry to attack from the west and the mounted troops from Es Salt from the south and east.

By the evening of May 1st food and ammunition were getting short, no vehicles could get up to the front and camels were out of the question. Each cavalry unit had a few donkeys used by cooks and batmen. About two hundred of these were collected at Ghoraniyeh and loaded with ammunition and stores. Marching all night they succeeded in reaching Es Salt by morning, they off loaded and returned safely to Ghoraniyeh; a double journey of forty miles over terrible country, with no sleep.

The R.G.H. was ordered to picket the Es Salt - Nimrin road, which was a good metalled one in a deep ravine. There was an abundant water supply from fresh water springs and terraced gardens leading up the hills. "D" squadron acted as advanced guard and made contact with the enemy half a mile north of El Howeij bridge so they took up a defensive position on the hills commanding the bridge, overlooking a stone barricade the enemy had erected across the road. At 9 o'clock the enemy started shelling this position, wounding four men. "A" and "B" squadrons took up positions to the rear, picketing the road. The G.O.C. visited "D" squadron and decided they must stand fast. At dusk the regiment withdrew to one mile south of Es Salt and bivouacked for the night. The Worcesters and Sherwood Rangers taking up the line.

Next morning "D" squadron moved back to take up the position of the previous day and found it occupied by the Turks. At 9.30 "A" and "B" squadrons dismounted and moved up to support "D" squadron which had meanwhile advanced to the same position it held the previous day. The Worcesters and Sherwood Rangers advancing on the left could make little progress because of the precipitous terrain. The G.O.C. decided that any further advance was impossible and the brigade was withdrawn to the previous night's bivouac.

The position of the force at Es Salt had now become precarious. The Beni Sakhr Arabs had failed to turn up and they were being continuously attacked from Amman and on the north and west from Turkish forces advancing from Jisr ed Damieh. Only the one convoy of ammunition had reached them, their corridor of retreat was very narrow, kept open by hard fighting. On the afternoon of May 3rd General Allenby ordered them to withdraw. During the night they came back down the Um es Shert track to the valley with little interference from the enemy. By the afternoon of May 4th the whole force had recrossed the Jordan by the Ghoraniyeh Bridge.

Our losses were 500 in the Mounted Division and 1,100 in the infantry. Close on 1,000 prisoners were brought away and enemy losses must have been heavy.

Extracts from Major Howard's diary read as follows: -

"We are told fresh troops are coming up. Captain Vines discovers a track out from the road to Track 13, this might be useful to let us out -- "D" squadron is at last relieved by "B" and they come back -- the situation becomes more and more critical. We settle down for the night and cook our dinner of mutton and cabbages, but before we have time to eat the Brigadier comes by and says "move in half an hour". We are moving back by the track discovered by Captain Vines -- every man is told to eat a good dinner and leave his fire burning. At 2.30 we move down the road and meet "A" and "B" squadrons, we are followed by the whole brigade, the line is nearly five miles long, after four hours we arrive at a spot overlooking Track 13. We had to wait till dawn, it was impossible to proceed further in the dark.

May 4th - At 4a.m. we start -- the track is in many places worse than going downstairs how men managed riding one horse and leading another I don't know, the horses have become like cats -- portions of the track were under artillery fire from the Turks -- eventually we reached the Jordan Valley where shelling increased but not being tied to one track I scattered the force and proceeded to Ghoraniyeh Bridge. We eventually arrived in camp at 12 o'clock very exhausted after a 36 mile trek. Our casualties were six killed, two died of wounds and eight wounded".

John Edmondson wrote: -

"In single file we rode down the track, steep hills rising on each side of us. A tearing sound and the noise of an explosion, had they got the big guns up; but then we heard the drone of an aeroplane overhead. They came swooping down on us but the ground formation saved us from the bombs bursting above us on the hillside. A few dropped in the track and men and horses were hit. Having used up their bombs the airmen tried to machine gun us and the bullets kicked up the dust half way up the hillside.

Eventually we reached the plain. The bushes were smouldering where shells had ignited them. A few desultory shells were bursting; we rode through them and recrossed the Jordan".

So far as its main purpose was concerned this attack across the Jordan was a failure, but it did fulfil its purpose of persuading the enemy that our main objective was Amman. Liman von Sanders the enemy commander was convinced that Allenby intended to break through to Deraa some thirty miles to the north, which was the centre of Turk communications to the east of Jordan.

Sergeant Fred Lewis didn't see it that way; in a letter home he wrote:-
"We have been into it again and the least said about the affair the better. We very nearly got to Damascus, but not quite the way we want to get there. At the moment we are right down in the Valley goodness knows how many feet below sea level. We are worried to death with flies by day and mosquitoes by night but in spite of it all we manage to keep merry and bright, although some of the remarks passed about this district are hardly in keeping with the traditions of the place. My officer went sick just before the stunt came off, we shall expect to see him when we get out of the line again. We lost one of our oldest and best sergeants a few days ago, Sergeant Roberts. He had been wounded three times and then got knocked out by a stray bullet. I had my usual luck, a shell fell just under my horse but luckily for me it was a dud".

It should be mentioned that the Beni Sakhr Arabs, who failed to put in an appearance at Es Salt, were not part of the great Arab army under the Emir Feisal. Colonel T.E. Lawrence writing in "Seven Pillars of Wisdom" had this to say:-

"Dawnay (Arab liaison officer) met me and we talked over our brief before going up to Allenby's camp. General Bols smiled happily at us and said, "Well, we're in Es Salt alright". To our amazed stares he went on to say that the chiefs of the Beni Sakhr had come into Jericho one morning to offer the immediate co-operation of their 20,000 tribesmen at Themed; and in his bath next day he had thought out a scheme and fixed it.
I asked who the chief of the Beni Sakhr was and he said 'Fahad', triumphing in his efficient inroad into my province. It sounded madder and madder, I knew that Fahad could not raise 400 men; and that at that moment there was not a tent on Thamed, they had moved south.
We hurried to the office for the real story and learned that it was unfortunately, as Bols said. The British cavalry had gone impromptu up the hills of Moab on some airy promise of the Zebn sheikhs; greedy fellows who had ridden into Jerusalem, only to taste Allenby's bounty, but had been taken at their mouth value".

154.

Bronze relief panels on the Regimental War Memorial illustrate:-
The R.G.H crossing the River Jordan   Watering Horses in Syria.

The Jordan Valley. Engraving from an original photograph by F. Mason Good

Chapter 18
In the Valley of Death

Jordan Valley must be held – Turks very active – God forsaken horrible spot
Line on Wadi Auja – high sick rate – scorching hot wind – this month flies die
Next month men die – horses lethargic – move to Bethlehem – Quartermaster

By mid July 1918 it was apparent that the German offensive in France had failed, but the demands of the Western Front meant that it had to have priority in manpower. General Allenby would therefore have to make do with the existing forces at his disposal, with fresh drafts from home to replace the casualties.

Although the Es Salt offensive had failed it succeeded in convincing the Turks that this was where the main thrust would come from, they accordingly strengthened the line of their defences in the Jordan Valley. Maybe they were lulled into a sense of security, because instead of concentrating their forces on the Palestine front they embarked on a number of futile expeditions into the Caucasus. Their high command failed to realise that with their uniforms worn out their troops' morale was low, and desertions were frequent.

Allenby made the best use of the next few weeks training his new arrivals from India and improving his lines of supply. His strategy demanded that the Jordan Valley must be held throughout the summer. Of the four cavalry divisions composing the Desert Mounted Corps two were normally in the valley and two resting in the hills, changing places every month; even though the official military handbook said:-

"Nothing is known of the climate in summer time, since no civilised human being has yet been found who has spent summer there".

In other words at 1200 ft below sea level it was as hot as a furnace. Even the Arabs refused to stop there and it was only occupied by a few degraded outcasts.

As one officer of the R.G.H. wrote to his family: -

"Of all the cursed spots of filthy, hideous, dusty country, give me the banks of the Jordan. Why John the Baptist ever selected such a God forsaken, horrible spot I don't know. The flies are simply unbearable. There is no air, and it is deadly hot. It is a loathsome spot".

The line of the British force in the Jordan stretched from the foot of the Judean Mountains, along the north bank of the Wadi el Auja to its junction with the Jordan. It then extended along the right bank of the Jordan to the Dead Sea, including the bridgehead at Ghoraniyeh.

On May 5th the R.G.H. were ordered to proceed to the Wadi El Auja to support the 4th battalion of the Imperial Camel Corps Brigade. Next day orders were received that they should relieve that battalion, but during the day owing to pressure from the enemy the situation became so critical that it was thought advisable that they should withdraw to a line further back. "A" and "B" squadrons were in their new position by morning but "D" squadron, which had been the last to leave the old position, did not appear. It was subsequently found that their pack horses had gone astray and all stores, Hotchkiss guns, ammunition and small arms ammunition had to be carried by the troops. After a strenuous night march they arrived just before dawn and reported that they had been in contact with the enemy and inflicted some casualties.

An officer's diary recorded: -

"May 5th - We got orders at 2 p.m. to move in three quarters of an hour. Everything seemed to be in a fearful hurry and we all thought there was another attack on. The C.O. goes ahead and I follow with the regiment as fast as possible. We arrive at Wadi Auja and are then guided up along to Wadi Mallaheh, where we eventually arrive at 5 p.m. I have to drop guides at every turn to bring on our rear parties to Wadi Mallaheh. The three squadrons are to take over from the I.C.C. at 3 a.m. next morning.

May 6th - Three squadrons go into line at 3 a.m. the camels remaining till night to come out. I take the led horses back to Wadi Mallaheh and pick a camp. The 9th and 18th Bengal Lancers arrive at 3 p.m. The Turks are very active, and altogether the positions are not satisfactory".

During the next few days the position of the line was adjusted and time was spent digging trenches and erecting barbed wire. Enemy attacks were hourly expected and they had to be constantly on the alert. As far as possible working hours were confined to the cooler times of the day - or more correctly the slightly less hot. These were from 4.15 to 7.15 in the morning and 6 - 9 at night. In the intervening time they tried to survive. Whether it was for humanitarian reasons or whether it was an attempt to get them out but Fred Lewis remembered that enemy aircraft dropped messages saying that it was impossible to live in the Valley. They did live but they found that the only thing that kept them alive and help them survive was to keep drinking tea. Even so the work of constructing fortifications in the awful weather was taking a heavy toll, diarrhoea and septic sores being frequent and there was a steady dribble of men to hospital. On May 16th the R.G.H. moved back to 5th Mounted Brigade

Headquarters - still in the valley - and next day were bivouacked in the bed of the Wadi Auja. Large working parties had to be found and admissions to hospital mounted at an alarming rate. An announcement that a certain amount of leave to Egypt would be granted gave a great boost to morale and reduced the casualty rate.

Frank Fox records that on May 26th the R.G.H. took over the line previously held by Hodson's Horse on the north bank of the Wadi Auja, work was continued digging trenches and constructing wire entanglements. The strength was 14 officers and 148 other ranks, so the month went wearily by. The effective strength of the regiment was 24 officers, 368 other ranks, 437 horses, 41 mules and 10 donkeys. Battle casualties for the month amounted to 10 and three officers and 113 other ranks were evacuated to hospital.

The men weren't the only casualties Lt Col R.M. Preston commented:-

"After about three weeks in the Valley the horses become tired and dispirited, though they had little or no work to do. They can scarce drag themselves to water and back. An unceasing campaign was carried out by the medical staff against malaria bearing mosquitoes, which infested the valley. In spite of all efforts the sick rate was high, curiously enough the Indian troops suffered more than the British".

W.T. Massey in his book 'Allenby's Final Tiumph' wrote - - "Here in a country where few white men have lived a large number of white troops endured the agonies of awful heat and blinding sun. Where the air was so dry, that a shirt washed at midnight was bone dry at daybreak. There were scorpions, tarantulas, centipedes and snakes. The horned viper bit some men and I heard we had deaths from snake bites. The heat was so fearful it killed the flies. The Turks sent an aeroplane over and dropped a message saying, 'this month flies die, next month men die'. The heat was responsible for most of the sick cases -- as a rule three weeks was considered the limit, beyond which the men could not remain and they were brought up to the hills south of Bethlehem where good water and a breeze made them fit again. It was dreadfully oppressive I never came out of it without a violent headache. The Dead Sea flotilla of motor boats, the transport drivers who suffered from choking dust as well as the heat and whose work was harassed by enemy bombing had a hard time, but so did everyone whose duty pinned them to the Valley".

Sergeant Fred Lewis commented in the same theme in his letters home: -

"The valley of the Jordan has certainly changed since the days of bible history, for there is no vegetation to be seen except a few stunted bushes and a few rushes down by the river. It may be a better place in the spring but at the present it is about the last place on earth that one would chose to live in. We are about five or six miles from Jericho, but as the town is out of bounds I have not had a chance to look around. From the outside it looks like any other village that one sees in Palestine, mud huts with a few stone buildings. I hope before long to get to Jerusalem for two or three days -- the articles in the Christian World about this country are very interesting and are read not only by me but other fellows in the Regiment -- Colonel Palmer left us a day or two ago to take up a staff position somewhere or other. He had stuck it very well for he was not a young man. Our new Colonel comes from the Warwicks, Watson is his name and I think will be very popular. At least the Warwicks give him a good name, he is a great footballer, having played for England; I think he used to play scrum half". (Lt Col A.C. Watson was a 7th Hussar)".

In a later letter he writes: -

"I do not feel in a letter writing mood. It has been a very hot day and this afternoon a scorching hot wind sprang up and just about put the finishing touch to it. We are still down in the valley and I think we have to stick it out for another fortnight. When our time is up I think we will be going back to Bethlehem for a rest at least that is what we hear. When we get back I hope to get in a few days in Jerusalem -- no doubt you saw in the papers about our latest "do" out here. It was about the most exciting five days that I have spent for some time and I can't say that any of us are anxious to repeat the dose". (The attack on Es Salt).

The highest reading during the month was 122f and the lowest 107f and in august at Ghoraniyeh it reached 130f on several occasions. Frequent patrols relieved a little of the tedium and made a change from digging trenches, they had always to be on the alert because in the jumble of hills and Wadis they never knew when they were being observed until enemy shells started arriving. On June 16th the regiment was relieved in the front line by the 18th Bengal Lancers and moved back to the horse lines. Then on June 23rd they were at last relieved by the 7th Australian Light Horse and moved back to Talaat - el Dumm, which was about 1000 ft higher than the valley, where the climate was very much more bearable. They were not allowed to remain idle, a reconnaissance party was sent out and did some useful work exploring the country between Talaat el Dumm and the Ghoraniyeh bridge in case they had to move back into the valley in a hurry. Five days later the regiment was ordered back into the rear end of the valley, where it was put on an hour's notice to move up to the front line.

At the end of the month they moved back to Talaat el Dumm where an officer and 76 other ranks left for a rest camp at Port Said and the remainder of the regiment moved to Bethlehem. They were much debilitated after their sojourn in the valley and there were frequent admissions to hospital.

Fred Lewis, who had taken up the post of quartermaster during this time, gives an interesting description of his work: -
"In my official position of quarter-bloke I am having a busy time now we are out of the line, the men have to be fixed up with new gear, all the losses accounted for and a hundred and one little things keep coming up that they expect me to know all about. The following are some of the incidents that occur any day –
"Please quarter I want a holdall".
Quarter - "What have you done with your old one".
"I lost it".
"How and when did you lose it".
"A shell dropped in my shack when I was out and I couldn't find it when I came back".
He gets the hold all and then up comes someone else.
"Please quarter can I have some money, I am going on leave".
"How much have you got to come"?
"Oh about eight pounds and I want to draw right up".
"Let me have your pay book".

Silence follows while the ready reckoner gets to work and after a great deal of adding and subtracting the ready reckoner - in other words me – comes to the conclusion that the man is two pounds in credit. He goes away with two pounds ten shillings cursing quarter-blokes and all their kind. Then an officer rushes up and wants to know the forage scale for the day, because the General is just coming round and he might ask and so the day goes on. I like the job and will be very sorry when I have to give it up for it is really a rest from troop work.
We are camping about half way between the city and Hebron (Solomon's Pools). I shall have things squared up about the middle of the week and then I am going to have a tour round. The climate here is great except that it gets very damp at night and is about two blankets cooler than the valley -- things are very quiet out here now, suppose both sides will wake up again when the cooler weather comes".
It seemed that the Jordan Valley was not going to let them go because on July 14th they were ordered to prepare to move down into the valley at

once. Three battalions of German infantry were preparing to attack, together with a large force of Turks. Their attack began at 3.30 in the morning and they succeeded in penetrating our outposts, cutting off our positions to the north of the line. For a while the position was dangerous but the outposts managed to hold and at 4.30 the 1st A.L.H. brigade managed to hold them off and drive them back, capturing 276 Germans and 62 Turks.

At the same time a strong Turkish force attempted to ford the Jordan half way between El Ghoraniyeh and the Dead Sea. The cavalry moved in to counter attack and managed to arrive within charging distance without being observed, about 100 Turks were killed and 97 captured. After these two defeats the enemy made no serious attempt at an attack.

After these two skirmishes to the regiment's relief the order was cancelled but two days later orders came to relieve the Anzac division in the valley. The brigade reached Wadi Nueiameh on July 18th, relieving the New Zealand Canterbury Rifles. They then took up the old routine of patrols and working parties.

During July 2 officers and 52 other ranks entered hospital. Casualties were made up with drafts from home and men discharged from hospital, so that the strength in the field was 18 officers, 352 other ranks, 406 horses, 55 mules and seven donkeys.

Engraving from an original photograph by F. Mason Good
The road from Jerusalem to Jericho.

Reproduced by permission of the Imperial War Museum

Australian Light Horse in the Jordan Valley near Jericho

Chapter 19.

The final Blow

Turk desertions – R.G.H. become 13th Cavalry Brigade of 5th Mounted Division pleasant ride in moonlight – prepare for advance up coastal plain – opening the gate – greatest adventure for cavalry – Turk trenches obliterated R.G.H. in vanguard – huge batches of prisoners – R.G.H. enter Nazareth

General Allenby continued his strategy of keeping the enemy's attention on the Jordan Valley and the eastern flank; whilst secretly building up his forces on the western flank. He noticed the progressive deterioration in their morale, evidence of which was the increasing number of desertions to the British lines. They were ill clothed, ill fed, their transport animals were in a wretched condition with forage often unobtainable. While the Turks fought bravely, the impression is that they would give up the fight if it were not for the German presence and influence.

With their lines of supply and communication in a state of collapse they were very much dependent on the railway. The main line came down from Damascus to Deraa Junction and continued on down into the Hejaz, where it was constantly being sabotaged by Lawrence's Arabs. From Deraa it branched, off crossing the Jordan to the south of Lake Tiberius and continued on to Haifa. About halfway between Lake Tiberias and Haifa there was a junction at El Afule, near Nazareth, which branched off to the south roughly followed the line of the coast, with branch lines to Nablus, Jaffa and Ramleh and on to Junction Station and Jerusalem.

On August 3rd the R.G.H., were relieved by the Worcesters after four months in and out of the valley. Leaving their post at Wadi Nueiamah they marched to Talaat el Dumm and the next day they moved to Solomon's Pools, picking up 57 reinforcements on the way. This was a permanent camp and a great deal of work was done making improvements. The better air and getting away from the stifling heat did wonders for the men's health and leave was given to visit Bethlehem and Jerusalem. Likewise the horses showed a remarkable improvement by being on good grazing land.

Sergeant Fred Lewis wrote a very cheerful letter home: -
"We have just moved into a fresh camp, I was informed last night that my leave has been granted, I just have to wait my turn, don't be surprised if you see me walk in one day -- we are out of the valley and back near Bethlehem in quite a good camp, 3000 ft above sea level, quite a change

after being 1000 ft below. The news from France is very cheering and before long we shall have some from this front, perhaps before you get this letter -- I have still got my job as S.Q.M.S. so expect I shall keep it till my leave comes through. We are living on the fat of the land in this camp what with eggs, grapes and tomatoes not to mention plums, peaches and apples".

For the next two weeks the regiment trained in musketry, the Hotchkiss gun, signalling, riding and squadron drill. There were also courses in observing and first aid.

On August 22nd the 5th Mounted Brigade left the Australian Mounted Division and became the 13th Cavalry Brigade of the 5th Mounted Division and they started to put in hand Allenby's grand deception plan to mislead the enemy as to where he was going to make his main thrust.

A dismounted party under Lt Wilson loaded all the baggage on to lorrys and moved it to the Wadi Heinan. The Regiment followed under cover of darkness, having a pleasant ride in brilliant moonlight, stopping for the day at Enab and continuing the following night. From this point on all troop movements that Allenby did not want the enemy to see were carried out by moonlight. Three complete mounted divisions, many gun batteries and other units had to be moved under cover of darkness from the Jordan Valley to the coastal area. The olive groves and orange trees north of Jaffa were used to hide the troops. For some time battalions in reserve had been accommodated between two half battalion camps, so the additional troops could be accommodated without any additional tentage. The dominance of the air force kept hostile aeroplanes from crossing the line and observing what was happening. Activity in the concealed bivouacs between the hours of 4.30 in the morning and 6 at night was forbidden. Special Police were on the alert to see that this order was obeyed, they also carried binoculars to be on the lookout for enemy aircraft; if one appeared they blew a whistle and everyone had to keep completely motionless.

The camps in the Jordan Valley that had been vacated were left standing and new ones pitched. Fifteen thousand dummy horses made of canvas filled the deserted horse lines. Sleighs drawn by mules raised the dust and made it difficult for the Turks to observe what was happening. A handful of men left behind tended cooking fires at night, outside old worn out tents that had been discarded. For several days troops marched down into the valley during the day and were driven out at night by motor transport, repeating the manoeuvre over and over again. Captured Turk guns were hauled down into the valley and blasted away into the Moabite hills. Agents were sent by Lawrence to Amman to order large quantities of forage, for the Arab force's camels, following a feint attack. So successful was the deception that German reconnaissance planes reported that two new divisions had been placed in the valley.

Allenby's plan was for the infantry to punch a hole through the Turkish front line in the coastal area. The 5th Cavalry Division would then pass through, following the coast up the Plain of Sharon then wheel round to the right. The 4th Cavalry Division would make for Tul Keram and carry on up the Dothan Pass to Jenin and Beisan. The infantry meanwhile would wheel round to the right pinning the Turks in the hills of Samaria.

Still further to encourage the enemy to believe that an attack would come from the east, the 7th Indian Division left the coast early in September and marched up the Jerusalem road as far as Enab. They marched eastward by daylight and returned at night. To prepare for the advance four new bridges had to be built across the river Auja which empties into the Mediterranean. To lull any suspicions the Turks may have for an advance along the coast, a bridging school was organised, which for six weeks spent their time building bridges and pulling them down again, making sure four were left standing the evening before the attack was launched.

Two days before the start time he arranged for Lawrence's Arabs to advance on Deraa and cut the railway to the north and west. The tribes of the Rualla and Howeitat rose up in support and after coming across atrocities committed by the retreating Turks, they gave no quarter; few prisoners were taken. The Royal Air Force bombed the railway line and station buildings on the 16th and 17th of September. At the same time the Arab column destroyed a bridge and section of railway 15 miles south of Deraa; completely cutting off the Turks in Palestine. As a result of these movements the Turkish army in the west was trapped, because their only way out would be to follow the Valley of Jezreel to the gorge of the River Yarmuk. The hills approaching the Jordan and on to the hills of Moab were roadless, except for goat tracks and were virtually impassable.

In the early hours of September 19th the headquarters of the Turkish 7th and 8th armies at Nablus and Tulkeram were bombed with a view to disorganising their communications. A big Handley Page bomber set out for El Afule, the Turks had their G.H.Q at Nazareth and all their signals had to pass through El Afule a few miles to the south. The bombs were dropped from a very low level and when the cavalry arrived they found in the three bomb craters the broken ends of practically every telegraph wire between G.H.Q. and the front.

To prevent enemy aircraft getting up from their aerodrome, two bombers taking turns to relieve each other remained constantly overhead and at the slightest sign of movement below dropped a bomb on the runway. By this means the enemy were kept on the ground all day, blinding and keeping them in ignorance as to where the strike would soon come.

The content of the following paragraphs are taken from Frank Fox: - At 4.30 a.m. 385 guns, accompanied by fire from destroyers anchored offshore, opened a fierce bombardment on the enemy's coastal front. For fifteen minutes they kept up an incessant bombardment and then the infantry moved forward. Meanwhile the 5th and 4th cavalry divisions moved up behind the infantry, ready to pass through after the infantry had punched a hole in the enemy defences. It had been expected that the infantry would have "opened the gate" by 10 in the morning but so overwhelming had been the attack, so complete was the surprise of the enemy that by eight minutes past five the front line had been taken. By 6 a.m. the infantry could wheel round and pin the enemy in the Samarian hills, leaving an open road for the cavalry.

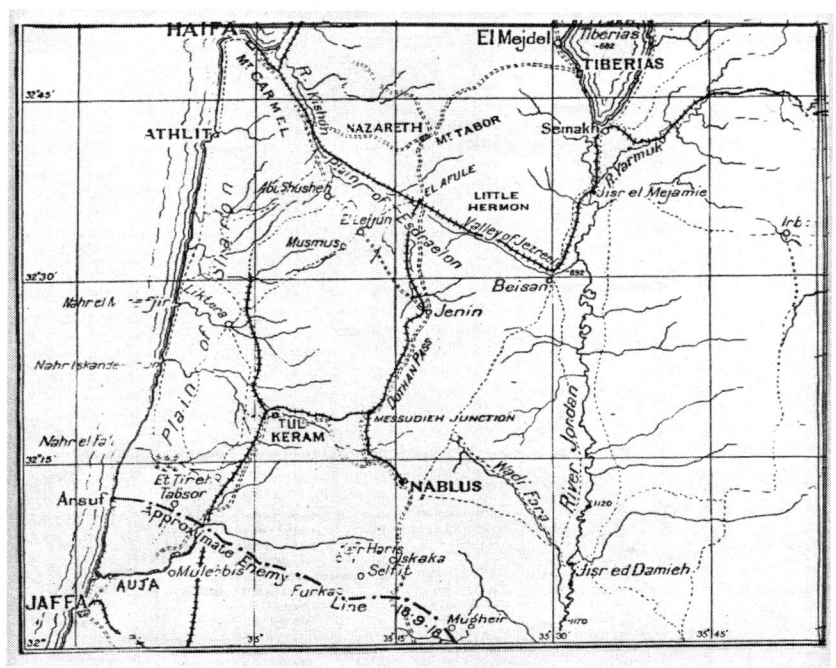

Northern Palestine

The R.G.H. rested hidden away in orange groves until the evening of September 18th, when with the rest of the 13th Brigade it marched to the sea coast and halted about one and a half miles south of Arsuf. Horses were watered from troughs erected during the day and lines were put down in column of troops. They were well sheltered by high cliffs giving good cover against enemy shells coming over. The enemy was in complete ignorance of the concentration of forces and nothing happened during the night. By midnight the whole of the 5th division had arrived at the assembly point and must have been an inspiring sight stretched for three and a half miles along the beach.

With the first roar of the guns, awe inspiring to those who had not experienced barrages in France, the regiment was keen to be off. A meal was served out but so great was the excitement it was hardly touched. Likewise the horses seemed to know that something was up and fretted to be off. At 5.30 a.m. the order to mount up was given and at 6 o'clock the advance commenced, long before the expected time.

This was a great moment for the R.G.H., they were the only British regiment in the vanguard. The disaster at Katia, the tedium and danger of the long march from the canal and the Jordan valley were all forgotten. They were embarked on the greatest adventure that fell to the lot of cavalry in modern times. As they moved forward signs of victory were soon seen in the numbers of prisoners passing to the rear. By 7 o'clock the Regiment had passed through the Turkish front line. Trenches had been completely obliterated and twisted barbed wire showed how effective the bombardment had been.

The head of the brigade cleared the beach and debouched into open country, a few shells came over at 7.50 a.m. but the shooting was very erratic and no casualties were inflicted. The 9th Hodson's Horse Lancers were leading the advance of the brigade and groups of dead Turks spoke eloquently of their lance work.

The regiment halted in the Wadi Ain - el - Yezek for about ten minutes at 9.40 a.m. to allow the advance guard to clear the village of Mukhalid, where a lively fight was in progress. This place was soon cleared and the regiment moved forward at the canter. Shell fire came from the North West and a patrol of four men under Corporal Wiseman was detailed to investigate. "A" squadron under Captain Butler was sent out as right flank guard to the brigade and succeeded in capturing a large number of prisoners, who were sent back under escort. They also rounded up a huge drove of camels, which they had to leave for others to secure.

The flank guard at this time went out a bit too wide and became engaged in a skirmish with the enemy. "D" squadron were sent out to do flank guard and "A" squadron was told to rejoin the regiment as soon as it was finished. Corporal Wiseman rejoined his squadron; he had found two enemy guns limbering up and charged them with his patrol. The officer in charge surrendered with twenty men. Private Forrest of "B" squadron saw a large enemy column moving away to the north. He galloped straight to the moving column, which halted and surrendered. The column consisted of 37 wagons, 4 officers and 100 men; Private Forrest turned them about and escorted them to the rear.

On the beach the going had been heavy and hard for the horses, but after turning into the plain the country was mostly turf and they simply cantered along, taking in their stride every obstacle that the retreating Turks had set up. They were constantly sending back huge batches of prisoners with the smallest of escorts. At 11.30 a.m. the brigade reached Liktera, taking by surprise a transport and supply depot chiefly manned by Germans. Sergeant George Castle rounded up several motor lorrys filled with Germans, which were escaping. 2nd Lieutenant R.U. White and his troop succeeded in capturing a complete training establishment, including the commandant, several officers and about 400 men, many of them Germans.

The brigade halted at El Hudiera at 11.50 a.m. where the horses were watered and fed and put under cover of some willow groves. Many huts and bivouacs were found as well as a large dump of small arms ammunition. Papers and clothes were strewn around in confusion giving signs of a hurried flight. However there was a price to pay for this remarkable advance, many of the horses showing signs of fatigue; five had died while 17 others had to be evacuated and afterwards destroyed.

The regiment paraded at 6 p.m. in rear of the 18th Bengal Lancers for the next stage of the advance, from Liktera to El Afule and on to Nazareth some 40 miles away. The going after the first few miles became very difficult, over rough and rocky hill country. Men and horses stumbled over the rough shale, where it was difficult for them to keep their feet and this resulted in the column becoming stretched out. At about 11 p.m. the Indian regiment in front lost touch with the rest of the brigade and were hopelessly lost. Patrols were sent out under Sgt Major Garret and eventually they were found.

Extracts from the second in command Major Howard's diary, give a vivid account of this incident, which occurred on the threshold of the Plain of Esdraelon (Armageddon).

"I discovered to my horror that the Indians in front of me, whom I was following, had lost touch with the main body at the critical moment, where the mountain track divided into four well worn paths across the vale in four different directions. I was furious with the Indians and cursed them up hill and down dale, that being of no avail I settled down to wait and dismounted. There were lots of Bedouin shacks about but having no interpreter it was useless to ask them. I sent scouts up the paths to east and west and they failed to make contact, by this time I had made up my mind that one of the two paths leading across the valley must be right. We went along and came across Major Mills the 2nd in command of the Lancers, who told me he had also lost the Brigadier and staff who had gone on in front. After half an hour we found the Brigadier near the railway, much to everyone's relief".

They pushed out on to the Plain of Esdraelon at 2.30 a.m. and reached El Afule without further incident. They hurried on leaving an R.E. detachment to blow up the railway. This awakened an enemy battery, who sent several shells over, most of which were duds. On reaching the village of Mejeidil the R.G.H. became advance guard to the brigade, leaving the 18th Bengal Lancers behind to occupy the village and deal with prisoners.

The brigade proceeded and the R.G.H. moving at a sharp trot pushed on and at 4.25 a.m. came in sight of Nazareth. 2nd Lieutenants Pretty and Cornwall were sent to occupy two tactical points covering the approach to the town and 2nd Lieutenant Greene with his troop were detailed to round up a large convoy of motor lorries that were seen to be leaving. Just on the threshold of the town a machine gun position was noticed on the right, it was rushed at the gallop and its crew of nine taken prisoner. With swords drawn the R.G.H. galloped into Nazareth, the streets of which were filled with the early morning bustle of an awakening camp. The enemy were taken completely by surprise; the soldiers both Germans and Turks were mostly unarmed. Some 1500 hundred of them surrendered, the German G.H.Q. was thus captured by a single regiment, only the brigade H.Q. was up with the R.G.H. to share this historic achievement. Lieut Inglis was sent with his troop to capture the enemy C in C, General Liman von Sanders, he entered several houses trying to find him and was told that he had left during the night. One account states that he was in hiding in the town, whether true or a rumour he managed to slip the net.

At about 8 a.m. the enemy made a determined counter attack. "D" and part of "B" squadron pushed forward inflicting severe losses on the enemy and our machine guns enfiladed the enemy advance, which broke down with further heavy losses. At 8.30 a.m. an enemy aeroplane came over and attacked the horses with trivial results. At 10 a.m. enemy heavy machine gun fire opened up from high ground, which we had been unable to make good and the regiment was ordered to fall back to the brigade reserve position.

Presently the enemy recovered his surprise, street fighting developed and the mounted men were at a disadvantage. The brigade had been weakened by a number of detachments, to guard positions captured, before reaching Nazareth and was not sufficiently strong to complete the occupation of the town. Having located the enemy headquarters and seized the most important documents in it, the 13th brigade retired on El Afule taking their prisoners with them. Many of the German prisoners taken at Nazareth were surprised at the rapidity of the advance and a staff major flatly refused to believe that the regiment had come all the way by land; holding that they must have been landed by ship from Haifa. It was indeed a tremendous achievement, having ridden at least sixty miles in two days, much of it hard going and showed great credit on the horsemanship of the regiment.

Next day September 21st it was decided to reoccupy Nazareth and the R.G.H. were given the task of leading the advance. They had not understood why the withdrawal had been ordered in the first place. The town was reoccupied without serious opposition.

There is the following entry in a squadron leader's diary.

"The Brigadier received a message to retire on El Afule, as he had a large outpost line to take up. This was a great pity because it was no easy job to get out, during the day we would have consolidated the position and the evacuation made a bad impression. There was only one road to get out by, 800 yards of which was under heavy machine gun fire -- a good gallop and no stopping was the only thing, the bullets were all splashing just in front of me, but did not appear to hit anyone. On turning the corner I found the C.O. and he showed me where we were wanted -- although the Turks made an immediate counter attack it was never pressed very seriously -- all units were very much scattered and many men could not find their horses -- eventually we got pretty well together and I went round the new line which our regiment was to hold until dusk while the rest of the brigade got back to El Afule.

The Line was a strong one, consisting of good positions on high hills with our horses in a ravine -- we were very tired, holding on till dusk and then retired slowly -- the way back down was one of the most ragged ravines I have ever seen -- after a weary effort we got to the Plain of Esdraelon below -- passing through the outpost line we got to camp at 8 p.m. and then had to go back a mile and a half to water from a muddy pool, most (horses) had not drunk since 3 p.m. the day before. No sleep for 42 hours so slept well.

Saturday September 21. Reveille at 5 a.m. we drew rations and forage at 10 p.m. and after watering moved off to reoccupy Nazareth. The track was a very tiring climb, most of us being dead beat on arrival. The Boche had evacuated and outposts were placed all round facing Haifa, Acre and the Tiberias roads, all regiments being required for the job".

After arrival at Nazareth, Lieutenant Greene and his troop were told to reconnoitre the Nazareth to Lake Tiberias road. Owing to a signals failure he was out all night. After passing through two villages he came to Kefr Kenna where the keys of the church, which was being used as a grain store, were surrendered to him. The German doctor in charge of the hospital in the Latin Convent was very courteous and did all in his power to make them comfortable for the night.

At about 9 p.m. information was received that a Turkish counter attack was expected from the direction of Haifa and "B" squadron were directed to cover brigade H.Q. At midnight the attack developed and was seen off by the 18th Bengal Lancers who made a splendid bayonet charge, killing about 180 Turks and capturing around 300. The attacking force was estimated at around 700, with a considerable number of machine guns, which the Turks abandoned when they retreated.

This action brought to an end the action around Nazareth; isolated pockets of prisoners were brought in during the next few days. Lieutenant Greene accounted for thirty of them. The local inhabitants made no secret of their relief at having got rid of the Germans and were pleased to supply the troops with plenty of fowls, eggs and other provisions.

The results of the action of the previous three days are best summed up in the following extracts from General Allenby's despatches:-

"The first phase was of short duration. In 36 hours between 4.30 a.m. on September 19th and 5 p.m. on September 20th the greater part of the Turkish 8th army had been overwhelmed and the 7th army were in full retreat through the hills of Samaria, whose exits were already in the hands of my cavalry -- practically the whole of the 7th and 8th armies were captured together with their guns and transports, as a result the Turkish 4th army east of Jordan was in full retreat.

The 5th Cavalry Division moved north, it then turned north east and riding through the hills of Samaria descended into the Plain of Esdraelon at Abu Shusheh. The 13th Cavalry Brigade (R.G.H.) was then directed on Nazareth, riding across the Plain of Esdraelon they reached Nazareth at

5.30 a.m. Fighting took place in the streets, some 2000 prisoners were captured, Liman von Sanders had escaped but his papers and some of his staff were taken".

The hills around Nazareth

The Plains of Esdraelon otherwise known as Armagedon, overlooked by the hilltop fort of Megiddo, which for over 6,000 years controlled the trade route between Egypt and Mesopotamia.

The above engravings are taken from original photographs by F. Mason Good

Chapter 20

Prisoners Galore

Coastal Plain cleared – Turk 8th army captured – 7th army scattered – prepare to March on Acre and Haifa – view Sea of Galilee – held up at Lake Hule – enemy Retreat to Damascus – Golan Heights, very cold, 3000 ft up – capture wireless Station – Arab village butchered – Turks and British combine – Damascus

The general position by the evening of September 20th was that the coastal plain was cleared of the enemy and that our cavalry was firmly established across the lines of his retreat. His rearguards were still giving stubborn resistance in the tangled hills and gullies of the Judean range but the Australian cavalry had them covered. The 21st saw the last serious infantry engagements of the whole campaign, when they advanced on to the high ground north and north east of Nablus.

The greater part of the Turkish Eighth Army was already taken prisoner they had been captured in the original assault in the pursuit up the coastal plain. The remnants of the eighth and the greater part of the Seventh Army set out from Nablus during the night of September 20/21st by a motor road, which the Turks had constructed down the Wadi Fara to Beisan and the Jordan. Near Nablus the Wadi Fara is a precipitous gorge, into the side of which the road was cut. At dawn on the 21st the air force found the retreating army and machine gunned and bombed the mass of Turks in the defile. The head of the column was soon blocked and the survivors dispersed in panic into the hills. Ninety guns, fifty lorries and a thousand other vehicles were found deserted in the defile next day. The demoralised survivors were scattered; a few escaped over the Jordan but the greater part were captured by the mounted troops. So perished Turkey's 7th and 8th armies.

On September 22nd the 5th Cavalry Division was assembled at Nazareth preparing to march on Acre and Haifa. The R.G.H. paraded at 4 a.m. next day ready to move off. During the advance they came across large numbers of dead Turk ponies and much discarded ammunition. At 9 a.m. a short halt was made at Shefr Amr and horses were watered and fed. The local inhabitants gave the troops a great reception and an English missionary who had been there four years said the Palestinians were glad to see the back of the Turks. He was anxious to know whether Nazareth, where some members of his family were living, was cleared of them.

After they had mounted up and moved forward, Haifa and Acre soon came into view. Haifa was being attacked by the 14th and 15th brigades and a great deal of artillery fire was heard. A light battery of Krupp guns from Acre opened up but no damage was done and they were quickly captured. The Brigade marched to the north of Acre and closed upon the northern side of the town. All enemy opposition had now ceased and "B" squadron were ordered to set up an outpost line half a mile to the north near a large mound. 2nd Lieutenant Gaydon and 40 men were detailed for police duty in the town. The men and the surviving horses were able to get a good swim in the sea and all ranks were cheered to hear that Es Salt, where they had spent a gruelling few days eighteen months ago, had now been taken.

R.G.H. casualties between September 19th and 23rd were 2 other ranks killed, one officer and ten other ranks wounded and 18 other ranks were treated for minor wounds. The horses were not so lucky 72 were either killed or destroyed.

The English had previous associations with Acre when it had been taken in 1104 during the first crusade, recaptured by the Saracens in 1187 it fell again to Richard Coeur de Lion in 1191. Because of Richard's neglect England entered a period of repression and hard times. These are chronicled in tales of fact and mythology, the country being left under the hand of his brother Prince John; giving rise to tales of the cruel Sheriff of Nottingham, Robin Hood and all that.

A diary entry reads: -

"September 23rd - Reveille at 2.30 a.m. Dress, cook and breakfast in the dark, everybody being hidden under a separate fig tree it was difficult getting started, however we got off to the starting point. The 18th Bengal Lancers are advance guard today; the road is strewn with overturned Turkish wagons. We follow the valley of the brook Kishon, the country on either side is covered with scrub. For the first time I saw pomegranate groves each side of the stream. By 10 o'clock we reached a village called Seframa, which was full of agriculturists busy harvesting. There are huge olive groves all round it and in front we see the huge, flat circular plain of Acre, with the town on a little promontory in the bay. We feed the horses and have lunch. Numerous gardens provide onions and tomatoes and the inhabitants performed with songs and dances for our amusement; there are some very pretty ladies here.

After half an hour we moved on again, Acre is surrounded by tall Palm trees, close to it is a little mound which the enemy would hold because it was the only tactical position anywhere near. The 18th Bengal Lancers galloped the mound and captured two field guns, we also captured 150 prisoners -- The town is probably just the same as it was 1,000 years ago, it has suffered 13 sieges which have not altered it very much. The streets are narrow, the walls high and the sea runs right up to the walls. Outside are large gardens rich with pomegranates, lemons, figs, dates and everything that is good to eat in hot weather. The plain of Acre is of fertile deep soil growing millet and maize, there are herds of very fine cattle and sheep.

The railway from Haifa has been taken up, the Turks had made dummy guns with two wheels and a stick and an iron pipe to represent the gun".

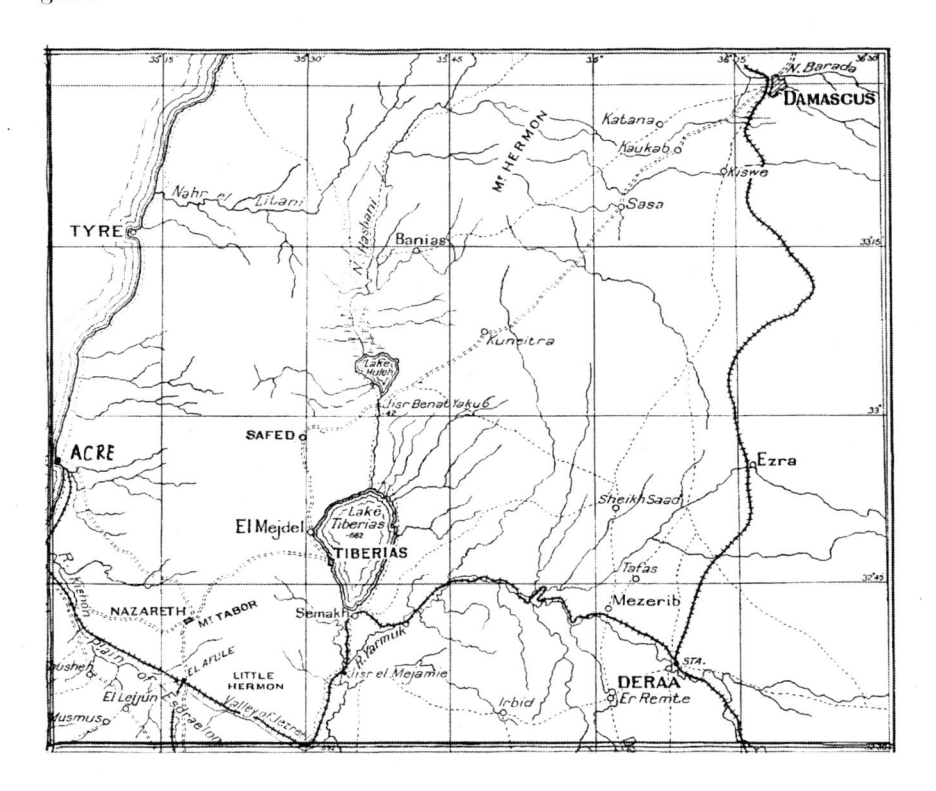

Map showing the road from Nazareth to Damascus

On September 25th Capt Lord Apsley took a troop to reconnoitre the coast road in the direction of Beirut, some forty miles to the north. After going eight miles he decided the road was impassable for motor traffic. In the evening orders were received for the regiment to march next morning on the road to Damascus. "A" squadron was to be left behind to garrison Acre until the infantry arrived to take over.

At 5 a.m. next day the brigade group assembled for the march to Kefr Kenna some 20 miles away. They halted at Shefr Amr to water and feed horses and have breakfast. Leaving the village they left the main road and branched off to the left, on to a track that crossed the hills in an easterly direction. The going was bad and they were in single file most of the way. At 2.30 p.m. reaching a point about one and a half miles north of Kefr Kenna they camped for the night. Watering was difficult and took several hours, being only obtainable in buckets from wells some three miles away.

Next morning they started off at 2 a.m. but not before a long and tedious delay, the whole division was on the move and there were frequent hold ups. After a brief halt on the road, Tiberias was reached at 8.30 a.m., after a march of some thirteen miles from the start point. They had a splendid view of the Sea of Galilee on the approach to the city. Upon arrival and after putting down the lines and watering the horses they lost no time refreshing themselves with a swim, after the long hot journey.

Engraving from a photo by F. Mason Good
Tiberias and the Sea of Galilee

They weren't allowed to rest for long and at 1 o'clock the brigade continued the advance towards the Jordan crossing at Kusatra, along the Tiberias - Damascus road. The country was very hilly and the going was bad, dead Turks and dead horses were frequently encountered, they halted a mile and a half beyond Kusatra and lines were put down for the night. The march had been hard on the horses, five were shot on the march and others died before the morning.

The 5th Cavalry Division were following the Australian Mounted Division, which was leading the way to Damascus. At the Jordan crossing south of Lake Hule the retreating Turks had made a show of resistance by blowing up the Jisr Benat Yakub bridge (bridge of Jacob's daughters) which crosses the Jordan about 2000 yards south of Lake Hule. They had also brought down 1000 German and Turk reinforcements from Damascus in motor lorries and some field guns to hold the crossing. A frontal attack was hopeless because the enemy were well hidden in a maze of boulders. The 5th A.L.H. brigade managed to swim their horses across the Jordan about two miles south of the damaged bridge. They attacked on the left flank and taken by surprise the enemy retreated back to Damascus. The 3rd A.L.H. brigade attempted a crossing at the southern end of Lake Hule but didn't manage to get across until after dark, when they pursued the retreating enemy, capturing 50 men, three field guns and some machine guns.

That was the position when the R.G.H. arrived at the blown up bridge on September 28th, straightaway they set about assisting the engineers repairing the bridge and making roads. There was a good crop of daru growing near the river and the horses were turned into it for a good feed. That and the availability of a good water supply undoubtedly saved at least half of the horses having to drop out during the next stage of the march. The bridge was made good and by midday wheeled traffic was able to cross. Enemy planes attempted to bomb the bridge during the day but did no damage. 100 men from the regiment were detailed to make a ford across some swampy ground by the river and by 1 o'clock pretty well the whole of the 5th Division were concentrated near the crossing ready to crossover.

At 5 p.m. the Brigade moved off to march to El Kunitra with the R.G.H. in the lead. With the Australian Division ten hours ahead of them they came across signs of enemy resistance. Numerous machine and camel guns with their crews lying dead beside them were frequently encountered, as well as batches of prisoners and wounded being treated by the roadside.

The Regiment arrived at El Kunitra at 11 p.m in the area now known as the Golan Heights and bivouacked for the night. It was very cold, a stiff north east wind was blowing and in the twelve miles they advanced they had risen to 4000 ft above sea level. The village was practically deserted, fortunately it contained a large quantity of hay and all the horses managed to have a good feed.

Extracts from an officer's (Major Howard's) diary read as follows: -

"September 27th - at 9 a.m. we arrive at Tiberias a squat thickly - housed town on the very edge of the Sea of Galilee, the road leading to it going down a steep hill. The last of the Australians were leaving when we arrived and as they were held up at the Jordan crossing this gave us time to off saddles, water and feed. This we did at the edge of the lake and of course we all bathed. It is a delightful sea with a stony bottom, in a deep basin, hot and very sultry.

At 1 p.m. we moved round the edge of the lake by Caperneum, of which there are very few signs left. The road seemed unending but after a long stiff climb we arrived at Kasra Atra (sic) in the dark and we just lay down and slept.

Saturday September 28th - Reveille at 4 a.m. and we move off at 9 a.m. for El Kunitra. On arrival at the Jordan crossing we have to set to work to make a ford for our guns to cross, this we do with brushwood and stones and after two hours hard work it is ready. We then get two hours rest so off saddle and graze our horses by the Jordan, the river here is not muddy and only about 30 yards across. Before moving off we left all the horses unfit to go on behind with Capt Gillholme, the divisional horse officer, much to his disgust. At 5.30 a.m. we set out along a road with very rocky country on each side and eventually arrived at El Kunitra, where we camped for the night. Found lots of hay in the village, which we borrowed, as the inhabitants were very hostile Circassians.

Sunday September 29th - Reveille at 5 a.m; we had all day to rest and did not move until 6.30 p.m. The country around is rocky with a good deal of short grass. It lies below Mt Hebron and is cold and desolate. We get plenty of water for horses and men. We are now 3000 ft up and the nights are very cold, we only have our drill jackets and no coats but use horse blankets as well as our own.

At 6.30 p.m. we move again but do not go very far because the Australian Division is held up and we are kept waiting and shivering on the road for four and a half hours. It was the coldest night we have yet experienced and many slept on the road".

It was so cold that the horses refused to drink from a wayside stream. As they advanced they kept meeting large batches of prisoners, including Germans and Austrians, being escorted to the rear. There were many dead lying around and wounded waiting to be treated by field ambulance. Field guns, machine guns and personal equipment had been abandoned to lighten the load of the retreating enemy.

At 11 o'clock the Regiment reached Khan Esh Shira and halted so that the horses could be watered and fed and the men took advantage of the respite to have a quick meal. Information came through that a large enemy force was advancing towards them and orders were issued to prepare to charge, but the enemy advance failed to materialise. At 1 p.m. the Regiment moved off as leading regiment of the brigade, to march on Kaukab (the reputed site of St Paul's conversion). With "D" squadron as advance guard, the Brigade proceeded at the trot over a rough and stony plain. About four miles from the town the Brigade was halted as Kaukab had already been taken.

Capt Lord Apsley was despatched with a strong troop to attempt the capture of a large enemy wireless station at Meidan. When they arrived at Kaukab they had seen the wireless masts and large columns of smoke rising nearby and one of the masts was seen to fall. The patrol pushed on to see how badly the station had been damaged and whether there was any possibility of salvaging the equipment. After encountering and dealing with scattered parties of the enemy, they entered wooded country west of the station and could see that the buildings were burning furiously and about 500 men were engaged in the work of destruction. The patrol formed up and charged, the enemy taken by surprise offered no resistance and between 150 and 200 were captured. After going a short distance the prisoners refused to accompany the patrol. Fire was coming from all directions and the patrol, out numbered by about 12 to 1, was ordered to charge. Three Germans and 12 Turks were killed with the sword and many more wounded, the Hotchkiss gun inflicting further losses on the enemy. One N.C.O. and two horses were wounded.

In the meanwhile the Regiment proceeded with the Brigade in the direction of Kiswe, because it was believed that large numbers of disorganised Turks were coming in towards Damascus. The position was that the 5th Cavalry Division (R.G.H.) had come up the west side of the Sea of Galilee and the 4th Cavalry Division had come up the east side. The Arabs advanced from Deraa up the eastern flank; all three forces aiming at Damascus.

The 2nd A.L.H. Brigade advancing up the eastern flank entered into negotiation with a Turkish force occupying Ziza. The Brigadier explained to them the hopelessness of their position and invited them to surrender. The Turks were willing to surrender, but were unwilling to lay down their arms until the British force was large enough to protect them. The Beni Sakhr, who it is remembered had failed to put in an appearance during the assault on Es Salt, had now arrived, outnumbering the Turks and were out for bloody revenge. So the Brigade commander was in the bizarre position of combining with the Turks to hold off the Arabs until next morning, when reinforcements arrived and the Turks could be relieved of their arms. (It should be mentioned that these were Bedouin Arab irregulars, not part of King Feisal's Arab army which was well disciplined).

The 13th Brigade made a wide detour but no enemy were met with in significant numbers. Horses and men were nearly done up as they had been on the move for 30 hours, without having the opportunity of a proper meal. At 7 p.m. they were just getting comfortable in their bivouacs when orders were received to set up an outpost line on the west of the road overlooking Corps H.Q. No fires or lights were allowed even though Corps H.Q. was brilliantly lit up. The night passed quietly but many fires and explosions were seen and heard in Damascus.

General Liman von Sanders after his narrow escape from Nazareth had issued orders for a defensive line to be formed from Deraa down the Yarmuk valley to Semakh at the southern end of the Sea of Galillee and thence west of the Sea of Gallilee by Tiberias to Lake Hule. His intention was to rally and re-organise his forces in these positions and give him time to organise the defence of Damascus. Such was the speed of our advance that he never had time for his orders to be carried out; in fact they never even reached the 7th and 8th armies. The Turkish forces had almost completely disintegrated and he was relying on German machine gunners to hold the line. They put up a stiff resistance at Semakh but the 11th A.L.H. approached the town by moonlight and attacked at dawn. On being received by machine gun fire they unhesitatingly formed line and charged. They then dismounted and a fierce hand to hand struggle took place amongst the substantial stone houses. The Australian losses were heavy with 17 killed and 61 wounded. They killed a 100 of the enemy and took 350 prisoners, 150 of them Germans.

Colonel T.E. Lawrence writing in Seven Pillars of Wisdom about another stand by the Germans said: - "he couldn't help but admire the Germans; they were two thousand miles from home, without guides in conditions bad enough to break the bravest nerves. Yet their sections held together in firm rank, sheering through the wrack of Turk and Arab like armoured ships, high faced and silent. When attacked they halted, took position, fired to order. There was no haste, no crying and no hesitation. They were glorious".

The 4th Cavalry Division moving up the east side of the Sea of Galilee advanced on and occupied Kunitra. Moving rapidly northwards from Deraa the Arabs and the Desert Mounted Corps occupied the railway stations of Ezra and Ghazale. With all forces pressing on by midday on September 30th the Australian Mounted Division had captured Katana and sealed the exits from Damascus to the north and the 5th Mounted

Division (R.G.H.) had reached the southern outskirts. Next morning it was occupied by the Desert Mounted Corps and the Arab army. For political purposes the Arabs were left in charge.

General Allenby's despatches comment on the capture of Damascus: -
"The advance to Damascus, following on the operations in the Plain of Esdraelon and the Valley of Jezreel had thrown a great strain on the Desert Mounted Corps. Great results were however achieved. On September 26th when the advance began some 45,000 Turks and

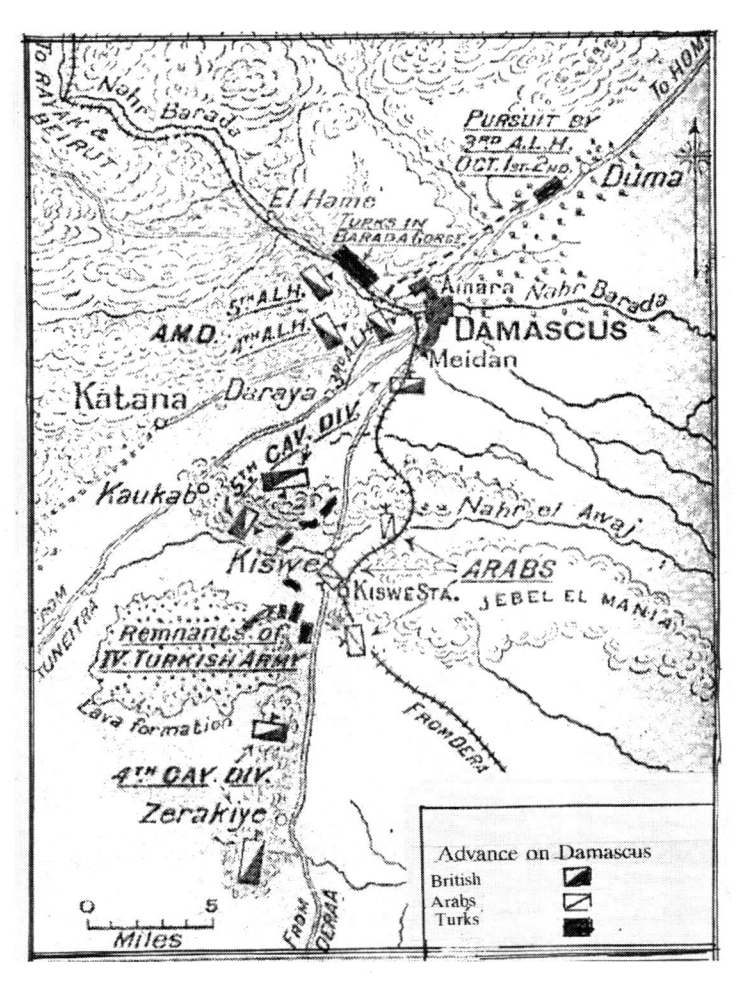

Germans were still in Damascus or retreating on it. It is true that all units were in a state of disorganisation, but given time, a force could have been formed to delay my advance.

The destruction of the remnants of the Turkish 4th army and capture of 20,000 prisoners prevented any possibility of this. The remnants of the Turkish armies in Palestine and Syria, numbering some 17,000 men, of whom only 4,000 were effective rifles, fled northwards a mass of individuals without organisation, without transport and without any of the accessories required to enable it to act, even on the defensive".

Major Howard's diary vividly relates what happened:-
"October 1st - On reaching the main Kiswe - Damascus road we met the Hedjaz troops, or rather numerous followers who had joined them. Galloping around wildly shouting, singing and letting off their rifles in the air - they were a most quaint and picturesque sight - gaudy, brilliant robes floating about in the wind, old men with long grey beards. They moved about in small parties of six to eight, all bent on loot and destroying Turks and Germans.

Finally the transport halted on a stream about eight miles out of Damascus, preparatory to bivouacking for the night. I made them form a square and had to dispose of my squadron all round them as night outposts. We got some good grazing and some fresh water and had a good meal. At 10 p.m. we received a fresh order to saddle up and march through Damascus to rejoin the division, which after being out of touch all day was found camped in the groves near the town. The town stands under a high range of hills running east and south west – really the Lebanon hills. To the east, north and south is a huge fertile plain, many rivers, trees and gardens growing round the town which obscured all troops and made it difficult to locate anybody. All the inhabitants had rifles and were firing them off continuously all night, which made one think that there was a battle still going on. We had a long trek right through the town, the dust was awful. Eventually we found the Regiment comfortably settled in a large walnut grove at 4.30 a.m. on Wednesday October 2nd. It was no good going to sleep, as we were to move again shortly. So we washed, shaved, had breakfast and got ready to move at 8 a.m. for a triumphal march through Damascus.

At 8.30 a.m. on October 2nd we moved to a rendezvous to take part in this triumphal march. To reach the place we had to go about 8 miles through the gardens, the dust was very bad and we could see very little. However it was interesting and we had a great welcome from the European and Syrian inhabitants. The prisoners and wounded were all in a very bad condition and great difficulties were experienced in dealing with them.

Lawrence on entering the hospitals discovered most appalling scenes of neglect and starvation. The dead had not been moved for days and it was difficult separating them from those still living.

Eventually we got to our camp area at El Judeida at 5 p.m. after marching all day. This was in a forest of orange trees, beautifully shaded and well watered. The camp was rather cramped but very pleasant. We settled down for a good rest not knowing when we would move on again.

From 5.30 (a.m.) on September 29th to 8 p.m. on October 2nd myself and the rest of the squadron had only slept nine hours in a total of 110 hours, so you can imagine we needed rest.

Thursday October 3rd - Reveille at 6 a.m.; we spent the day resting, washing, re-organising and writing reports. Managed to get a good supply of beautiful grapes, eggs and vegetables, several horses had to be evacuated. Also men started to fall sick, mostly with malaria caught in the Valley of Esdraelon or the Plain of Acre. One or two officers came round from the 4th Cavalry and we related our experiences to them".

The strength of the regiment at this point was 17 officers, 283 other ranks and 335 animals.

Photo by permission Imperial War Museum
General Harry Chauvel Commander 5th Mounted Division enters Damascus
Accompanied by representatives of units under his command

Chapter 21

Aleppo and the Armistice

Influenza and Malaria – 5th Cavalry Division marches on Aleppo – feed off country Nahar – Zaan Valley – invited to feast by local Pasha – R.G.H. enter Baalbeck, enter Homs – hostile villagers – Arab army enter Aleppo – 5th Cavalry Division completes march of 500 miles in less than six weeks

The strength of the whole of the Turkish armies in Palestine and Syria was estimated at 100,000 when Allenby's attack commenced on September 19th. Only some 17,000 escaped north, without artillery, without transport and without organisation. Their actual strength was estimated at 4,000 rifles, the remainder were a disorganised rabble.

General Allenby also had his problems in that his supply bases were some 150 miles from Damascus. He decided to advance to a line Rayak - Beirut. The occupation of Beirut, which was a good port, would ease his problems substantially. The 7th Meerut Division had already occupied Haifa and leaving that town it marched via Tyre and Sidon and reached Beirut on October 8th. On arrival they found French warships anchored and armoured cars from Rayak, which had been occupied by the 4th and 5th Cavalry Divisions two days earlier.

A severe attack of influenza and malaria hit the 4th Cavalry Division and put them out of action at Damascus. This only left the 5th Cavalry Division to advance on Aleppo, completely unsupported except for an Arab force and some Armoured Car Batteries; Aleppo being over 300 miles from the former front line. The Division's lines of communication were very much extended and they would have been vulnerable to a determined attack. Such was the estimated deterioration in the Turkish force that it was thought the task was well within their capability.

An officer's diary entry reads as follows: -
"We moved across rough mountain country till we struck the main road at Rayak. Here were many signs of the retreating Turks, dead men, horses and camels everywhere. They had been severely handled by the Australians and our aeroplanes. Just before the capture of Damascus, von Sanders had collected about 7,000 men, which he put under a Turkish commander to defend the city. The Turkish commander put these men in indefensible positions where they could get no water, then he galloped off himself and surrendered to General Barrow, telling him exactly where his men were.

We moved via Khan Dimez to Khan Meizulun, where we arrived at 2 p.m. It was not a good camping ground but there was a fair amount of water. During the march from here to Aleppo we fed entirely on the country except for sugar, milk and bacon, which we got where we could. The method was this: before starting, a party of about six men went in advance with the supply officer, who had to requisition mutton or beef, barley and wood near each camp site. The sheep were driven in, killed and butchered. If we had time we always boiled the mutton and had it cold next day, otherwise each man had to fry his own. On arrival in camp 75% of the men had to go off with sacks and blankets to collect barley for the horses. Others were sent to gather green millet stalks and others to forage for wood, which was always the greatest difficulty. We often had to pull down windows and doors of houses to get enough to do our cooking. After a 15 or 18 mile trek the real work was only just beginning and everybody was busily engaged till dark; hardly a horse was groomed. Each regiment took it in turn to do advance guard and outposts for the night.

October 6th - Reveille 4.30 a.m., move off at 6.30 a.m. preceded by the 14th Brigade. After a long trek through a waterless country with deep ravines and gorges, in any of which we might easily have been held up by the Turks, we arrived at the beautifully cultivated and rich valley of Nahr Zaarn, between the Lebanon and anti Lebanon hills. It is about six miles across, all corn in the valley and all vineyards on the hillsides. The red soil intermixed with the green barley and green trees, with here and there a few villages. Built in sheltered nooks on the east side of the Lebanon they created a beautiful picture, which an artist could make the most of. We got good water and proceeded on to Rayak, the important railway junction between Aleppo, Beirut and Damascus. Here the broad gauge from Aleppo shifts into narrow gauge to Damascus and a rack railway to Beirut. It was used as a centre by the Turks for repairs and making engines, also a large aviation park. The machinery captured here was worth over a million pounds.

We were overtaken by a thunderstorm and got wet through. On approaching Rayak an immense fusillade was going on and I thought we were in for another battle, but it turned out to be only the inhabitants, all of whom were armed with Turkish rifles taken from the retreating Turks, showing their joy by letting them off in every direction. The ride through narrow streets was most dangerous, little boys of six or eight letting off rifles from about two feet away. We eventually settled down near the aerodrome, which is now a complete wreck with about thirty burned aeroplanes. We got lots of wood, had a large bonfire and a sing song and got more or less dry before going to bed.

Monday October 7th - Had a day of rest and gave the horses some good grazing. Brig Gen G.A. Weir turns up to take command of the Brigade; he is an old Harrow man and reported to be a great thruster.

Tuesday October 8th - During breakfast, over came a Taube with bombs, of which we got three. Private Kendall was blown to pieces and I had two horses killed and one wounded, we were lucky to get off so cheap.

Charles Turner and I were invited with 18 other officers to a feast given by the local pasha in a village called Bethnail. We rode to the outskirts of the village where we were met by the pasha's son, who gave us an exhibition of horsemanship on a beautiful Arab mare. Also a most brilliantly dressed Arab appeared who spoke English very well, having been in America for some time. On the arrival of the G.O.C. in his car this man jumped in and led the way, firing off his rifle all the time. Outside the village we were met by the inhabitants, who each let off about 30 rounds more or less into the air. We eventually brought up at the pasha's house, small but comfortable in a secluded ravine. Here we had coffee and cigarettes and sat down to a good feast of seven courses; excellent bread, wine, grapes and some very good meats and vegetables. We all ate till we were nearly bursting, not having had such a good feed since September 20th. Afterwards our servants were entertained until they also nearly burst and then we rode off amongst more fusillades and feux de joie".

On October 9th the R.G.H. were ordered to move forward to Homs, the Desert Mounted Corps was much weakened by malaria and having to guard prisoners, this only left the 5th Division to move on Homs said to be occupied by 2,000 Turks. After moving about eight miles north and resting for a day, the 4th Division being still too weak to move they were ordered to push on to Aleppo via Baalbeck.

On October 11th as leading regiment of the 13th Brigade the R.G.H. entered Baalbeck. Here they had a great reception and the inhabitants raised triumphal arches in their honour. The town was very little damaged and there were good possibilities for shopping and exploring one of the most ancient cities in the world. The ruins of the temple of Jupiter being comparable to the ruins of the Acropolis in Athens. It lies on the ancient caravan road between Tyre and Palmyra and was one of the chief cities in the time of Alexander the Great.

The regiment were detailed to organise the prisoners of war into working parties to clean up the town, another task given them was to collect grain for the brigade horses. The following day, October 13th, the regiment paraded to march on Lebwe about 18 miles away. "D" squadron under Major Howard acted as advance guard to the Brigade. The going was very bad through rough and stony country. They reached Lebwe in the afternoon and again had a very friendly reception. Four officers of the regiment dined with the local chief who told them that the villagers had killed 120 of the retreating Turks and Germans and many of their horses. The consequent stench and visual evidence confirmed his statement.

Next day the regiment acting as leading regiment of the Brigade entered Homs and had a terrific reception from the inhabitants, who turned out in thousands to welcome them and five officers were invited to a banquet given by the Mayor. They stayed in Homs for four days and camped on the banks of the river Orantes, the bridge having been destroyed. Here they had good grazing for the horses and the men were able to bathe. The rest and the grazing had a tonic effect on both man and beast, not least because their rations could be supplemented by fresh vegetables and fruit. Even so Major Turner and no less than 16 other ranks had to be evacuated to hospital. The rapid advance and strain of the last few weeks was having an effect on their health and there was a constant dribble of casualties through sickness; dysentery and malaria being a persistent problem.

Even though they were rested for a few days, 40 horses had to be left behind when on October 22nd, the bridge having been repaired for road traffic the regiment moved on to Shakihun, leaving the Orantes behind. The going was good across an undulating plain but the only water available was from wells in the villages they passed. After some rather dull marching they eventually arrived at Maarit el Naman on October 24th, where the villagers were hostile so the regiment helped themselves to some excellent figs growing there. The hostility may have been due to a reported force of a thousand Turks at Hamidada station and an outpost group was posted to watch them. The strength of the regiment was now down to 15 officers, 153 other ranks and 225 horses and this may have had some bearing on the attitude of the local inhabitants.

It was reported that there were some thousands of the enemy still in Aleppo and General MacAndrew, the divisional commander, sent an officer with a flag of truce to demand the capitulation of the city. He was most courteously received but was sent back with this letter: -

"The commander of the Turkish garrison of Aleppo does not find it necessary to answer your note".

However after making this bold reply he began to get uneasy and during the night of October 25th he started to withdraw his forces and form a line about 20 miles to the north. In the morning the Arab Army forced its way into the city and the next day the armoured cars of the 15th

Brigade moved round to the west of the town. The Turkish rearguard consisted of some 2,500. The enemy was charged but our forces were not strong enough to overcome them and they withdrew until a stronger force could be assembled. The 5th Mounted division being too weak to attack confined themselves to covering the roads into the city until the 4th Cavalry Division arrived. Before they arrived the enemy sued for peace, and on October 31st the war in the Middle East was over.

On October 27th 1918 the R.G.H. entered the city, their strength being 14 officers, 142 other ranks and 214 animals. Of this number 58 had left England with the Regiment on April 9th 1915.

W.T. Massey in his book Allenby's final triumph wrote:-
"The 5th cavalry division had now completed a march that will be numbered as one of the finest in the annals of war. From September 19th to October 20th they had marched and fought over 500 miles of country and during this period they had captured 52 guns, 6 German officers, 273 German other ranks, 371 Turkish officers, 11,191 Turkish other ranks and 151 Bedouins. The towns the division occupied included Nazareth, Haifa, Acre, Zahle, Moallaka, Baalbeck, Homs, Hama and Aleppo. All this had been accomplished at the cost of 39 killed, 160 wounded and 9 missing".

Sadly General MacAndrew was badly burned when he met with an accident in Aleppo and although his wounds responded to treatment his heart gave out and he died, before he could fully savour the rewards of his triumph.

An interesting inscription was cut on the rock cliffs near Beirut alongside those of Ramases 11, Nebuchadnezzar, Sennacherib and other early conquerors of Syria, it reads : -

The British Desert Mounted Corps aided by the Arab forces of King Hussein captured Damascus, Homs and Aleppo.
October 1918

One member of the R.G.H. recalling the Biblical story of Nebuchadnezzar being turned out to grass commented that he hoped the grazing was better in those days.

Chapter 22.

Home

Turk detachments troublesome – welcome Katia released prisoners – General Allenby warns Turk commanders – farewell to first demobilisation party – Lectures for civilian life – R.G.H. not eligible for demobilisation transfer to Sherwood Rangers – R.G.H. cadre leaves for home.

During November the regiment remained on outpost duty, having to be constantly on the alert because isolated Turk detachments were inclined to be troublesome. The weather was cold and wet and they were relieved to get winter clothing after having had to survive in summer drill without any greatcoats.

In the middle of the month they moved to some Turkish barracks to the north of Aleppo. Unfortunately they were full of vermin and in such a filthy state that they could not move in for some few days, until they had been cleaned up. This they managed to do in time to welcome nine members of the regiment, who had been captured at Katia. To give the Turks their credit these men rejoined the regiment in good condition, the different prison camps varying tremendously. They certainly fared better than English prisoners captured during the Crusades; Church vestry records frequently record payments made to "soldiers who had their tongues cut out by the Turks".

To relieve the inevitable boredom, football matches and race meetings were organised. In early December Major Turner and Captain Butler went to Katina to take over surrendered Turkish guns and report on the facilities for a cavalry camp. Also on December 10th the regiment provided a guard of honour to welcome General Allenby when he arrived by rail and again a day later when he made his victorious entry to Aleppo. Christmas day celebrations helped relieve the cold, wet conditions which were not helped by the impassable state of the roads. To cheer things up a leave roster to Egypt was commenced.

The British forces had to be constantly on the alert because early in the New Year General Allenby had to give the Turk commanders a stern warning that the armistice terms must be obeyed. There were outlying groups that had not yet been rounded up and disarmed, giving rise to a grave risk that hostilities might start up again and the troops had to be in a constant state of readiness.

During January the regiment was reduced in strength by detachments from the regiment being required for special duties. Fortunately the horses could be stabled in the Turkish barracks, but this still meant that those remaining with the regiment had their hands full, with the reduced manpower to look after them.

On January 12th a farewell dinner was given to the Regimental Sergeant Major, the Regimental Quartermaster and nineteen others who were leaving in the first party for England and eventual demobilisation. They were followed by others at infrequent intervals, the regimental strength being made up by new arrivals and units that had been disbanded.

At the end of January "A" Squadron; strength 3 officers and 68 other ranks, was ordered north of Aleppo to Katma for patrol work, Captain Lord Apsley reported: -

"At Katma horses in brick and plaster sheds - good stables, warm but plenty of air. The men are in tents, squadron office in wooden hut. Two hundred demobilised Turks and 43 Armenian refugees are in sheds between the stables and camp. Have re-allotted billets to them and made them clean the ground. Hope to get rid of majority of Turks and Armenians today, but the train service is irregular. I have to feed the Turks and Armenians from store dump. Supplies are working well. We are getting meat bread and vegetables from Killis, tibben and barley from supply dump Khan Afrin, requisition own tibben and meat. I supply Khan Afrin with with vegetables, bread and barley; health of troops good.

At Mejer horses are in stables but not dry or good lying. Men in barracks, clean camp site. Telegraph line frequently broken by camel convoys. At Khan Afrin horses are in good stables; men in bivouacs. Ruined Khan affords good defensive position.

At Khan Beiram Lieut White on my orders left one section - N.C.O. and six men to act as relay post in case of breakdown of telephone and to assist in patrolling wire and neighbourhood. It is a disused Khan and before the arrival of troops was used by bandits, who waylaid several convoys here; stables good and airy. Men billeted in top story of Khan, which they could defend against any force with guns. Telephone communication to Katma and Khan Afrin. Clear running stream and good grazing".

Lectures in various subjects were organised to prepare the men for civilian life when they were eventually demobilised. There was still work to be done however and on February 10th the regiment moved north to Killis reaching the town on the 13th having bivouacked at Khaian and Mejer in miserably wet conditions on the way. On arrival they were unable to occupy the allotted billets because of the insanitary conditions, so they camped on some waste ground until the camp could be cleaned up. They had to be constantly on the alert because large numbers of Turks who had not surrendered their weapons were wandering around the town. They were pleased when on February 19th a draft of 65 arrived and the following day they were able to move into the Turkish barracks, which had been cleaned up. With constant signs of unrest amongst the Turkish inhabitants they made a great effort to make their presence felt and trouble was avoided.

So they continued throughout April, May and June doing police and patrol work, parties were constantly leaving for home and demobilisation; the regimental strength being kept up by fresh drafts so that there were very few of the original regiment left. At last on June 24th 1919 the Sherwood Rangers arrived at Killis to take over the R.G.H. position. Four officers and 143 other ranks that were not eligible for demobilisation were transferred to the Sherwood Rangers and a cadre of 8 officers and 19 other ranks left for Aleppo and home.

This may be taken as the final chapter in the R.G.H.'s part in the war. Although the regiment went on to give distinguished service in the Second World War and is still doing so, it was also the final chapter in mounted cavalry actions that started when men first went to war on horseback. Mechanisation had started to take over as was seen when armoured cars reached Beirut and Aleppo ahead of the mounted cavalry. This is not to belittle their achievements, no force other than men on horseback could have covered the terrain they encountered or advanced so quickly.

As in days of old, when the development of the Longbow was responsible for the emergence of the Yeoman as a separate class of warrior, they acquitted themselves nobly. Those old Yeomen would travel mounted on a pony together with their accoutrements, taking their continental enemies by surprise at Poitiers and Agincourt, where the continental crossbow was no match for their rate of fire. The yeomen were held to be the real strength and defenders of the nation. In Starkey's England he writes:-

"If the Yeomanry of England were not in time of war we should be in shrewd case. For in them standeth the chief defence of England. Other nations had no such middle class, but only an oppressed peasantry and the nobles and men at arms who robbed them".

These Yeomen of England, always amongst the first to volunteer, proved that they possessed the finest quality of manhood, charging entrenched positions, facing rifle and machine gun fire, armed only with drawn sabres. To get into that position, slashing and thrusting, neither giving nor failing until they had won through. This the Gloucestershire men did in full measure, giving no heed to the cost, as they did in the days of old.

Their achievements are best summed up in extracts from two despatches, firstly that of General Allenby: -

"Perhaps the most striking feature of the operations has been the variety of the terrain and of the nature of the fighting. There have been periods of desert warfare; of fighting in difficult hill country and in open cultivated plain. There have been periods of trench warfare alternating with periods of rapid movement with no fixed defences. Troops have been exposed to the sand and glare of the trenches, to the tropical heat of the Jordan Valley and to the bitter storms of the Judean winter.

Such conditions have called for great powers of endurance and cheerful adaptability; of quick conceptions of the varying tactical circumstances on the part of the leaders and of rapid improvisation, these qualities have never been lacking.

That the health and morale of the men was maintained was due to their own inimitable spirit and willingness; to the constant care and foresight of the medical authorities; and to the organisation, official and private, which provided in spite of all difficulties for the comfort and recreation of the troops.

The experience gained in the varied forms of warfare which have fallen to the lot of the Egyptian Expeditionary Force has proved the soundness of the principles on which our army was trained before the war and above all the value of the cavalry arm to confirm and exploit a success".

To this may be added a contemporary comment by "Q.L." in the Journal of the Royal United Services Institution".

"It seems most extraordinary that so little notice has been taken of this campaign in Palestine and Syria, a campaign and a victory that are without parallel in modern history. General Allenby with a force of inferior strength, in five weeks had not only severely defeated, but absolutely destroyed and annihilated an army of 100,000 men - no horde of undisciplined savages, but an army well led, well trained and amply provided with all the munitions of modern warfare. And this he had done entirely by the skilful and daring use of his magnificent cavalry, for after the first shock of battle had opened the way for his horsemen the infantry took but a very small part in the fight.

The result of this great victory was by no means confined to the East; its earthquake shock was felt throughout the whole theatre of war and it brought down in utter ruin the entire edifice of the alliance of the Central Powers. The collapse of Turkey was inevitably followed by that of Bulgaria. The defection of Bulgaria gave the final blow to the already shaken military power of Austria; and with the fall of Austria vanished the last hope of German victory. General Allenby and his horsemen thrust victory into the arms of the allies and precipitated the end of the greatest war that the world has ever known".

Between September 19th and October 26th the Egyptian Expeditionary force had captured 360 guns and 75,000 prisoners, of whom 200 Officers and 3,500 other ranks were Germans or Austrians. The front had been moved forward over 350 miles.

The 5th Cavalry Division with the R.G.H. very often in the van had actually marched 600 miles in less than six weeks, capturing 11,000 prisoners on the way. This would have been a remarkable achievement for a mechanised force. For a force whose mounts had to be cared for and fed off the country, it reflected great credit on the horsemanship shown by those involved. Yes the horse casualties as seen from a modern viewpoint, 1,920 out of 8,971 killed or evacuated, might appear heavy. But such was the acceptable mode of warfare of that age.

At this distance in time, almost a century later, the extraordinary achievements of this advance must surely rank with those of Crecy, Agincourt and Waterloo.

OOOOOOOOOOOOOOOOOOOOOOOOOOOOOOOOOOOOOOOOOOOO

Chapter 23

Epilogue

On April 29th 1922 the new Regimental War Memorial was unveiled on College Green, just below the west door of Gloucester Cathedral, by Lieutenant General Sir P.W. Chetwode K.C.B., K.C.M.G., D.S.O. Three steps lead up to a platform on which stands an eight sided stone, which carries on alternate faces bronze relief plaques, depicting actions in which the regiment participated. On the faces between the plaques are engraved the names of the Gloucestershire Yeomen who fell and would remain for ever on the field of battle. After the 1939 - 45 war an additional plaque and names of those who died in that conflict were added.

The following year on the anniversary of the Battle of Katia a handful of the survivors, without any prior arrangement, happened to meet at the memorial. Thus starting a tradition that has been continued up to the present day; by representatives of the regiment, old comrades, relatives and friends.

The ending of the 1914 - 18 war brought to an end the Regiment's role as mounted cavalry and heralded the introduction of a mechanised force; it also signalled the end of the old feudal system of raising an army and the loosening of the tie with the agricultural industry. Taxation and modern emancipation of the individual hastened the process. Up to the time of the Peninsular wars many tenanted farms had to supply a man and a horse in times of emergency. What this meant in practice was that the local nobleman, who in all probability was the landlord, would lead this little army to wherever it was required. We saw a survival of this autocratic command when the then Duke of Beaufort issued an ultimatum that his tenants must resign from the Berkeley squadron or loose their tenancies.

Although they substituted their mounts for mechanical forms of transport, it was far from being the end of the R.G.H.; in fact the ending of the war marked a new beginning. Trained as a mechanised force the regiment divided into two lines at the beginning of the 1939 - 45 war, the second line was sent to the 8th army in North Africa, where after suffering heavy casualties and winning further honours the 2nd regiment was disbanded.

The first line took on the important work of a training regiment, eventually becoming part of the European invasion force and army of occupation. Today they are the R.G.H. squadron of the Royal Wessex Yeomanry and train as an armoured replacement and reserve force.

So what became of those men who brought glory to the Regiment? Some signed up again when the Regiment was reformed after the war as an armoured car company, this being more appropriate to the cavalry "spirit".

When war broke out in 1939 Hugh Lefaux and Charles Turner commanded Home Guard battalions. Hugh Walwin returning to his photographic chemist business joined the Royal Observer Corps, Harry Colburn became a director of "Townsend's of Stroud", George Castle became kennel huntsman to the Duke of Beaufort's hounds, Charles Lovell rose to the rank of Major in the Home Guard and was much loved and respected by all serving and past members of the Regiment. Fred Lewis became the local Air Raid Warden, Eddie Tippet went into practice as an estate agent at Bourton on the Water, Bert Troughton, George Hyett, Andy Andrews and Frank Hopkins returned to their farms, Lord Apsley was killed in a plane crash when serving in the East Riding Yeomanry.

Shep Sheppard tried to fiddle his age and rejoin the R.G.H. at the outbreak of hostilities in 1939. Mathematics were obviously not his strong point because after he had recounted his previous military experience, including South Africa, the recruiting officer asked him "how did you manage to join the R.G.H. at the age of eight"? He regularly attended the Katia memorial services until one year he failed to turn up, like all old soldiers he simply faded away.

195.

Royal Gloucestershire Hussars War Memorial

Appendix "A"

KEY PLAN TO NON-COMMISSIONED OFFICERS ROYAL GLOUCESTERSHIRE HUSSARS.

1. Corporal Kingston.
2. Band Sergeant Green.
3. Sergeant E. Gibbs.
4. Corporal Yeend.
5. Corporal Bennett.
6. Corporal Ball.
7. Corporal James.
8. Corporal Philpots.
9. Corporal O. R. C. Larner.
10. Squadron Sergeant Major Gravenell.
11. Sergeant Pearce.
12. Sergeant Cypher.
13. Sergeant Welch.
14. Sergeant Goodwin.
15. Sergeant Cornock.
16. Sergeant Derrett.
17. Corporal Vezey.
18. Corporal Worlock.
19. Sergeant Farrier Jenkins.
20. Corporal Trumpeter Mills.
21. Corporal Phelps.
22. Corporal Barber.
23. Sergeant Ratclift.
24. Sergeant Farrier Spreadbury.
25. Corporal Hadley.
26. Corporal Kilminster.
27. Corporal Akerman.
28. Corporal Harris.
29. Sergeant Hatherall.
30. Sergeant Bridgeman.
31. Sergeant Gould.
32. Corporal Lord.
33. Corporal Mansell.
34. Corporal Hillier.
35. Sergeant Pullen.
36. Sergeant Young.
37. Quarter Master Perris.
38. Quarter-Master Voyce.
39. Trumpet-Major Hewitt.
40. Sergeant-Major Henderson.
41. Sergeant-Major Parker.
42. Sergeant-Major Cope.
43. Regimental Srgt.-Major Hayward.
44. Major & Adjut. W. H. Wyndham-Quin.
45. Sergeant-Major Brill.
46. Sergeant-Major Whitehead.
47. Sergeant-Major Holderness.
48. Quarter-Master Limbrick.
49. Quarter-Master Parker.
50. Quarter-Master Bennett.
51. Quarter-Master Bastin.
52. Sergeant Cummings.
53. Sergeant Burrow.
54. Sergeant H. Davis.
55. Sergeant G. Adams.
56. Sergeant A. Adams.
57. Sergeant Phillips.

Appendix "B"

References

For the tactical appreciation of the Palestine Campaign I have drawn heavily on "The Palestine Campaigns" by Lieut General A.P. Wavell and The Royal Gloucestershire Hussars Yeomanry 1898 - 1922 by Frank Fox. Other references include - Pembrokeshire by R.M. Lockley, The Yeomanry Cavalry of Gloucestershire and Monmouth by W.H. Wyndham Quinn, Three into One by John Lewis, Silent Fields by Roger Lovegrove, a series of magazine articles entitled "I was There" edited by John Hammerton, A Pot of Smoke by R.M. Lockley, Weather and Warfare by John Tyrell, The Anzac Book, Reminiscences of a Naval Surgeon by Surgeon Rear Admiral T.T. Jeans, Gallipoli by John Masefield, "Gallipoli the Fading Vision" by John North, The Suvla Bay Landing by John Hargrave, The Gallipolian magazines especially No's 38 & 41 edited by David Saunders and numerous other Gallipoli works, Seven Pillars of Wisdom by T.E. Lawrence, Winston S. Churchill by Martin Gilbert, History of the English Speaking Peoples by Winston Churchill, With Lawrence in Arabia by Lowell Thomas, extracts from the Cheltenham Chronicle and Gloucestershire Graphic, The Life of Christ by Frederic W. Farrar, The Road to En-Dor by E.H. Jones.

ISBN 142514103-X